FIVE LANTERNS AT SUNDOWN

Evangelism in a Chastened Mood

Alfred C. Krass

William B. Eerdmans Publishing Company
Grand Rapids, Michigan

Copyright © 1978 by Wm. B. Eerdmans Publishing Co.
255 Jefferson Ave. S.E., Grand Rapids, Mich. 49503

Library of Congress Cataloging in Publication Data

Krass, Alfred C.
Five lanterns at sundown.

1. Mission of the church. 2. Evangelistic work.
I. Title.
BV601.8.K67   269.2'09   78-6181
ISBN 0-8028-1738-6

Unless otherwise noted, Scripture quotations in this publication are from the Revised Standard Version of the Bible, copyrighted 1946, 1952 © 1971, 1973.

Those quotations marked TEV are from The Good News Bible, *The Bible in Today's English Version,* copyrighted 1976, American Bible Society.

Permission has also been granted to quote from the following:

Christ the Meaning of History by Hendrikus Berkhof. © 1966 SCM Press Ltd. Used by permission of John Knox Press.

The Crucified God by Jürgen Moltmann. Copyright © 1974 by SCM Press Ltd. Reprinted by permission of Harper & Row, Publishers, Inc.

Foundations and Perspective of Confession. © 1955 by New Brunswick Theological Seminary.

The Technological Society by Jacques Ellul, trans. by John Wilkinson. © 1964 by Alfred A. Knopf, Inc.

To Mike . . .

I will not be so fatuous as to say the future belongs to you. I'm rather moved to ask: "Do you belong to the future?"

CONTENTS

FOREWORD

A book is not written in a vacuum. Nor could a book like this one have been written in a library. This book has emerged out of continued dialogue—in meetings, at conferences and consultations, in classes, on field trips in the course of my work as Evangelism Consultant for the United Church Board for World Ministries from 1971 to 1976, in letters, in close interpersonal relations.

These years have been a time of continuing stimulation. I remain thankful for the ongoing friendship of those with whom I have been sharing the stimulation: Alan McLean and Richard Griffis, David Stowe and Lawrence Henderson, Stephen Knapp and Orlando Costas, Roger Hull and John Poulton, Jeff Utter and Bill Webber. Traveling along the same road as they, I have found myself with them in what Nathan Detroit would have called "a permanent, floating seminar"!

But this book has more specific origins as well: my participation in the growing dialogues of the world church about evangelism, and my studies in comparative historical sociology at the New School for Social Research.

I would like to thank those people who have meant a great deal to me as partners in the reconceptualization of evangelism in which we are all engaged these days: those who met under the "Kairos" clock at Lausanne, the Jesuits who so graciously received a number of us into their missions conference in St. Paul, Thomas Stransky, Joan Chatfield, Gerald Anderson, the members of the American Society of Missiology, Emilio Castro, M. M. Thomas, Rajendra Sail, and Lesslie Newbigin. I would also like to thank the pastors of the United Church of Canada (and their Evangelism Secretary, Norman MacKenzie) with whom I spent a formative week in Toronto in 1974, Jim Wallis and Wes Michaelson and the whole crew at *Sojourners,* Gabriel Fackre, the faculty of the Fuller School of World Mission, Dean Kelley, Lucius Walker, Jitsuo Morikawa, Grady Allison, and the Evangelism Working Group of the National Council of Churches. And—of course—for helping me to reflect on all this and adding their own perceptive insights, I must thank Orlando Costas and Larry Henderson.

On the sociological side of my life the list is headed by Professor Benjamin Nelson, who finally convinced this man of little faith of the ultimate world-historical significance of the theological concerns which, though I was partial to them, I had been too ready to consign to the realm of "the parochial," of interest only to Christians. To Dr. Nelson I will be forever grateful for opening up to me that heady mix of Durkheim, Weber, and other "civilizationalists" which he calls "the comparative differential sociology of historical-cultural process." He has given me a frame for the study of missiology which I lacked before; I hope that this beginning attempt at using such a frame is helpful both to sociologists and to theologians.

Professors Robert Canfield, Charles Kraft, Richard Mouw, Charles Taber, Charles Forman, and Max Stackhouse have been helpful to me in integrating my socio-anthropological studies with theological and missiological concerns, as have Joan Chatfield and Stephen Knapp. Opportunities to read papers to the Fuller School of World Mission faculty and the Symposium on Christian Faith in a Religiously Plural World at Washington and Lee University, as well as to give four lectures at Milligan College and one at Yale Divinity School, and to participate in courses at United Theological Seminary of the Twin Cities, Eden Theological Seminary, and the Overseas Ministries Study Center at Ventnor, New Jersey, have given me a chance to develop these approaches in the context of living dialogue. I am grateful that I had the opportunity to lead a family camp for the Penn Central Conference for several weeks, and also to lecture for Makiki Union Christian Church.

Isaac Rottenberg of the Reformed Church in America has given me invaluable help in synthesizing theological and historical-sociological approaches; no one has helped me more. It was he who directed me to the *Foundations* document and the works of Van Ruler and Berkhof, without which I could not have completed this book. Professor Roger Shinn of Union Theological Seminary

and Dr. Edward Huenemann of the United Presbyterian Church
have helped me understand the significance of Calvin's treatment
of the ascension and the Kingdom of Christ.

The "Forepiece" was done for the Springfield (Mass.) Pastors'
Conference.

Michael Clark assisted me with Chapter 6.

Denis Goulet kindly led me to the writings of L.-J. Lebret. His
own writings have been a particularly enticing frosting on Lebret's
cake!

Dr. Walter Wink has given helpful counsel on biblical interpretation. My wife Susan Krass has sought to direct me away from
eisegesis to exegesis. Her painstaking scholarship is a continual
example of what I ought to be doing. Doug Macneal suggested the
title.

I am grateful to Jitsuo Morikawa and Rajendra Sail for their
examples of an evangelism which integrates word, deed, and
presence. Their contributions have been an inspiration to me, and
have opened doors which I did not see before.

I recognize that in the foregoing list are to be found only two
women's names, and that in a book about ten women! That is to
underrate the immense contribution made by the women's
movement toward raising my consciousness. Some of the best
feminist theology I have seen has, however, been the product of
groups, rather than of individuals, and I cannot easily name
names. This work has been some of the best theologizing I have
seen, overcoming the subject/object dichotomy, challenging all
forms of elitism, working for the total liberation of the people of
God. I think of the work of the Evangelical Women's Caucus and
the Task Force on Women in Church and Society of the United
Church of Christ. I also think of the contributions of women on the
Council of Theological Students of the United Church Board for
World Ministries. Without their insights, I would be much the
poorer, and this book would not have been what it is.

The book finally got out of the conference hall and into the
streets when I participated in the Campaign for Global Justice at
the Eucharistic Congress in Philadelphia during the summer of
1976. The contributions of that close fellowship of women and
men in helping me live what I had written and understand it anew
give the book whatever integrity it has.

The final product is, of course, my own. I bear full responsibility for all its undoubted shortcomings. If it can be of some use in helping people to relate things they have previously kept separate, then my prayer for it will be answered, for I am convinced that we must begin right now to take seriously what the writer to the Ephesians says is God's intention, in "the fullness of time," to "bring all things together with Christ as head" (Eph. 1:10).

Thomas Luhrman showed great skill and devotion in transcribing and typing the manuscript. Without his help this book would have been much slower in emerging.

Advent 1976

PREFACE: Of Moods and Prospects

This is a book about discipleship, and calling people to discipleship. It is, in other words, a book about evangelism. But the evangelism is set in the context of contemporary history, which is, for the eyes of faith, itself set in a larger context—that of God's history.

To use theological language, the context in which we call people to discipleship is that of the *eschaton*, the "last days." The context is "eschatological": the evangelizer calls people to serve a God who is in the process of bringing all things to completion, of making all things new. The evangelizer calls people to the service of the one who is, in our own day, through people's response to him—and beyond and in spite of their response—fulfilling his ancient purposes. The evangelizer plays a role in God's historical and trans-historical re-creation of the cosmos.

The book is called *Five Lanterns at Sundown,* and the somber impression which that title makes is confirmed immediately by the subtitle. The title conveys my belief that we have no right to anticipate the future toward which contemporary history is rushing as a time of bright light. And yet the specific biblical passage on which the entire book is fashioned—the Allegory of the Ten Young Women (Matt. 25:1-13)—deals with the night in the Bible's characteristically paradoxical way. The night is the time of darkness, but it is also the time at which the wedding takes place.

For the pre-modern world, night is that part of the day most difficult to measure, to divide, to gauge. It is therefore the time of unexpected events—the thief surprises the householder, the master surprises sleeping servants. Most peoples of the ancient world would subscribe to the view of the night expressed in the Chokosi proverb I learned to appreciate when I lived in Northern Ghana: "Night falls—then trouble!"

For the ancient Hebrew, however, there was a strange wrinkle in this way of thinking: each day begins with the night (cf. Gen. 1:3,8, etc.). Therefore in reading the Allegory of the Ten Young Women, which takes place at night, we are hearing about a time which is not the end-time but the beginning. At the midnight wedding-feast the prelude to the next day occurs. The feast is the beginning of the marriage.

And so it is with this book. If it is written "in a chastened mood," that does not mean that it is written in a pessimistic mood. As far distant as the biblical message is from naive optimism, that far is it distant from pessimism and cynicism.

Why do I describe this as evangelism in a chastened mood? An author must work within a given cultural context. The context in which American evangelism has developed and which it has helped shape—and which has marked my work until recently— has been that of evolutionary optimism, theological Arminianism, and pragmatic activism. I must speak to that context. (Were the book written in Germany it might well have a different subtitle.)

To an American audience which expects to see evangelism associated with growth and visions of the New Jerusalem, the biblical evangelist must address the question: Have you really caught the drift of the biblical message? Have you appreciated how counter-cultural it is? Or have you reshaped it to conform to the millennialism of your culture? Are you aware of the break between your highest visions and God's promise?

The context in which the Bible places evangelism is one in which night is understood to be hastening on. The call of an American evangelist, if he or she refuses to take part in the great bipartisan cultural project of mystifying the public, must be "Prepare for night." In the New Testament view this is true of all times; I believe there is a sense in which that somber reality has a particular truth and urgency today. There is a sense in which the world is heading for a time of increasing unrest, injustice, violence, repression, suffering, and inability to cope with the basic human needs of exploding populations, and I cannot be optimistic about "the human prospect."

Still, the evangelist's call is not just "Prepare for the night," but "Prepare for the night in which the wedding will take place; prepare for the night which is the prelude to a new day." (Otherwise the speaker would not be an evangelist but—were there such a word—a "malangelist," an announcer of bad news.)

This means that the news which the evangelist has to announce is not just news of the human prospect. The future about which he or she speaks is not just an extrapolation from current tendencies and directions. For it is not just we who move toward the future. There is also a future which moves toward us. It is the future of God, a future which introduces a true *novum* into the human prospect: a marriage.

I believe the world is simultaneously moving toward that future—God's future—and toward a time of great stress—humanity's prospect. The contrast is not between what humanity does and what God is doing, not between "earthly" and "heavenly" events, but between two kinds of events—two different processes—taking place on earth today. But were I to say more about that now, I would steal the subject matter of this book.

FOREPIECE: A Parable — "Ten American Suburban Women"

It all started—it all was decided—the essential things took place *before* the sun set. It appeared to us later that the important events were the ones which took place at midnight, but now that we look back at it, we have to recognize—when our heads are clear and it's cool enough to think—that nothing happened at midnight that *had* to happen that way. The events in the middle of the night, on which we tended at the time to place so much emphasis, could've been foretold before six o'clock or even earlier. There was nothing at all surprising about them. They were, as some of our friends say, "in the cards." But not in the way our friends mean, for we ourselves had set up the deck.

When we were inveighing against the "selfishness" of the five who got in, it seemed to us more than just making them our scapegoats. Why in hell, we asked, wouldn't they share what they had with us? Anybody could make a mistake! How were *we* to know he would be so late coming? Anyone could make a mistake like that, and—what with the price of oil the way it got to be in those last months—who would willingly buy more than was needed? I mean, you've got to eat, too! And you've got to buy clothes, and if you put all your money into oil, it's not going to leave you with very much on hand for necessities, much less emergencies.

But that's what was different about them. They never seemed to do things the way everyone else did. For example, they were never in style—"couldn't afford to keep up with the fashions," they said. They never, I must admit, seemed any the less happy for that. How sublime they were! They never seemed to have any consciousness of what they looked like. As for me, I couldn't go around looking like that. The impression a woman makes is an important part of her character and personality. People just know if you haven't taken time to take care of yourself.

1

I once said to Helen, "Don't you ever look in a mirror?" She just smiled and didn't reply. I went on, "You know you look just like my grandmother. Don't you realize styles have changed? People don't wear their hair that way anymore. And your shoes! Straight out of *Vogue* 12 years ago." She just smiled. I got mad. "Don't you speak the same language everyone else speaks?" I asked. "Don't you see what the world is like today?"

She retained her composure, but her smile started to change, into . . . well, I guess it was a look of pity. "You really irk me, Helen," I said, "you and your damned friends. The way you go around wasting your time with those nothings, people no one's ever heard of, and all that do-goodism you get into—baking pies for kids on probation, taking in mending from the prisons, and putting up derelicts in your house. God! what they must do to your sheets! *I* wouldn't want to sleep in your house with all those tramps having been there."

But it was no use. She just sat there, a look of incomprehension on her face. Then some of her friends came along and said it was time to go make another one of those damned church dinners for the migrant workers or whoever—when I'd had an extra ticket for the matinee and some nice folks had invited me in for a drink afterwards, asking me to bring a friend along if I liked. I'd been thinking of Helen, but the hell with it! She wouldn't have gone. Why did I waste my time on her? She was just incorrigible.

The day it all happened I was walking past Helen's place, too, on my way to my encounter group, and I saw that some of Helen's friends were there. As I passed the window I heard one of them say, "We'd better get on down to the store to buy some extra oil, just in case the marriage is delayed," and I thought, "Isn't that just like those diddies? 'Waste not, want not!' 'An ounce of prevention is worth a pound of cure.' 'Be prepared'—and all that crap!" But I did ask myself, I remember, whether I'd put aside enough oil for my lamp and for once I was glad to remember that I had some at home. Not at all like me, you know! I'm always buying things at the last minute. I remembered it would be enough to last even until 10 o'clock—and whoever heard of a wedding starting later than 10 o'clock? So I felt pretty pleased with myself, and I strutted on down to the encounter group.

As I think it about it now, hadn't I done pretty well? I mean, I hadn't forgotten about the wedding. I'm always forgetting dates, my calendar is so filled. But I hadn't forgotten about the wedding, and I had bought a quart of oil when I went to the A & P last week, and we had only used a little bit of it one night when we thought we heard thieves trying to break into our house. Ever since we bought those expensive paintings we don't sleep well at night for fear someone will break in and take them. And they're our nest egg, after all! (Barney says you can't get enough interest in a bank these days to keep up with inflation!)

Oh, for a moment I forgot. I thought it was back then again. I wish it were. I wish it were. If only we could turn the clock back. . . .

That's how all the trouble came—over clocks and over time. His time just wasn't like our time. He never kept schedules—he was never on time—*our* time, I mean. He always did things his own way, at his own time. Well, yes, he'd said he would do just that. He told us he couldn't say when he'd come for the wedding, that we'd just better be ready. I said to Phyllis, "What kind of a way is that for anyone to do things?" She said, "I bet we'll die before he comes." None of us thought of the wedding possibly coming at any date we could point to. So I said to Phyllis, "We'd just better carry on as if it'll never come to pass, just live our own lives, have some fun, not worry too much about the future. If he comes, we"ll certainly be around—or near at hand—and we can kind of hustle things together and make do."

And why *shouldn't* it have been enough? I mean we *had* oil. We weren't bad people—no saints, of course, but who would want to be a saint? Gad!

I guess, now that I mention it, I just wasn't his type. I don't know that I could've lived with him. I couldn't have stood him—so righteous, so good, so loving, so kind—it would've been too much! I must admit his looks always got to me, kind of sent chills down my spine.

But the way he acted that night was just so typical! "I'm here, and it's time to start the wedding. Come on, girls." And we all woke up and the five of us saw with horror that our lamps were out—it must've been past 12! And there he was going in with Helen and her friends and, and—they were shutting the door! I ran to the door and stood there with my hand against it.

"Helen," I said, "give me some of your oil!" But she just looked at me, and at my lamp, and hers, and at her oil bottle and quietly shook her head. "There isn't enough for both of us," she said. "Maybe you could run down to the 7-11 Store and get some—maybe they're still open."

But that was just a lot of crap. The 7-11 isn't still open at midnight! She knew that. (I guess she was just trying to be kind, so we wouldn't see the door shut.)

And so I grabbed Phyllis and the others and we ran, FOR NOTHING! FOR NOTHING! Down to the 7-11. And the bridegroom shut the door. And he shut it forever, for . . . ever, FOREVER!

You see, I still get all riled up when I think about it. I kind of lose control. In my more objective moments, I recognize that what happened that night made no difference whatsoever. The essential things—the decisive things—had happened before sunset, before that day even. The events of that night were only the logical conclusion to the deep decisions the five of us—and the five of them—had made long ago.

1: THE WEDDING-MAKER

> And I will betroth you to me forever; I will betroth you to me in righteousness and in justice, in steadfast love, and in mercy. I will betroth you to me in faithfulness; and you shall know the Lord.
>
> —God, to Israel, sometime in the eighth century, B.C. (Hos. 2:19f.)

THE SUBJECT OF THIS FIRST CHAPTER IS GOD. GOD CAN BE and has been described in many ways. Sydney Carter has described him in a popular hymn—accurately, I believe—as a dancing God. (Sam Keen has done the same in a book.) I shall here describe God as a wedding-maker, a giver of feasts, one whose profoundest hope for the whole creation is "that they'll really have a ball."

I can claim no originality for my image of God, for I am using Jesus' image. Old Testament and inter-testamental scholars will add that Jesus was not original either: to describe God as a giver of festive celebrations and weddings is an analogy with a long history in Israel.

The history goes back at least as far as Isaiah of Jerusalem, who, in the eighth century B.C., prophesied that on Mt. Zion "the Lord of hosts will make for all peoples a feast of fat things . . . of wine on the lees." With this imagery, Isaiah was speaking of the future salvation of Judah, but he saw that her salvation would be universal good news. God, he said, "will wipe away tears from all faces" and "it will be said 'Lo, this is our God; we have waited for him, that he might save us' " (Isa. 25:6-9).

Isaiah was not alone in the Old Testament in having a vision of God's giving a feast for his people. The Psalmist (in Ps. 81:16) hears God saying to his people, "I would feed you with the finest

of the wheat, and with honey from the rock I would satisfy you."
The image of God feeding his people with the very best became,
in the tradition, a metaphor for salvation. This tradition may date
back to God's feeding of the people in the desert.

The imagery continued in post-exilic times. At the time of the
return from captivity in Babylon, Zechariah remembers that
Jeremiah had not only prophesied Judah's exile, but had pointed
beyond Judah's immediate calamity to her ultimate salvation. He
had prophesied a new covenant ("I will make a new covenant
with the house of Israel and the house of Judah . . . and I will be
their God and they shall be my people" (Jer. 31:31, 33).
Zechariah hears God telling him to reaffirm that earlier prophecy:
"I am jealous for Zion with great jealousy . . . ," God says. "I will
return to Zion, and will dwell in the midst of Jerusalem. . . . I will
save my people from the east country and from the west country
and bring them to dwell in the midst of Jerusalem, and they shall
be my people, and I will be their God, in faithfulness and in
righteousness" (Zech. 8:2, 3, 7).

But what images does Zechariah find to express the new relationship between God and his people? He uses images of abun-
dance and nourishment: "The vine shall yield its fruit, and the
ground shall give its increase, and the heavens shall give their
dew; and I will cause the remnant of this people to possess all
these things" (Zech. 8:12). And he uses metaphors of feasting:
"The fast of the fourth month, and the fast of the fifth, and the fast
of the seventh, and the fast of the tenth [month], shall be to the
house of Judah seasons of joy and gladness, and cheerful feasts"
(Zech. 8:19).

As prior to the Exile, so once again after it, the imagery is found
to be suggestive. For a nation whose religious observances were
often rites of communal eating and drinking, the imagery of the
feast was a natural one for a prophet to use to speak of God's
eschatological salvation. Zechariah recognizes that, when Judah is
saved, holding feasts will be a sign for the whole world to see that
God is with the people (see Zech. 8:23).

The imagery of the feast of God for his people is found in
inter-testamental literature as well. This time the feast is en-
visioned as taking place in heaven (see Midr. tehill. 14:7). Fourth
Ezra envisions the completion of the roll of the saints at the end as

the prelude to a heavenly marriage-supper (IV Ezra 2:38-41). He describes the heavenly, or new Jerusalem as a woman, probably a bride (IV Ezra 19:38ff., 10:25-30).

The New Testament inherited a tradition, therefore, in which the salvation of the end-time was already pictured in the imagery of feasts, weddings, and banquets. For that reason we should not be surprised to find God pictured in the New Testament as one who is planning a cosmic banquet ("a celestial fish-fry," the people in *Green Pastures* would have called it, a generation ago).

Let's begin with references in the gospels to God as a giver of feasts. Perhaps we should start with what John calls Jesus' first sign: turning water into wine at the wedding in Cana of Galilee (John 2:1-11). John wants us to recognize that it is not just ordinary wine into which Jesus turns the water (or even the best contemporary wine, as the man in charge of the wedding mistakenly concluded) but the wine of God's coming Kingdom. John conceives of God as preparing a salvation for his people which he can describe by the human analogy of a feast. Similarly, in one Johannine resurrection account, the disciples recognize Jesus because he provides, first, a miraculous catch of fish, and then a feast of bread and fish. In all of these instances the linkage between salvation, the Savior, and feasting is assumed.

Perhaps the fact that John chooses the metaphor of bread to describe Jesus—he is "the bread of life" (John 6:25-59)—shows how central God's feeding of his people is as an analogy of salvation.

In Luke's Gospel as well there are many references to show how God's future salvation is interpreted as a feast. In chapter 16 we note that, when Lazarus died, he was carried "to Abraham's side, at the feast in heaven" (v. 22, TEV). In chapter 22:14-10 (= Matt. 26:26-30) we find Jesus speaking of the passover being "fulfilled" in the Kingdom of God (Matthew has him say he will "drink the new wine in my Father's Kingdom"). In chapter 22:30 Jesus tells the disciples, "You will eat and drink at my table in my kingdom," and it is characteristic that, in the account of the journey to Emmaus (Luke 24:30ff.), the disciples recognize Jesus when he breaks the bread for them.

There are many other instances we could cite, in Luke and the other Synoptic Gospels, where God is spoken of as a giver of feasts. But what about God as a wedding-maker? Certainly this is the image behind the Allegory of the Ten Young Women in Matthew 25:1-13, but this allegory is best approached not directly, but from the total tradition of God as wedding-maker.

In addition to this allegory, the wedding imagery is most fully developed in the Book of Revelation. There (Rev. 19:1-10 and 21:1-9ff.) the coming salvation is pictured as "the wedding feast of the Lamb." "Happy are those," John hears the angel say in his vision, "who have been invited to the wedding feast of the Lamb" (Rev. 19:9, TEV). Here is the place to look at the imagery in its totality and in its individual elements.

Much interlocking imagery is found in these verses: a feast, a feast-giver, a bridegroom, invited guests, various traditional liturgical forms of rejoicing. We should not try to ascribe fixed meanings to each image, as if we had a single, well-constructed allegory. Jesus, for example, is called the bridegroom (as in John 3:29) and the Lamb interchangeably. God's people are spoken of at different times as the bride (as in II Cor. 11:2 and Eph. 5:25, 32), as the invited guests (Rev. 19:9 et al.), and as the new Jerusalem (Rev. 21:2).* The images are complementary and, at times, overlapping.

Each of the images has a long history. In the Old Testament God is identified as Israel's bridegroom, or husband (e.g., Hos. 2:16 et passim, Isa. 54:6, Ezek. 16:8ff.) and Israel as God's wife—a faithful bride (usually an image for past relationships) or, more frequently, a faithless harlot (cf. Isa. 1:21, Jer. 2:2, Hos. 1-3). The future reconciliation between God and Israel is spoken of as a new betrothal (Hos. 2:14f., 19ff.; Ezek. 16:59ff.).

What is the crux of all this wedding-related symbolism? Why did it exercise continuing appeal over the centuries? Let's answer by trying to assess why John used it in the Apocalypse.

John wanted to describe, in contemporary, historical, and eschatological terms, the relationship between Christ and his followers. He knew this relationship was intimate and indissoluble (e.g., Rev. 7:17, 14:1). Yet at the same time he recognized that it had

*That is why it is not clear in the Matthaean allegory either whether the ten young women are invited to be guests at a wedding or partners in a (polygamous!) marriage. It is pointless to nit-pick here—the new Jerusalem is both God's bride and God's guest.

not yet been consummated: salvation was still a hope; the disciples to whom he was writing were confronting extreme forms of suffering and persecution; and yet he knew that God would turn that around.

In the image of God's people as an affianced virgin he found a symbol adequate to describe both the love and devotion existing between Christ and his people, and its needed—and promised—future consummation, an image of present faithfulness and expectation as well as of far greater future joy.

Such imagery, John knew, would console and fire the hope of the believers, while at the same time encouraging them to continue to exercise repentance and faith—so that they might respond to the "invitation" to the wedding feast by bringing forth the fruits of faith (as in Rev. 2:2ff., 9, 13, 19).*

John believed himself called to summon the early believers to good works and vigilance. But note that in Revelation 19:8 John says it is *granted* to the bride to be clothed with fine linen, that holiness is God's gift. But, he adds, the fine linen is at the same time the life the bride lives, her righteous deeds (Beasley-Murray: "the holy life of the Redeemer in the redeemed"). As in Philippians 2:12f., that which is received by grace is acted upon in faith—the bride who is made ready also makes herself ready. The fine-tooth comb of Reformation polemic about works and faith is unknown here and we do wrong to try to introduce it. We are not studying a theological treatise but a piece of symbolic religious literature written in a pastoral context.

The question we are asking is why John chose the wedding imagery. I think we have by now appreciated how rich in possible associations the images are, how appropriate the analogy of betrothal and marriage is to describe an eschatology in the process of realizing itself, how suggestive the bride/bridegroom image is to describe the relationship between Christ and the church. But let us not underestimate the importance of the total image of the wedding as we analyze its elements. The fundamental association is certainly that of joy and celebration, but it is a particular kind of joy. It is not the comfortable, sentimental, commercial joy of our

*This is the significance of the five wise young women "procuring oil" in our foundation allegory.

vacation resorts or TV variety shows. It is not what, following Bonhoeffer, we might call "cheap joy." It is costly joy.

John indicates this by making clear that the central figure of the section, as of the whole Apocalypse, is the Lamb. The wedding-supper to which the believers are invited is the wedding-supper of the Lamb. The Bridegroom whom the bride will marry is the Lamb.

We are probably correct in seeing Passover imagery here, as in I Corinthians 5. (But we should not rule out the imagery of the Day of Atonement either.) The new relationship between God and his people is made possible because of a sacrifice. As Paul writes, "Christ, our Passover lamb, has been sacrificed. Therefore let us celebrate our Passover" (I Cor. 5:7f., TEV). In the time between the two comings of Jesus this festival is celebrated, Paul says, with the unleavened bread of "sincerity and truth." One senses that Paul would have found the liturgical formulas of the Apocalypse dangerously "enthusiastic."

John probably captures more clearly than Paul the spirit of Christ's own ministry, an enthusiastic spirit of joyous celebration, but in order to clarify that statement I must return to the Synoptic Gospels. In the following exposition I hope to clarify my reasons for choosing the wedding imagery as the central imagery of this book. Also, I hope to show why, if this book has a "doctrine of God," it is of God as the wedding-maker.

Scholars tell us that in the parables of the unshrunk cloth, the new wine and the old wineskins, and the friends of the bridegroom (Mark 2:18-22= Luke 5:33-35= Matt. 9:14-17) Jesus was contrasting the joyous time of the announcement of the Kingdom—the new order which had broken in upon the world in his ministry—with the time which had preceded it. The comment added at the end of the Parable of the Bridegroom's Friends— "the time will come when the bridegroom will be taken away from them, and then they will go without food"—has probably been added by the early church. It was Jesus' intention when he spoke these parables to answer the complaint of his opponents that he and his disciples were not properly "religious" and earnest. It was not his intention to comment on the future, but only on the time of his ministry.

That time doubtless was a time of celebrative feasting. That is part of the reason why, in a time of great moral earnestness, Jesus caused such an affront, why he was called "a glutton and a wine-bibber" (Luke 7:35ff.). His attendance at the feast in Levi's house (Luke 5:29ff.) is not intended by Luke to depict an isolated event. Wherever Jesus went, there was feasting and celebration, as befitted his proclamation of the coming of the Kingdom. That is why he himself used the imagery of a wedding party. His disciples, he said, knew the joy that the friends of a bridegroom know at a marriage: they had been called to be involved in a celebrative, festal event. A radically new time had come—a new order had broken in upon the world. It was as different from the preceding order as new wine is from old, as unshrunk cloth is from often-washed cloth. The new wine was no longer to be seen as entirely future, reserved for the Last Days. The Last Days had begun!

Nevertheless, just as Jesus differed from the earnest Pharisees, so he differed from the Zealots and other enthusiasts of his day: he affirmed the "not yet" character of the Kingdom as well as the "already." "Happy are you who hunger now," he preached, "for you shall be filled" (Luke 6:21). The uniqueness of the formula lies in the juxtaposition not only of present hunger with present happiness—which, by itself, might amount to a kind of spiritualizing—but in the juxtaposition of the two (present hunger *and* happiness) with future filling. God, he was saying, was acting concretely as well as spiritually to bring about an order in which the hungry will be filled (cf. Luke 1:53). That time has not yet come, but it is coming, he was saying.

When Jesus fed the five thousand (Matt. 14:13-21 = Luke 10:12-17 = Mark 6:30-44 = John 6:1-13ff.), in what has been described as "an enacted parable," he was once again likening God's future salvation to the feasting of God's people—and inviting a comparison to God's feeding of Israel in the wilderness. Had the Kingdom fully come, such a "preview" would have had no significance.

The present time, Jesus said, is—for those who can read the signs of the times—a time of fervent celebrative expectation. We are like servants waiting for our master to return from a wedding. He may come at any time. We should therefore be prepared (Luke 12:36-40). But notice! When the master returns *from* a wedding feast, at midnight, he tells his faithful servants to sit down and *he* makes a feast for *them*! That tells us something about the spirit in which we prepare. It need not be one of joyless earnestness. He who knows a celebration is coming will be celebrative, not dour, in awaiting its coming. (Or have you never seen a child's face as he wakes on his birthday morning? The party may not be till four o'clock, and the presents till five o'clock, but the joy is there with the dawn.)

We must recognize that the question of the relation between the present time and the future was one of the most difficult aspects of Jesus' teachings and ministry for people to accept. Jesus radically lessened the distance between the two. He didn't remove it, but he reduced the seeming opposition between the present time of expectation, and that future which was expected.

Much of our recognition of our foundation allegory's meaning (Matt. 25:1-13) rests upon whether we will appreciate how time is collapsed in the allegory. As I sought to bring out in my Forepiece, the crucial events take place long before night falls. The difference between the wise and the foolish young women lies in the ability of the former to read the signs of the times—to know that *this* is the end-time—and act eschatologically in the present. To wait till the announcement that "He has come" before acting is to guarantee that we will not get in to the wedding.

This is more than the trite counsel to "Be prepared" which our culture recommends. That counsel rests on other trite observations, like "You never know what'll happen" or "You never know when you might need one." Jesus was not teaching human folk-wisdom. He was announcing the Kingdom. The five wise young women were the ones who heard the announcement and took it seriously.

In the Parable of the Wedding Feast (Matt. 22:1-14 = Luke 14:16) Jesus says invitations to the feast (=God's Kingdom) are going out right now (in his calling people to discipleship). Now is the time to accept the invitation—even though the event to which the invitation is given is still around the corner (slightly!). One accepts the "invitation" by becoming a disciple. And note that a disciple is, once again, a member of a wedding-party!

Luke puts the parable in a redactional context which makes its significance clearer (Luke 14:15). Jesus, he says, was moved to tell the parable when a man at a feast he was attending misunderstood what he was teaching about the Kingdom. The man heard Jesus teaching about the Kingdom and assumed (a) it was very distant, and (b) that knowledge of its coming was an occasion for a pious response. So he said, "How happy are those who will eat bread in the Kingdom of God!" (On the face of it, that was an unexceptionable statement, quite an orthodox affirmation, as we saw above.) But the Kingdom Jesus announced was neither that distant nor did it require such a "spiritual" response. The Kingdom, Jesus was saying, is not that far different from life today. God is working in the midst of present events to establish his new order, which he will complete when the time has come. By our actual, lived responses to his leading we are either part of the making of his Kingdom—part of "the God-movement," Clarence Jordan would have said—or part of its opposition. Just as the opposition does not wait till Armageddon to reveal itself, so the supporting team does not.

"Eschatology" is taking place right now. God's Kingdom is at this very moment locked in combat with the empire of evil, and God is seeking to liberate his people from evil's grip (see Mark 3:22-27, Luke 11:20, etc.). He calls people to become members of his Kingdom-community. When they accept the invitation they enter upon a qualitatively different life. They are children of a radically new age (see Matt. 11:11).

The radical otherness of it can be reduced. Perhaps it always will be—the church seems unable to bear too much realized eschatology. It prefers to retreat into otherworldliness. It finds God's remoteness—where he can be objectified—more comfortable than his presence.

But this was not Jesus' style, nor was it his message. It was not the life he offered his disciples. Joachim Jeremias has argued that the central idea of the Lord's Prayer ought to be translated "Give us this day our bread for the morrow"—and that the "bread" is salvation. According to this way of thinking, Jesus was thus instructing his disciples to use a terribly bold petition in their daily prayer: "Give us today the salvation you promised for tomorrow." But it is bold only if we are Thomases, who think that even after knowing Jesus, we do not yet know the way to God, or Philips, who do not recognize that the life we have with Jesus is already eschatological life (see John 14:8-11).

But if we have truly heard the kerygma, then we recognize that the boldness is not our own but God's: he wants to give us our "bread for the morrow" today. Not only John, but also Paul (see especially II Cor. 6:2), the letter to the Hebrews (ch. 4), and the Synoptic Gospels affirm this.

There may be arguments about the relative degree of "future" and "realized" eschatology in various New Testament strata, but on one thing there can be no argument: the scandal of the kerygma lay in Jesus' proclamation that the future had been brought drastically closer to the present, the divine into immeasurably more intimate relationship with the human, and the sacred into much greater oneness with the secular.

All this from God, the wedding-maker, the giver of feasts, the one whose highest hope for all creation is "that they'll really have a ball."

> Ho, every one who thirsts,
> come to the waters;
> and he who has no money,
> come, buy and eat!
> Come, buy wine and milk
> without money and without price. . . .
> Hearken diligently to me, and eat what is good,
> and delight yourselves in fatness. . . .
> And I will make with you an everlasting covenant . . . (Isa.
> 55:1-3).

2: ON GETTING INVITATIONS TO FUTURE EVENTS

AS SHE APPROACHED THE GRAY BORDER BETWEEN "YOUNG adulthood" and "the middle years," Janet Peterson Comstock still kept the figure that she had had as a senior at Smith. Those who jested that she looked like "a Geritol ad" were not all wrong, for, deep down, she admired "people who took care of themselves." She watched the cholesterol level in her husband Gerald's diet, and it was a source of pride to her, as she watched her children go off to school in the morning, that they had had a high-protein breakfast, that her kids didn't eat "junk foods."

She needed that peace of mind, for, as soon as the kids were off in the morning, she had a lot of things to do. She did secretarial work for the United Nations Association and she was involved in a telephone campaign for Common Cause at the moment, trying to get people to support legislation to establish a primary election process in the state. At noon she would have to be off to the Episcopal Church for the Church Women United luncheon to hear a speaker from the Nader organization telling about the latest developments in the fight to restrict nuclear power plant development in the area. It took a lot of concentration, and it helped to know that she and her family were well-nourished and in good health.

Janet had succeeded as a Peace Corps volunteer in Nigeria in the early '60s where others had failed, largely, she believed, because she took such precautions with her health. She had served her two years with distinction, having not only taught general science fairly commendably— "despite that archaic British system of education"—but also established the school's first lab.

It was a bit difficult finding her "niche" when she returned home, but she had never really had any doubt but that eventually she would. ("The Petersons always find their place," she told Gerald.) Until his retirement two years ago, her father had been

15

chairman of the humanities department at a small liberal arts college in upstate New York, and he was one of the leading citizens of the Four County Area—trustee of the summer arts festival, head of the United Way, moderator of the Congregational Church, you name it.

Her mother had set a good example for Janet, too. Though not terribly involved publicly (she sometimes wondered "whether I've made the best possible use of my college education"), she was a real regular citizen—a member of the Faculty Dames, superintendent of the Sunday School Junior Department, a first-class housekeeper and manager, and a sympathetic and efficient mother to four children, all of whom—thanks in part to Mom, Janet thought—had done pretty well for themselves.

She turned on the dishwasher, hung up her apron, and went over to her desk. It was going to be another good day. Actually every day was. Life was exciting. She flipped on the FM radio and tuned in to the local classical music station to get some peaceful background music for checking through address lists. It was a Bach chorale. She sat down and began to work.

All of a sudden the music stopped and the announcer's voice came on—a strange voice. Before he had spoken a sentence—about some revival meeting—she recognized what was the matter. She had gotten that new "Christian family station" by mistake. Irritated, she stood up to correct the dial, but she bumped the flower vase on the way, spilling water all over some books. She ran into the kitchen to get some Bounty towels.

The announcer introduced the preacher of the morning. He had a nasal twang. "It will be as in the days of Noah," he said. "A lot of folks are going to be mighty surprised when they see the Son of Man come in his glory with the holy angels, and they won't be ready to join the Lord in the clouds—"

She turned the radio off, terribly upset. "Why do those people keep propagating those out-of-date fundamentalist doctrines!" she said out loud. She saw the photograph of her father on the shelf. She remembered how he used to talk about "those holy rollers down at the gospel hall."

He was right. How grateful she was that she had been raised with a modern religion, a faith for today. Long before it was fashionable, Dad had been a liberal. He was a great devotee of

Fosdick, Hocking, and William James. "Eschatology and apocalyptic," he used to tell his family, "are children's clothes that a religion has to shuck before it can become adult. They are children's dreams that the powerless must invent to console themselves. But in modern society the citizens have the power, and we can work for a better world here, not just 'pie-in-the-sky-when-you-die'."

And that, Janet recognized, was what she was trying to do. She finished mopping up the water, turned the radio to the correct station, and went back to her address lists. But before she got far, she made an entry in her diary: "Tuesday, January 17. The Kingdom of God is not in the clouds. It's here, in the United Nations, in Common Cause, and in the Sierra Club, AND I'M WORKING FOR IT!"

*   *   *

The people in the adjacent booth at the coffee shop were surprised to hear what they called "words of testimony" coming from such a disheveled person, wearing dirty jeans, her hair looking as if it hadn't been brushed in a week, a cigarette going constantly back and forth to her mouth. But they distinctly heard her say to her "equally radical hippie-type companions," "That's the hope Jesus awakens in me, and that's why I need that word of resurrection—in order to keep on going. Without that all my effort would seem futile."

Her "hippie" friends would have been equally surprised to hear "words of testimony" coming from Elise, had they not heard them often before. They remembered when they hadn't heard them from her. They'd been with her a long time—through the sit-ins of the Vietnam era, the street theater, the women's collective. Wherever they'd been, Elise had been. And in the midst of it she'd gotten her Christianity back.

In many ways she was more radical than they. Some of them got the distinct impression she admired the Weather Underground. That's what freaked them out—you could expect Christian preaching from types like those in the next booth (who probably sported a "Honk if you love Jesus" sign on their car bumper), but not from radical counter-culture types like Elise.

The daughter of a low-ranking U.A.W. official, Elise Sullivan was born in 1950 in Youngstown, Ohio, where her family, living in a ticky-tacky suburb on the instalment plan and Fulton Sheen's TV preaching, spent the '50s and '60s trying to get solidly into the middle class. They were sanguine about America ("land of opportunity")—and about the economic system ("partnership between labor and management, beyond barren ideology").

Elise absorbed their ideology with her mother's milk, and if she had any uncertainty about it, it was just a nagging question why you had to be so darned earnest about becoming what the ideology said you already were.

It wasn't till she got to Bowling Green that she met anybody who questioned the system, and most of them only mildly. She joined a sorority, majored in sociology, attended the Newman Club, and, sexually, graduated from holding hands to heavy petting. In her sophomore year she got pinned to a downy-faced, but serious-looking fraternity "man" from Shaker Heights named George McKenna. It was a source of pride to her that she had out-upward-mobilitied her family. ("Wow! Won't Dad be impressed if I marry someone from Shaker Heights!")

When she was 18 years old, a Catholic who had made it even farther than Shaker Heights—to the U.S. Senate—got her to start questioning "the system." As Eugene McCarthy rode his white horse through a losing campaign, Elise responded with all her awakening being, first with idealism and expectation, and then, when he lost, with a sense of treason.

At the same time in her class readings she discovered Herbert Marcuse and C. Wright Mills. For the first time, she became a self-motivated student, reading till the early morning hours, constantly arguing with fellow students about whether there was a "power elite" and the like, and spending evenings and Saturdays trying to recruit voters.

George didn't go for it much—he didn't think a woman should get involved in politics—and their relationship came apart. Elise hardly noticed. For a time she had an affair with a Black athlete from Hough. "From Shaker Heights to Hough in one semester! How's *that* for social mobility?" she mused, delighted with her sense of irony. Her sorority sisters thought it was the wrong direction to be mobile and Elise found herself in need of housing.

She moved into a newly-formed women's collective, taught
sociology in the free college they ran that summer, and was
instrumental in starting a food co-op in the poor section of town.
She didn't go home during vacations, except for a few days at
Christmas. ("The UAW used to be a union when Walter Reuther
was around," she told her father then, "but now it's just the other
side of the coin of management, part of the capitalist system.")

Later, as she saw the Movement fall apart and many of her best
friends cop out and buy into the system, Elise's cynicism peaked.
But then it began to decrease, as she grew in realism and patience.
Upon graduation she decided to teach high school and to study
law at night. She became active in NOW. On a fluke, one empty
weekend, she attended a Newman Club conference—she had
been attracted by a poster which spoke of "Christian Feminism."
Mary Daly was the speaker. She turned Elise on. From that she
was led to read Rosemary Reuther, and, learning of a progressive
Catholic community a few miles from her home, she started
attending their liturgy. A number of members of the community
called themselves "Christians for Socialism."

In a short time she recovered her Christian faith—in fact, she
had never really rejected it. But it was a different faith from the one
in which she had been brought up. When she recited the Mag-
nificat now, it no longer seemed just "spiritual" to her. It was a
political statement. As she was telling her friends in the coffee
shop that night, "The coming of Jesus means God has decisively
intervened in human history on behalf of the poor, to work toward
the establishment of a classless society where there will be justice.
The resurrection means that the future is open to human creativity, to our shaping of a new order."

Elise hoped, after getting her law degree, to join a poverty law
center.

*   *   *

Meeting Jeanne Anne Singer was enough to make you love her.
People had felt that way about her when she worked as a waitress
at the Burger Supreme in Bethesda during high school, and they
felt that way about her when they met her in the Towson elemen-
tary school now. She was the kind of person who made you glad

to be part of the human race—golden hair, absolutely clear complexion, tidy, neat figure (though she had been putting on some weight lately), hardly any make-up, a smile on her face.

It was true Jeanne Anne didn't have many friends—or, perhaps, any, if you define that word narrowly—but she was never lonely and never really alone. She was always in the middle of "groups of nice people doing fun things." And, even if she was from time to time alone, she wasn't really alone, because—as she told her landlady—"You're never alone if you have Jesus." The landlady, a Jehovah's Witness, merely said, "Hmphh." Jeanne Anne was the first tenant she had not been able to out-talk, and she'd lost all hope of getting her to become a Witness. Jeanne Anne *had* all her answers already, and she could quote you—wrongly, her landlady believed—chapter and verse.

Jeanne Anne hadn't just come to this belief recently, the way some people in the charismatic fellowship she attended had. She'd been in Youth for Christ in high school, and her family attended an evangelical United Presbyterian Church ("Yes, there *are* a few of those, though most United Presbyterian churches have not got Bible believing pastors"). In teachers' college she had been in Intervarsity. So she had had good Bible teaching right along. It was just the second baptism which she hadn't received earlier, and now that she had it—"Well, my heart just began to sing, that's what it did!"

She was accused by some of her secular colleagues at school of being "too good for God" (and, as she would be the first to affirm, she had never "cohabited with a man") and of being unconcerned about the matters of this world (it was true she didn't vote), but Jeanne Anne had her social ministry, one she felt the Lord had called her to, tutoring ghetto children. ("I may not be able to change the economic system or residential patterns in this city, but I can help some of these kids get ahead.") She was quite effective. The kids—particularly the younger ones—liked her immensely, and she had, as she said, "been able to lead some of them to the Lord" (which, she was sure, was much more to the point than a changed political or economic system, or even better grades).

In 1976 she did finally register to vote, however, because there was a referendum on ERA coming up, and she wanted "to cast my vote with the Bible." Of late she did that also on Saturday afternoons, picketing the medical center with the Right to Life committee.

If some detected a growing hardness in Jeanne Anne as she passed 30, it reflected her conviction ("from reading the signs of the times—wars and revolutions and violent insubordination and famines and pornography, the gay movement and false teaching and lack of faith") that the End was approaching. "When Jesus comes," she said, "I want to be ready." She wanted *the world* to be ready, but frankly, her hope for that had lessened of late. Her proper concern should be that Jesus would find her "fighting on the Lord's side."

* * *

"It's just too quaint down here to be true," Carol Miller wrote on the picture postcard she was sending her daughter Wendy from the motel in Tennessee, where she'd spent the night on her "tour of the Bible belt." "Every five miles you come up to a big cross with the words 'Get right with God' on it. I sure hope you're right with God! (And don't forget to take your pill!) We'll stop off at Hood on our way home. Will look forward to seeing you then."

She finished her coffee, took out her compact, and checked her face. She'd need to get her hair done when they got to Nashville— the grey roots were showing again. She gave a deep sigh, closed the compact, put away her pen, and got up from the table. When she got to their room, Phil was still on the phone to New York. His papers were spread out on the bed. From the conversation she could tell he was on that shareholder disclosure action again. The company was being challenged for not providing equal pay for Blacks in South Africa and now, it seemed, one of the church groups was challenging them to disclose their political contributions in El Salvador as well. What a bother!

Carol listened to Phil search for words and then blurt them out: "Tell them management has initiated—a long-range study—of the ethical principles determining the corporation's involvement in developing nations. Cable Johannesburg—tell them to make a large contribution to—some mission school. And get press coverage!"

Carol could remember the times Phil's attitude was less cynical, when he really seemed to believe in the company and what they were doing. Ever since he became a vice-president it had seemed different. He didn't share his dreams with her the way he once did. Maybe he didn't dream anymore.

She didn't. Life seemed not a matter for dreaming but one of trying to keep from being bored. There was a time when reading a sexy novel was all she needed, and then a time when treating their supper guests to a little cocaine provided a little excitement. It was all very chic. But that hadn't lasted either. When she started reading about "bisexual chic," she thought maybe a relationship with another woman might be the answer. She had tried that, too, with an *au pair* girl they'd had on Fire Island, but it had never really seemed to be her thing.

Nowadays, it was mostly travel—South America, the Soviet Union, the Caribbean every winter, and occasional short trips with Phil around the country, which he could charge to his expense account, since the corporation had offices just about everywhere.

Sometimes she envied her eldest daughter Becky, living with some guy whose last name Carol didn't even know, in Berkeley. Becky didn't have any money—and that would be hard—but she didn't seem bored.

Carol took her morning Valium. She flipped through the pages of *Viva*, as she waited for Phil to get off the phone. How she hated the smell of his cigars! But they were the less bother. She was far more concerned about his need, of late, to take a shot from his flask before they set off every morning. The way he drove, they sometimes nearly had accidents.

"The world" didn't know Phil Miller the way she did. He was always "Mr. Clean, Vice-President for Social Responsibility," Treasurer of the county Republican organization, "valued counselor" of the Secretary of Commerce, trustee of Holy Cross.

She'd been hard-pressed to explain to her Lutheran parents why she'd chosen to marry a Catholic, and it had been hard for her to sign the agreement when they got married that the kids would be raised Catholics, but religion didn't seem that important. All the kids had left the church anyway, so what difference did it make? Phil himself rarely went to church anymore. Ever since they'd started using birth control he'd felt hypocritical about going to mass, he said. The parish priest still cited him as "a fine example of the apostolate in the business community," and, as he was willing to serve on the fund-raising committee for the diocesan high school, no one raised any questions about his personal religious habits.

Religion should be to help you, Carol thought, to help you in this life. She doubted that there was any other. "But if Mommy and Daddy were right, and there is an after-life," she mused, "I'm quite sure I'm right with God." She chuckled.

*   *   *

In the first chapter of this book, I tried to describe how the Bible portrays God as a wedding-maker, a giver of feasts, one who wishes the creation to share his joy. Inseparable from that portrayal is a definite eschatology, with present and future dimensions, a certain conception of history which sees the present time as a time in via, a time into which a new time is breaking, a time in which a new order is being established.

I tried to show how Jesus identified that order as the Kingdom of God and said that, in his ministry and that of his apostles, the invitation was going out to become part of that new order, to become part of God's future.

At the end of the chapter, I suggested that many of the people of his time rejected Jesus' message because they found it too threatening to believe that God's future began today. For them it was more comfortable to keep separate the future and the past, the secular and the sacred. The proper response at this time, to the sacred and to the eschaton, was a "spiritual" response, they felt.

The desire to keep God and his Kingdom remote, to objectify them as somewhere "out there," to reduce their immediacy is not characteristic of Jesus' time alone. It belongs to all times and places. Similarly the attitude of the Zealots of Jesus' day—a too ready identification of proximate causes with ultimate goals, a subordination of divine eschatology to human projects and of divine wisdom to human party platforms—is a temptation in all ages. Our own age is not immune to either temptation.

In the current debate and dialogue between "conservatives," "liberals," and "radicals," between "social actionists" and "seekers of the transcendent," the ancient battle is re-joined. Yet it can be just a cynical way of dismissing that battle to say, "We've had all that before." To accept that "above-the-noise-of-battle" posture is to assert, ultimately, the futility of history, to say that nothing really has happened, that humankind just repeats the same errors over and over again, that the history of the church is just a pendulum motion from one extreme to another, generation after generation, "a tale told by an idiot, full of sound and fury, signifying nothing." ("There's nothing new under the sun.")

I take the current theological debate with the utmost seriousness, both as signifying historical direction and movement, and as having crucial consequences for the history of God's Kingdom. I do not believe it is a matter of indifference—like the debates over how many angels can dance on the head of a pin*—whether one takes an "evangelical" or a "conciliar" or a "fundamentalist" position, whether one separates this world and God's Kingdom into two different realms or holds them together, whether one makes a response to the Kingdom by withdrawal or by engagement, whether one seeks God in "the beyond" or in the present. I do not believe it is of indifference either to the progress of the Kingdom or to the ultimate well-being of Christ's would-be disciple. If, as the centurion recognized, we are "set under authority" (Luke 7:8), then the response we make to that authority cannot be a matter of indifference or "religious preference." The song "I Cannot Come to the Wedding" is not just cute and contemporary—it concerns the rejection of discipleship. God, the wedding-maker, is calling us to the wedding. He is calling us to discipleship.

The English word *disciple* can best be understood correctly—not in the snide or nonchalant way in which it is used in everyday parlance ("He's a disciple of Ralph Nader")—by relating it to its cognate *discipline*. *Disciple* translates the Greek *mathetes*, which means "learner," and the type of learning intended is the committed, regular learning of one who studies, walks, and eats with a teacher (a Hebrew rabbi).

Each of the first three characters I sketched in the beginning of

---

*And scholars tell us that debate had the utmost significance, too, in its time, as telling whether divine being was material or not.

this chapter lived under a recognizable discipline, involving a definite life-style, a personal commitment to Christ, a conception of proper goals to be attained, and a sense of responsibility or accountability to God for their lives, as well as a sense of how crucial for their own fellowship with him was their faithfulness to him. (The last figure, Carol Miller, differed from these three in living an entirely anomic, undisciplined life, recognizing no authority beyond that of the self, no goal higher than that of "the kick.")

The three probably could not have spoken meaningfully to one another, however. It is not even certain that they would have accorded to each other the recognition "sister in Christ." It is far from my intention to say with these sketches, "That's how it is in the pluralistic church of today. Let us rejoice in our differences, for we complement one another." What goes by the name of "pluralism" can, sometimes, be a cop-out, a refusal to think out and critique the varying life-styles suggested to us in the course of seeking to work out our own discipline and life-style in response to the announcement of the Kingdom.

I do not intend to leave the matter by "affirming pluralism." It will be my endeavor in the remainder of this book to try to ascertain what God is saying to us about a Christian life-style for this time in history. My intention in this chapter is only to introduce the question of discipleship and its contemporary meaning.

I would like to say three things before concluding that introduction. First, Janet Comstock, Elise Sullivan, and Jeanne Anne Singer each had an understanding of the Kingdom of God. For Janet it was a more perfect world and it would come about through the gradual, evolutionary working of God's Spirit in humankind. For Elise it was a radically different world (still, however, another version of *this* world), and it would come about through a process of liberation of the oppressed and the unmasking of the present powers-that-be. For Jeanne Anne the Kingdom of God was another world entirely, and she could live in it by life in the Spirit now while anticipating its coming, at which time she could anticipate a form of existence without analogy in the present.

Second, the life-style each adopted was related to and determined by a distinct conception of the Kingdom. For Janet what was required was long, steady, earnest work, stalwartness of purpose, and a Puritan ethic. Elise, on the other hand, rejected any association between the Puritan ethic ("the class ethic of bourgeois society") and the values of the Kingdom ("It's not thrift, earnestness, and moderation we're called to, but justice, love, and solidarity"). Jeanne Anne, on the other hand, could remain unconcerned, to some extent, with what happened in this world: her proper endeavor, she believed, was to keep herself beyond reproach, to seek to get others to commit themselves to her Jesus, and to make a public witness against sin. The Bible, she believed, depicted a world which was ideal, and today's world would be secure if it went "back to the Bible."

Finally, each of them had developed or received a hermeneutic, a principle of interpretation of the scriptures. For Jeanne Anne it was a kind of "Biblical literalism." Elise referred to hers as "Biblical radicalism—going back to the root meanings of scripture." Janet employed a kind of "cultural hermeneutic," in which "dated" ideas are interpreted in the light of humanity's most highly developed ideals. Only Janet would have admitted she was looking at the Bible through a filter of extra-Biblical ideas, yet Elise's Marxism and Jeanne Anne's modern individualism and mechanistic world-view served the same role.

In the course of this book I, too, will develop a hermeneutic. Such a task cannot be avoided, for we do not have immediate access to the world—or worlds—of the scriptures. The scriptures were written for people who lived in definite places and at particular times and, often, in highly specific contexts. By saying they were inspired writings, the church was saying they were the right message for the right people at the right time.

We are not those for whom the scriptures were first written. We live in different places, and in different times. Our specific contexts may, at most, be comparable to those in which the original audiences lived. Just as the word of God had to be encoded in a form appropriate to the first hearers, so it must be encoded again now in a form which will enable new receptors to hear and comprehend it.

In the process of that encoding a hermeneutic is involved. It will either be explicit or else it will be implicit and unexamined. The question is not whether to have a hermeneutic, but what kind to have, whether it will be examined or unexamined, and—the crucial question—whether it will be a medium to open the ears of contemporary people so that they may hear what God is saying to us through the scriptures.

In the course of working out a hermeneutic, I will also be developing an understanding of the central question of the Kingdom of God, as well as of a life-style appropriate to it. As I do this a conception of evangelism will emerge. I cannot pretend that it will "spring full-blown" from the scriptures themselves. It will be a product of my perceptions, in the Spirit, of what God is saying to us in our times, and my understanding, in prayer—*fides quarens intellectum*—of the meaning of the word.

In his great wisdom God does not make it easier than this for us. The tasks he gives his church, in every age, are to answer the questions which he asks it *in that age* (not just "in general"), and to give account to the people among whom it lives of "the hope that is in you" (I Pet. 3:15).

The answers I saw Janet, Elise, and Jeanne Anne giving—in their words and in their life-styles—reflect not only some of the understandings of scripture I find today, but also some of the questions I hear the church being asked today: about the meaning of life, about ultimate purpose, about the transcendent, about the efforts of people to shape a better human order, about the struggles of the poor, about human dignity, about the responsible society, about Jesus and spirituality, about God and change and constancy, about morality and human community.

I must now begin to answer some of those questions myself.

3: ON WAITING, or THE DIFFERENCE BETWEEN WISDOM AND FOLLY

> Faith is always imperiled on the one side by despair, and on the other side by optimism. Of these two enemies of faith, optimism is the more .dangerous.
> —Reinhold Niebuhr, *Beyond Tragedy*

> For I heard a cry as of a woman in travail, anguish as of one bringing forth her first child, the cry of the daughter of Zion gasping for breath, stretching out her hands, "Woe is me! I am fainting before murderers!"
> —Jeremiah 4:31

WHAT DO THE YOUNG WOMEN DO AT NIGHT? THEY WAIT. What is it that they wait for? The marriage supper. For that they wait.

Five of them are foolish, and five of them are wise.

*   *   *

One of our less sung Advent hymns is Bowring's "Watchman, Tell Us of the Night." It is one of the hymns which the American composer Charles Ives frequently weaves into his symphonic music. I believe I had sung "Watchman" fewer than three times in my life before I discovered Ives. Ives opened the hymn up to me. The questions it asked about the future were questions Ives asked, through using it, of America's future.

I had thought "Watchman" dealt with the expectation of the first coming of Christ, that it was an application of a vision of Isaiah (21:11f.) to Christ's birth.

Ives saw in "Watchman" (a hymn sung constantly in his time as an Advent hymn or a hymn about missionary work) a kind of key to America's self-understanding in history. Juxtaposing it with "Columbia, the Gem of the Ocean" and other national and martial music, Ives (a Congregational and Presbyterian organist) heard this hymn express America's attitude toward the future:

> Watchman, tell us of the night,
> What its signs of promise are.

To late 19th and early 20th century America the future was a time of promise—but a promise not yet fully revealed. There was reason to look to the future with hope, but that looking was done in the midst of night, and what was seen was not yet daylight, but a star:

> Traveler, o'er yon mountain's height,
> See that glory-beaming star.
> Watchman, does its beauteous ray,
> Aught of joy or hope foretell?
> Traveler, yes, it brings the day,
> Promised day of Israel.

In keeping with a symbolism already commonly accepted, American congregations—and certainly the establishment ones for which Ives played—understood Israel to symbolize America ("a Christian nation"). Just as the star of the magi did not light Israel alone, but the nations, so the new star of technological and commercial progress and liberal democracy would be "a light to the nations."

> Watchman, will its beams alone
> Gild the spot that gave them birth?
> Traveler, ages are its own;
> See, it bursts o'er all the earth.

Through both the religious and the secular mission of America (not two separate things to American Christians) the world was in the process of being saved:

> For the morning seems to dawn.
> Traveler, darkness takes its flight.
> Doubt and terror are withdrawn.

What John Bowring intended when, in England in 1825, he wrote "Watchman" was somewhat less. His first reference for the

hymn was to the England of his day, and the hymn expressed his
hope that the reform movement there would undo the damage of
the early industrial revolution and bring a more humane Britain
into being. As the century grew older and the hymn emigrated to
America, the capacity of congregations to relate its words to
openly expressed hopes grew. In Ives' Connecticut and New York
Protestantism in the early 20th century it would not have seemed
strange to sing "Columbia, the Gem" and "Watchman" with the
same spirit. Theology even seemed to legitimate it, for American
post-millennialism—the belief that Christ's Kingdom was finally
being revealed in America (and perhaps in Western Europe)—
was in its heyday.

It was a daring idea. Jonathan Edwards, in 1739, had been the
first to suggest that, through the American Second Great Awakening, Christ's Kingdom might be dawning. ("Perhaps never were
more of the prelibations of heaven's glory given upon earth.")
"There are many things," Edwards wrote, "that make it probable
that this work will begin in America."[1]

Samuel Harris went much farther by 1870, when he published
a series of lectures on *The Kingdom of Christ on Earth*:

> God has always acted by chosen peoples. To the English-speaking
> people more than to any other the world is now indebted for the
> propagation of Christian ideas and Christian civilization. It is a re-
> markable fact in this day that the thinking of the world is done by the
> Christian nations; that the enterprise and energy of the world are
> mainly theirs. They alone are colonizing, and by their commerce and
> enterprise pushing their influence throughout the world. So also the
> political condition of the Protestant nations is that of constitutional
> government, popular education, and a growing regard for the rights
> and welfare of the people.
>
> These are conditions more favorable to the advancement of Christ's
> kingdom than have ever before existed. And in view of both the
> thinking and the practical life and character of the age, I believe that
> no preceding age has presented conditions so favorable to the
> advancement of Christ's kingdom and so encouraging to faithful
> Christian effort.[2]

Secretary Clark of the American Board of Commissioners for
Foreign Missions expressed it popularly when he spoke of America's "special trust within the economy of Divine Providence":

> There was to be developed in this land, thus prepared of God, a chosen people, a peculiar nation, with a growth in numbers and power unrivaled in the annals of time. Through a baptism of fire and blood it was to purge itself of the last remnant of the old-time civilization, and then press on to a career of national prosperity that should be at once the despair and the wonder of the civilized world, which all men, of whatever land or race, should see and feel to be due to the freedom of a life begotten and energized by the gospel of Christ.[3]

This was not just rhetoric. Clark believed America's qualifications for a special role in God's work could be empirically examined. It was obvious, Clark believed, as he surveyed the American scene, that America was worthy of the trust. Anyone could see

> an advance in public morals, in Christian activities of all kinds, in keeping with the growth of the church and of our educational institutions. The very atmosphere is charged with moral and religious ideas; the common sense of the average American represents an amount of knowledge and moral perception quite unknown to the average man of any other age or country; it is so far Christianized that thousands of men and women outside the pale of any existing church are an honor to the institutions amid which they live.[4]

A review committee of the Board, that same year, seconded Clark's understanding of America's mission:

> Our Christian institutions are to be reproduced in other lands. The eyes of the world are upon us. What an impressive thought that America is expected to set the fashion for the world in the transcendent business of building a Christian civilization![5]

The future was looked toward, in late 19th and early 20th century America, with great expectation. The literature of the day contains countless references to "the darkness' and "the clouds" dispersing, to "the new day" dawning, to "curtains" being opened—so many images of light triumphing over darkness. This way of thinking was common to the leading religious and secular thinkers of the day.

If we were to place the people of that day on a time-line according to where they perceived themselves to be, it would be at dawn. As another hymn of the day expressed it:

For the darkness shall turn to dawning
  And the dawning to noon-day bright,
And Christ's great kingdom shall come on earth,
  The kingdom of love and light.

*   *   *

It is at night that the young women wait. Five of them are foolish,
and five of them are wise.

*   *   *

In 1974 a thinker in America who directed himself toward the task
of "inquiring into the human prospect" could write:

> There is a question in the air, more sensed than seen, like the
> invisible approach of a distant storm, a question that I would hesitate
> to ask aloud did I not believe it existed unvoiced in the minds of
> many: "Is there hope for man?"
>
> In another era such a question might have raised thoughts of man's
> ultimate salvation or damnation. But today the brooding doubts that
> it arouses have to do with life on earth, now, and in the relatively few
> generations that constitute the limit of our capacity to imagine the
> future. For the question asks whether we can imagine that future
> other than as a continuation of the darkness, cruelty, and disorder of
> the past; worse, whether we do not foresee in the human prospect a
> deterioration of things, even an impending catastrophe of fearful
> dimensions.[6]

"The spirit quails and the will falters," Robert Heilbroner wrote.
"We find ourselves pressed to the very limit of our personal
capacities."[7]

A more radical change of mood in America from Ives' time one
can hardly imagine. It is no longer at dawn that Heilbroner stands,
but at the proverbial "eleventh hour"—without having passed
through the fullness of the day. His main question is not even the
one many doom-sayers ask, "Can we survive?" It is more than
that. He asks, "Do we have the will to survive?" For to Heilbroner
it is not just that the problems are immense but that, without the
will to solve them, no problems can be solved.

To solve the problems before us as a civilization, we will need to
make sacrifices, we will need to change our life-styles, our fundamental assumptions. Heilbroner doubts, however, whether we

have the will to change. There is ample evidence, he believes, that knowledge of the threats to our existence from environmental degradation and from unequal justice between nations, to take two examples, has not moved us to change. Like the cigarette smoker who knows the connection between smoking and lung cancer, we continue smoking, we continue to use limited resources at a suicidal rate, we continue to industrialize, we continue without question to seek economic growth.

Heilbroner writes:

> Will mankind survive? Who knows? The question I want to put is more searching. Who cares? It is clear that most of us today do not care—or at least do not care enough.
>
> If mankind is to rescue life, it must first preserve the very will to live, and thereby rescue the future from the angry condemnation of the present.[8]

What Heilbroner sees ahead is not, we must be clear, doomsday, but a "death sentence." There is a chance, he says, just a chance, of moving beyond doomsday. The death sentence is better viewed, he says, as "a contingent life sentence—one that will permit the continuance of human society, but only on a basis very different from that of the present, and probably only after much suffering during the period of transition."[9]

*   *   *

What do the young women do at night? They wait. Five of them are foolish and five are wise.

*   *   *

What does it mean for us to live in this time? According to the America of Charles Ives, it is to wait for the coming of the Kingdom of God on earth. According to the America of Robert Heilbroner—or at least an increasingly large part of its intellectual elite, as of the European intelligentsia—it is also to wait, but for a secular eschatology. According to our foundation allegory, as well, the meaning of these times is to be found in waiting, but for what? For weal, or for woe? For judgment, or for salvation?

"Read the signs of the times," Jesus said (Luke 12:54-13:5). In them you can see how God's eschatological action has already begun. "Do you mean that we should look for religious events?" we ask. "No, quite secular ones," he replies—the murder of some Galileans by Pilate, the death of 18 people when a tower fell (Luke 13:1-5)—it is by such events that we can read the meaning of the times. In them God is giving us signs. He is warning us: "If you do not repent, you will die as they did." The time of judgment has come. The present time is therefore to be understood as a time to act decisively.

> Why do you not judge for yourselves the right thing to do? If someone brings a lawsuit against you and takes you to court, do your best to settle the dispute with him before you get to court. If you don't, he will drag you before the judge, who will hand you over to the police, and you will be put in jail (Luke 12:57-58, TEV).

The situation is critical. Jesus almost sounds like John the Baptist:

> The ax is ready to cut down the trees at their roots; every tree that does not bear good fruit will be cut down and thrown into the fire (Luke 3:9, TEV).

But then Luke affixes a parable which again shows how we are wrong whenever we see too much similarity between John and Jesus (on that point see Matt. 11:11):

> Then Jesus told them this parable: "There once was a man who had a fig tree growing in his vineyard. He went looking for figs on it but found none. So he said to his gardener, 'Look, for three years I have been coming here looking for figs on this fig tree and I haven't found any. Cut it down! Why should it go on using up the soil?' But the gardener answered, 'Leave it alone, sir, just this one year; I will dig a trench around it and put in some fertilizer. Then if the tree bears figs next year, so much the better; if not, then you can have it cut down' " (Luke 13:6-9, TEV).

This is a time, Jesus is saying, for fruitbearing. God is gracious. He has suspended his judgment. He is patient. That does not give us reason to be Pollyannas. The situation is no less critical for all God's patience, but God's patience shows us that the proper response to the crisis (in the sense of the Greek *krisis,* a judgment we ourselves pass on our destiny) is neither suicidal indifference (in its secular or Pentecostal forms) nor mindless panic, but fruitbearing. To use our earlier imagery again, as we wait for the Bridegroom's coming, we are to procure oil—to perform good works. This is the difference between the wise young women and the foolish ones—the wise ones get more oil. Their salvation, and the rejection of the others, is meant to be a warning for us. As Karl Donfried writes:

> Matthew composed the allegory of the virgins as a warning to his congregations not to be caught short for lack of sufficient oil, a symbol we understand from the context of Matthew's Gospel to mean "obedience to the will of the Father," specifically, the performance of καλὰ ἔργα [good works]. This exhortation is urgent not simply because the parousia was delayed, but especially because many were now becoming aware that they might well die before the end. Thus, simply because the end was not to come necessarily during their lifetime is not to excuse them from obedience and the bearing of fruit, since at the resurrection only those who have performed καλὰ ἔργα, only those who have sufficient "oil," will be accepted through the narrow door to the wedding feast.[10]

> Once this identification of "oil" with "good deeds" is clear it becomes most intelligible why the five wise virgins would not transfer their oil to the five foolish virgins: it is impossible to transfer "good deeds" or "obedience" from one person to the other and it is equally absurd to purchase good deeds from the dealers (25:9).[11]

We are all called to personal accountability. But we are called to be concerned not just for the salvation of our own souls but for the salvation of the commonwealth. As God said to the Jewish exiles in Babylon through Jeremiah: "Build houses and live in them; plant gardens and eat their produce. . . . Seek the welfare of the city where I have sent you into exile, and pray to the Lord on its behalf, *for in its welfare you will find your welfare*" (Jer. 29:7). And the converse is clearly implied: "Apart from its welfare you will find no personal welfare."

A modern-day Jeremiah, fourth grader Dorothy Frazier, who attends a Harlem school, understood the same lesson:

> The world is a ghetto, everybody is
>   doing their own thing.
> That's why there will always be war
>   and never peace.
> People are always envious of the other party.
> That's why there will never be peace.

There will always be junkies on the streets
   digging in the garbage cans.
Beating up priests 'cause you ain't got a dime;
They beat you up and kick you around.
It's like a ball of fire that won't flicker.

The World is a ghetto where I live,
   'Cause I live in Harlem
Where just because you're black or white
   don't mean you always gotta fight.
I see gangs on the street:
Black, white and Puerto Ricans
   fighting against each other.
They have chains, knives, guns.
Everybody gonna get hurt.

The world is a ghetto and I'm not kidding one little bit.
We better get on the go before we're
   gone, gone, gone with the wind.
The world is a ghetto.

                            Right On.
                            The End.

"We better get on the go before we're gone, gone, gone with the wind"—Heilbroner's conclusion, in essence. It's because "everybody is doing their own thing," Dorothy writes, that "the world is a ghetto." We've got to overcome our hyperindividualism and come to understand that it is in the welfare of the city of humankind that we will find our welfare.

Thomas Herzog, in a look backwards at the '60s, surmises that that was the fundamental issue beneath most of the surface issues:

> What was really at stake in the sixties was a new vision of human selfhood as corporate selfhood—not identification with success but solidarity with the poor.[12]

The psychologist Kenneth Clark, who teaches just a few blocks from Dorothy Frazier's school, believes the survival question comes down ultimately to a question of the ability of human beings to transcend self and empathize with others:

> The essential for hope is to be found in that critical minority of human beings who insist upon being unrealistic, who for some still unknown set of reasons continue to argue that human beings are somehow capable of the possibility of empathy, compassion and

sensitivity even as cruelty and hostility and insensitivity and rationalized dishonesty now dominate.[13]

To Heilbroner this ability to transcend one's self and one's group is one of the big question-marks over the future (cf. pp. 113f.). Clark is more optimistic about the possibility of such transcendence:

Fortunately for the future of a civilized society there exist these human beings who remain concerned about moral and ethical values and justice in the affairs of men.

They also seem to have the courage to risk the repeated expressions of their concern and thereby serve as a gnawing and irritating conscience to those who have attained success.

In the final analysis only these individuals provide the hope for that ultimate type of realism that is defined by the capacity of a society to survive rather than to be destroyed eventually on the altar of human barbarity.

For Christians, however, the ultimate weight in the balance is neither optimism nor despair, but prayer emerging from the heart of the action, such as the prayer used at the Fifth Assembly of the World Council of Churches in Nairobi:

Leader: The old order is passing away; your new order, Lord, has already begun and we are numbered among its signs. Through your Spirit in our hearts you have set us free and taught us to call you Father.

People: You have called us out of darkness into your marvelous light.

Leader: You have opened our eyes, given us hope that we shall live in the glorious liberty of the children of God. . . . But not alone, Lord; not while others remain poor, brokenhearted, imprisoned, blind and bruised. Yet . . .

People: You have called us out of darkness into your marvelous light.

Leader: So, Lord, we pray for our brothers and sisters, your family, oppressed by ignorance and poverty, caught in a web of injustice and apathy, cut off from one another by language, culture, colour, class and creed.

People: You have called them out of darkness into your marvelous light.

Leader: Through education may the powerless be led to self-discovery, the despised find new dignity, the dispossessed

> be enabled to claim their place in the community of free people.
>
> People: You have called them out of darkness into your marvelous light.
>
> Leader: Give to your Church a vision of the total liberation of humanity. Grant us the wisdom to hear the voice of the foolish of the world, the strength of the weak, that through those who are nothing we may understand the word of Christ.
>
> People: You are calling us out of darkness into your marvelous light.
>
> Leader: But we tend to love darkness rather than light. We shrink from the responsibility of freedom, the uncertainty of the desert, the conflict of the Cross. We keep turning back, preferring the security of slavery to the adventure of the promised land.
>
> People: Call us out of darkness into your marvelous light.
>
> Leader: Call us, Lord Jesus Christ, that we may follow. May we follow you not only as one who goes ahead but as one who journeys with us: Lord Jesus Christ, freeing us, uniting us! Let us be content to learn the meaning of your way as we walk in it.
>
> People: Amen.

To sum up, boundless optimism is no longer an option—nor would a proper reading of the signs of the times have made it seem so in Ives' day (Ives himself was skeptical of the "American dream"). But cynical pessimism is the ultimate attitude of selfish indifference. Is a chastened, tentative optimism, then, our alternative? It *is an* alternative—the "liberal" alternative, if you will. It is based, however, not on the way in which God's future breaks in upon our present but on the possibilities inherent in the present order and on human activism. It is Janet Peterson Comstock's way.

Many real-life Christians choose this alternative. It may seem more intelligible than the kind of waiting Jesus counseled: fruitful waiting, waiting for the Bridegroom, waiting for God's marriage feast.

But it may not assess deeply enough the radical fallenness of the present order. It may underestimate the depth of sin and the extent of the world's captivity to what Paul called "the principalities and powers." But many of those who speak of the principalities and powers use that as an excuse for non-involvement ("It's all out of our hands—all we can do is pray and trust God. This world is done for.")

Jan Lochman suggests an alternative "style" of "waiting" and a different way of understanding our activity:

> Human action is a secular activity and it's not the soteriological act, the process of self-redemption. In the biblical conception man is not burdened with a soteriological mission. He does not have to perform this "mission impossible." . . . (though) he is very much engaged in an effort to build a human secular city. In this he is asked to deploy all his energy because the new Jerusalem is not the tower of Babel. We need not climb into the heavens. We may remain . . . on the earth. The New Jerusalem is coming down.[14]

What, we will then need to ask, effectively distinguishes the New Jerusalem from Babel? What is the criterion for distinguishing between idolatrous human action and obedient human responsiveness?

Dale Brown agrees with Lochman that there is a difference. He uses temporal instead of spatial imagery to point to it:

> The vision of a God who pulls from ahead should free Christians from fatalism and utopianism and release them for permanent revolutionary activity.[15]

It should, but it may not. There are powerful forces working in the opposite direction. Even Peter, James, and John fell asleep.

What is the "permanent revolutionary activity" to which we are called? How do we work with God in the revolution he is bringing about?

Here we do not have time to resolve these questions, only to hint, as we have done, at some answers. Before answering more satisfactorily, we need to take a more serious, analytical look than we have taken at our times and what human action in such times cannot mean and what it may, by God's grace, mean.

4: AN EXCURSUS ON NIGHT

(1) The Darkness Deepens

> For the Lord of Hosts has a day
> Against all that is proud and lofty,
> Against all that is lifted up and high;
> Against all the cedars of Lebanon,
> Lofty and lifted up;
> And against all the oaks of Bashan;
> Against all the high mountains,
> And against all the lofty hills;
> Against every high tower
> And against every fortified wall;
> Against all the ships of Tarshish,
> And against all the beautiful craft.
> And the haughtiness of people shall be humbled,
> And the pride of humankind shall be brought low;
> And the Lord alone will be exalted in that day.
> And the idols shall utterly pass away.
> —Isaiah 2:12-18

AT A LUNCHEON IN 1975 CBS NEWS CORRESPONDENT DAN Rather was asked to speak about "Broadcasting's Role in America's Future." He did not feel qualified, he apologized, to make lofty pronouncements. "I'm no expert on anything." A TV news correspondent, he said, is "a generalist," someone who "knew a little bit about a lot of things." He explained that TV reporters have to cover a broad spectrum of stories and can only rarely do any follow-up or in-depth investigation.

He then went on, however, to speculate on what he thought must be "the best story of our time—the question of whether Western civilization, faced with a number of crises, is on the threshold of immense change. The basic principles of our government and civilization are challenged" by problems of food, energy, finance, and population. These aren't new problems, he said, "but they run deeper this time."[1]

*   *   *

In a dialogue sermon with the Vicar of Great St. Mary's in Cambridge, England, in 1975, Robin Day, the leading British TV interviewer, was asked, "What do you feel are the important things which ought to be said in British society at the present time?" Day replied:

> I think that everything else is subordinate in importance to the maintenance of parliamentary institutions and the rule of law. . . . Ten years ago, I wouldn't have bothered to mention this, because it would have been rather like talking about the need for fresh air. But . . . this is absolutely fundamental now.

He went on:

> There are many other detailed problems about the economy, social problems, etc., and we all have different views on how these should be solved. But the main thing we have to guard against is the collapse of our parliamentary system and the total disappearance of things which until very recently we have taken for granted.

He explained what he meant:

> This doesn't only mean parliamentary institutions and the rule of law, but also the climate of society which went with those institutions. One might perhaps term this "the reasonable society"—not a perfect society in which there was no injustice, but a society in which there was tolerance, a recognition that views should be changed by persuasion rather than force, and a reliance on the processes of reason rather than the processes of violence.

He concluded by confessing his fear that television itself contributed to the reduction of reason and the increase of force through the way in which it portrays events.[2]

It is at night that the young women wait. They wait at night.

*   *   *

A coincidence? Two unrelated prophecies? Two "nervous Nellies" 3,000 miles apart? Two newsmen surprised by deeper news than either ever expected to report about, each one in an uncanny way confirming the other's surprise and deepening each other's suspicion?

Their theme—"The Decline of the West"—is much older than Dan Rather and Robin Day. Oswald Spengler and Hermann Hesse, among others, taught many to intone that theme toward the beginning of this century. Despite that, we might be moved to react, the Western world is still the most powerful sector of the globe. It seems to have even survived the onslaught of OPEC rather well. Is there any reason to be as nervous as Rather and Day? Is there any *reason* to think of the present time as "nightfall"?

There certainly seems to be a growing consensus that the problems the world is confronting may, in one sense or another, be eschatological. If at one time the only people saying we were in ultimate crisis were fundamentalist apocalypticists speaking about the "end of the world" or Marxists speaking of "the death throes of capitalism as it confronts its own contradictions," nowadays they are joined by, to name just a few, anthropologists worried about whether the continuance of human society and culture is possible with the vast problems of scale in today's world; sociologists, concerned about the inherent dynamic of technology; social psychologists, writing about "future shock" and the sense of alienation which people in mass societies experience; and ecologists, speaking of the death of the environment.

Many rational, common people—middle-of-the-road liberals and moderates—are expressing these days the same question raised by Rather and Day, who are themselves not radicals: How long can this thing we call "Western civilization" go on? Fears about the imminent collapse of our civilization are widespread.

The explanations different people give for what they see as our society's imminent collapse are varied. Some say the basic reason is the problem of scale: the inability of society to cope—and cope quickly enough—with the sheer magnitude of its problems. It is a managerial problem, an organizational problem. They doubt that there is any fundamental problem in the structure of society, the mode of production, or in our social, political, or economic systems. Our society has just not planned far enough ahead, they say, for the changes which have come upon us, and there will be a time of "lag" till the systems of society "catch up"—if they shall—with the physical world. The best analogy for their model is the way in which the ticker gets behind on Wall Street on days of heavy trading.

That is not to belittle the gravity of their analysis, for many people who accept the present system are quite concerned about its survival. They wonder whether we will marshall the resources we need with sufficient alacrity to confront the vast crises of population growth, unemployment, hunger, and pollution. They don't doubt that liberal democracy and the free enterprise system can cope. They fear that a persistent unwillingness to do more than just contain immediate emergencies—an oil shortage, a Watts, a nuclear power plant accident, a recession, an ozone watch, a crime wave—will impair the ability of society to deal with the underlying problems which cause such outbreaks.

In addition, they worry about the rapidity of change in modern society and what that does to human psyches. They call for a balance between tradition and modernity, an intentional slowing down of the processes of change, an attempt to consolidate our position. They fear that, unless society stays on an even keel, extremists of the left—or right—may profit from its weakness to subvert its fundamental institutions.

The people we have been speaking of fear that a conspiracy might take over. As Henry Kissinger, certainly one of their number, told the press during one crisis, before departing on a round of "shuttle diplomacy," dislocations caused by OPEC policies might lead to human unrest which—in pre-Nazi Germany—could lead to impatience with democratic forms of government. Kissinger feared that under such circumstances a *coup d'état* might take place in the United States.

There are people in our society, however, who are convinced that—far from its being a question of a conspiracy taking over—a conspiracy already rules our society. Where the first group is wrong, they say, is in imagining that the institutions of our society are neutral, that it's simply a matter of who controls those institutions and how to make sure the control is democratic, that all sectors of the population have equal access to the use of power. This is a superficial analysis, they say. The existing institutions have been developed by those who have achieved power, they claim. The institutions exist in order to maintain the power of those same people and to continue to oppress those under them. They are not, in other words, neutral institutions. "Free enterprise" is an economic system geared to free the capitalist class from any effective challenge to its control. "Liberal political institutions" exist to mystify the populace into believing that it controls a social order to which it is, in fact, alien. "Equal opportunity" and the "equal protection of the law" are myths promulgated by those who deny others equal opportunity and protection and want the others, not themselves, to bear the sense of guilt for that, by being forced to think of themselves as "poor achievers" or "culturally deprived" rather than as exploited. Recessions are not just kinks in the economic system. They are contrived by those who control power to weaken the bargaining position and destroy the solidarity of the working class.

Such analysis is no longer the sole property of card-carrying Communists. Indeed, those who make it are just as likely to be damnatory of the Communist Party and of the Soviet Union as of the Republican Party and the United States of America. As just one example of how widespread such analysis is becoming, take the following statements from a meeting of church people in Green Bay, Wisconsin, in September, 1975. They were consulting on domestic hunger in the USA. They began by indicating how, though they had tended to view the problem as one that could be approached from within the system, they had been led "to conclude that the commonly accepted analysis of the problem, and therefore the solutions that were sought for it, have all been faulty." We now need, they said, to take "a critical look at the structural arrangements in our society for distributing wealth, income, power, work, and status, and to the underlying values and assumptions that have generated these arrangements and kept them operative.

"Our society's assumption has been that a competitive pursuit of private gain will work to provide the best possible life for all. Our examination of hunger in the US convinces us that it has not provided the best possible life for all but has resulted in exploitation of the many for the sake of the few and the Third World for the sake of the First World."

They therefore concluded that "there will be no eradication of poverty and hunger either here or abroad within the present economic/political system. . . . The contradictions are too apparent, and we are forced to confess our complicity, whether through ignorance, apathy, fear, or deliberate venality—with a system which is basically unjust." The solution to the problem of domestic hunger was therefore far more complicated than they had anticipated: "To end hunger, then, means to work for radical change in the economic, political and religious values and institutions of this society."[3]

A third group of analysts of our civilizational crisis says the problem is more profound than either of the first two groups imagines. It is not a matter of the inability of those who run our technological and social institutions to manage massive and rapid change, nor is it a matter of the need to wrest control of those institutions from a "power elite," nor is it a matter of devising new structures of government and economy which will be democratic and just. The problem lies deeper: in the nature of technology itself. It is from the pervasive control of technology over our society that our civilization—and life itself—is threatened, and it is from that control that it must be liberated.

The French sociologist Jacques Ellul has probably been the most famous of the critics of technology (*la technique*).

> Technique has become autonomous, it has fashioned an omnivorous world which obeys its own laws and which has renounced all tradition. Technique no longer rests on tradition, but rather on previous technical procedures; and its evolution is too rapid, too upsetting, to integrate the older traditions.[4]

As a result, Ellul claims:

> In the modern world, the most dangerous form of determinism is the technological phenomenon.[5]

or again:

> Technical progress today is no longer conditioned by anything other than its own calculus of efficiency. ... The individual participates only to the degree that he is subordinate to the search for efficiency.[6]

He explains:

> Let no one say that man is the agent of technical progress ... and that it is he who chooses among possible techniques. In reality, he neither is nor does anything of the sort. He is a device for recording effects and results obtained by various techniques. He does not make a choice of complex, and in some way, human motives. He can decide only in favor of the technique that gives the maximum efficiency. But this is not choice. A machine could effect the same operation.[7]

He goes on:

> Technique's proper motion ... tends irresistibly toward completeness. To the degree that this completeness is not yet attained, technique is advancing, eliminating every lesser force.[8]

Ellul speaks of technique's ability of "self-augmentation"—"it is being transformed and progressing almost without decisive intervention by man."

"Whenever a new technical form appears," Ellul writes, "it makes possible and conditions a number of others."[9] The progression of technique is therefore geometric, not arithmetic— "Every invention calls for other technical inventions in other domains."[10]

But, the reader is moved to ask, can technique not be controlled? Certainly there are abuses, but are there not also sound uses? Ellul responds:

> It ought never to be said: on the one side, technique, on the other, abuse of it. There are different techniques which correspond to different necessities. But all techniques are inseparably united. ... There is an attractive notion that ... it is not the technique that is wrong, but the use men make of it. Consequently, if the use is changed, there will no longer be any objection to the technique.[11]

But, says Ellul, this "attractive notion" "manifestly rests on the confusion between machine and technique. A man can use his automobile to take a trip or to kill his neighbor. But the second use is not a use; it is a crime."[12]

But we cannot suppose, he goes on,

that men orient technique in a given direction for moral, and conse-
quently non-technical reasons. . . . A principal characteristic of technique . . . is its refusal to tolerate moral judgments. It . . . eliminates
them from its domain. Technique never observes the distinction
between moral and immoral use. It tends, on the contrary, to create
a completely independent technical morality. . . . Technique pursues
no end, professed or un-professed. It evolves in a purely causal way:
the combination of preceding elements furnishes the new technical
elements. There is no purpose or plan . . . there is not even a
tendency toward human ends. We are dealing with a phenomenon
blind to the future. . . . To propose a direction for technique is to
deny technique and to divest it of its character and its strengths.[13]

Ellul quotes Jacques Soustelle's comment with reference to the
atomic bomb, "Since it was possible, it was necessary." For Ellul
technique is a whole—each part supports and reinforces the
others. They together constitute "a coordinated phenomenon, no
element of which can be detached from the others." It is therefore
"an illusion . . . to hope to be able to suppress the 'bad' side of
technique and preserve the 'good'. This belief means that the
essence of the technical phenomenon has not been grasped."[14]
"It is necessity," Ellul says, "which characterizes the technical
universe."[15]

Ellul's notions have become attractive to many in our day.
Robert Heilbroner, from whose *Inquiry into the Human Prospect*
we quoted earlier, is almost as pessimistic as Ellul about the
prospects of humanizing technology.

Modes of production establish constraints with which humanity
must come to terms, and the constraints of the industrial mode are
particularly demanding. The rhythms of industrial production are
not those of nature, nor are its necessary uniformities easily adapted
to the varieties of human nature. While surely capable of being used
for more humane purposes than we have seen hitherto, while no
doubt capable of greater flexibility and much greater individual
control, industrial production nonetheless confronts men with
machines that embody "imperatives" if they are to be used at all,
and these imperatives lead easily to the organization of work, of life,
even of thought, in ways that accommodate men to machines rather
than the much more difficult alternative.[16]

Similarly, the American sociologist Robert Bellah observes that
an economy founded on the type of industrialization on which
ours has been, under the control of corporate capitalism, has

wedded technology to profit in such a way that human beings cannot make decisions:

> Our economy can only survive through constant expansion, whatever the ecological and social consequences of that expansion. Thus in any economic crisis it is not possible to say: we are rich enough, let us consider the conserving of resources, more adequate repair of present equipment, improved quality but reduced quantity in our style of life. No; the economy is like a heroin addict; only another shot of the very profit narcotic that creates a recession will get us out of it.[17]

And Bellah is worried:

> How many more belts of uncontrolled economic expansion will we be able to absorb before the social and ecological consequences totally undermine our democratic society, not to speak of our physical health?[18]

In an interview with *Right On!* magazine, Bellah was even more graphic:

> I feel that the structures that have been built up out of the modern capitalist economy and the large-scale bureaucratic government have a kind of life of their own, that basically they move without any kind of human control at this point, that the pressures to maximize the power and wealth of large corporate structures or large government structures pull us along. It's like being possessed by demons, if you want to use the biblical metaphor. I don't feel human beings are in control of it.[19]

It might seem that this kind of analysis is recent. Quite the contrary. As long ago as 1905, the German sociologist Max Weber foresaw what Ellul and Bellah now lament:

> The tremendous cosmos of the modern economic order . . . is now bound to the technical and economic conditions of machine production which today determine the lives of all the individuals who are born into this mechanism . . . with irresistible force. Perhaps it will so determine them until the last ton of fossilized coal is burnt. . . . Material goods have gained an increasing and finally an inexorable power over the lives of men as at no previous period in history.[20]

In seeking to explain our contemporary lack of freedom, Heilbroner, Ellul, and Bellah assign different weights to the search for profit and a commitment to technology. Yet all agree that these are the three elements of the equation, and that neither the restructuring of institutions founded on this technological base nor the guarantee of democratic control of the institutions will in and of itself be sufficient to bring about human liberation. Contrary to the propaganda on behalf of technology, that it will introduce "a new era of liberation," human freedom is, under technology, reduced to a new low.

With the coming of the computer, technological determinism has increased geometrically. Not just industry, but society and culture are much more amenable to technological control. A case in point is the use of technology today in broadcasting, an appropriate instance to pursue in a chapter which began with a consideration of two broadcasters' views. Perhaps many of us are unaware that when we turn on the TV news we are watching a product not just of the day's events and the minds of reporters such as Rather and Day but of sophisticated technological "consultants." One such consultant is Frank Magid of Marion, Iowa. Referred to as "Mr. Magic," Magid is the President and sole owner of the largest broadcasting consulting firm in the United States, with clients, in 1975, in one hundred television markets (out of a possible 224). Magid's technique is to make house-to-house surveys of viewer interest and likes with an IBM 1130 computer and come up with recommendations which will increase a program's audience ratings and thus the station's advertising revenues.

Magid has been responsible for the shape—among other programs—of many of our news broadcasts, the substitution, for example, of a "team presentation" for an "anchor man" and the introduction of "action news" in which the maximum length of a story without accompanying film footage is 15 seconds while that with it is 90 seconds.

"The anchor man was not received positively," Magid says, "so he had to be changed." He is upset that some people have criticized the shorter news stories as a "rip'n read" sort of thing. "They didn't understand," he says, "that what we were attempting to do was to deliver more news than people had ever seen in that period of time."

But less and less time is reserved for hard news. Many of the items on these programs are pre-tested "service items" like "Dollars and Sense." As one departing disgruntled, prize-winning investigative reporter commented, "It's the kind of thing that weighs the priorities against investigative reporting. You've got to fill up the board with a whole horse load of stories."

Richard Salant, President of CBS news, considers the "newscast doctors" an "abomination":

> To the extent that they take a look to see how you can better your external cosmetic look—you know, a set that isn't distracting or graphics that are helpful—I think they're all right. But to the extent that they get into news content—telling you how long stories should run and what should be covered . . . I think they're an abomination. They're there to advise you about how to increase your audience and performing a proper journalistic function is not necessarily consistent with increasing your audience.[21]

Weber called technology "instrumental rationality." One wonders whether anyone in an economy such as ours can hold out against what produces profit so long as the "instrumental rationalists" of technology produce profit—and they do. It is harder and harder to resist them. If the tool is there, Ellul says, it must be used. Contemporary fights against the B-1 bomber, nuclear power plants, the SST, the plutonium economy, and strip mining are examples of the difficulty of resisting "the logic of technology." The proposed or actual use of compulsory sterilization, tranquilizing drugs for "hyperactive" children, elaborate techniques of surveillance and torture and subliminal advertising are examples of the intense pressure of technology to expand into what were once "non-technical fields," as is the difficulty of resisting "life-preserving" techniques in hospitals an example of the lack of freedom we already have in one of those areas. And over us hangs the specter of "genetic engineering," which even has its own technicians running scared over the immense ethical questions it raises.

*   *   *

Whether one listens seriously to those who find the source of our troubles in our inability to manage our economy and society properly and democratically, or turns to those who see the source of the problem in inherently unequal institutions of society, or gives one's credence to the analysts of technology itself, one is not going to sleep well. All agree in a disturbing way that the problems of our day and of our civilization are immense, threatening, and only with difficulty—if at all—amenable to control. In this present day we are confronting multiple major crises, threatening our whole past way of dealing with things. There is no appropriate historical paradigm of how a civilization anywhere at any time successfully confronted such a mega-challenge, and this one may just overwhelm us.

"Solutions" are cheap and, because of the complexity of the problems, probably all of them are at least plausible: economic "solutions," political "solutions," technological "solutions." It is not the task of the theologian to add to the already high number of "ways out." A theologian's task is different from that of a "Mr. Magic." He or she is charged to "read the signs of the times" and to "proclaim the manifold wisdom of God" (Luke 12:54-56; Eph. 3:10).

That is what I will try, in the next sub-chapter, to do. I call it a sub-chapter because it cannot be separated from this analysis just completed. A theologian does not put aside economic, technological, and political analyses, but seeks to read them *sub specie aeternitatis,* in the light of eternity—eschatologically, not in the abstract. As readers will see, for me this means to read the analyses historically, in the light of the Kingdom of God. This is, in addition, a social metaphor.

My analysis will therefore be both theological and sociological. I shall attempt to use a (primarily) Durkheimean sociological analysis as a hermeneutical key to the re-presentation of biblical eschatology. It is my hope that a comparative, historical sociology of cultural and inter-civilizational process will provide a useful vantage point for examining the relationship of the Kingdom of God to human history at this time of great crisis.

(2) Dwelling in the Darkness

Life was in him, the light which was light for people, the light which shines in the darkness, and which the darkness has not overcome.
—John 1:4-5

MOST SOCIOLOGY CAN BE CHARACTERIZED AS THE SOCIOLO-
gy of what is. That is, most sociologists have as their goal an analysis
of the present order—how does the social system work? Who
holds power? What functions do the various institutions serve?
Which roles are played by whom? According to what norms and
values?

Functionalism is one such type of sociology. It is sometimes
called structuralism or structural-functionalism. The late 19th-early
20th century French sociologist Emile Durkheim is usually called
"the father of structural-functionalism," and it is probably correct
to call him that. Yet structural-functionalism, as it has developed,
has been prone to a legitimate criticism which no knowledgeable
person could apply to Durkheim. The criticism is that structural-
functionalism is biased toward continuity and equilibrium and
does not know what to do with the phenomenon of change.

Durkheim, however, was at least as much concerned to describe how societies come together over time and how, over the
course of time, they change as to describe how they function at a
given point in time. Durkheim was, it may be said, a sociologist of
socio-cultural process. His sociology was less a sociology of what
is than a sociology of what is in process of becoming. In this
sub-chapter I hope to present Durkheim as the sociologist of an
emerging world order. I believe that he has much insight to offer
us as we seek to understand the troubled times in which we live.

*   *   *

Let us think for a moment of the analyses of today's world which
we encountered in the last sub-chapter. A central question they
raise is: to what extent is today's world continuous with the world
we have known, and to what extent can we expect that tomorrow's world will be like today's? All three analyses describe the
present world as a world in crisis, but with different meanings. The
Marxist analysis says that what we witness today is the end of the
previous order—capitalism in its death-throes is marked by accel-
erated exploitation and oppression of the people, but the people
are arising; tomorrow's world, therefore, will be totally different
from today's—it will be a world of peace, justice, and harmony;
power will truly belong to the people.

The analysis associated with Ellul says that change is not tomorrow but yesterday, that the decisive *novum* has already entered the scene with the coming of technology, that today's world is already qualitatively different from yesterday's, for it is no longer subject to human control. Ellul foresees no comparable change in the future, barring unexpected massive resistance to technology, but a deepening of today's crisis, an even greater threat to authentically human existence.

The first analysis, however—the "managerial approach"—emphasizes the sameness of today's world and yesterday's, and it does not anticipate, barring breakdowns, that tomorrow's world will be radically different from today's. Fundamentally what is at issue today, in this analysis, is what has always been: how to manage society efficiently so as to provide the goods and services that people need. Technology, it is believed, if it is managed properly, can solve many of our age-old problems and provide a more satisfying life for more people. For the moment, granted, there is a crisis; somehow, strangely, the gap between the rich and the poor is growing rather than decreasing and the quality of life is declining rather than advancing, but this must be a temporary phenomenon. History does not make leaps, nor does it contain insoluble contradictions.

There are ineradicable differences in these positions. They cannot be harmonized. Yet, somehow, in our popular reading, all three become meshed. The average person, who is not bound to take any party-line position, can be forgiven if his or her attitude toward our contemporary crises is a kind of amalgam of these three positions, if he or she ends up feeling, along with Dan Rather and Robin Day, that things are falling apart, that we may be witnessing the death of civilization as we have known it. Many respond, not by following the prescriptions of any of the three analyses, but by a kind of nostalgic looking backward at the world from which we have come as somehow a better world, a more stable world, a simpler world. One cannot criticize them too severely. It is an understandable psychological reaction. It is a reaction of fear. Since the dominant image we have of the present world is one of breakdown and disintegration, we look for our salvation to a return to the *status quo ante bellum*. Such a knee-jerk reaction fails to consider, however, that there are other possible readings of the situation.

A central concept of Durkheim's thought was that of *anomie*.

By *anomie* (from the Greek *nomos,* or law) Durkheim described a state of normlessness which occurs between two orders of society. *Anomie* is a Janus-like concept, looking backward to the past order of society, as well as forward to an order still to emerge. The trouble with our analyses of society, Durkheim would have said, is that most of them lack this future dimension—they only look backward at what has been; they therefore understand the present as a time of disintegration, instead of seeing it as a time of new birth as well.

If the times in which we live are characterized by social turbulence and moral darkness, Durkheim suggests that the darkness has a pre-dawn character as well as a post-sunset one. To cure our limited vision he would have us ask, "What new order is being born?" as well as "What old order is dying?"

The following quotation, from a 1914 essay, is a striking example of Durkheim's approach:

> The old ideals and the divinities which incarnate them are dying because they no longer respond sufficiently to the new aspirations of our day; and the new ideals which are necessary to orient our life are not yet born. Thus we find ourselves in an intermediary period, a period of moral cold which explains the diverse manifestations of which we are, at every instance, the uneasy and sorrowful witnesses.
>
> But who does not feel—and this is what should reassure us—who does not feel that, in the depths of society, an intense life is developing which seeks ways to come forth and which will finally find them?[22]

Anomie is the intermediate condition which he thus describes, the state of a society in the throes of transition. It is a pathology, a sickness, containing great danger so long as it lasts, but also containing within it—if we know how to look—signs of health, for in *anomie* is expressed not only the dysfunctionality of outmoded orders but people's striving for an order which has not yet emerged.

In what sense is *anomie* a social sickness? A society characterized by *anomie* is sick because it does not give clear cues to its members as to how to act:

> Social man necessarily presupposes a society which he expresses and serves. If this dissolves, if we no longer feel it in existence and action about and above us, whatever is social in us is deprived of all

objective foundation. All that remains is an artificial combination of illusory images, a phantasmagoria vanishing at the least reflection; that is, nothing which can be a goal for our action. . . . Thus we are bereft of reasons for existence; for the only life to which we could cling no longer corresponds to anything actual; the only existence still based upon reality no longer meets our needs. . . . So there is nothing more for our efforts to lay hold of, and we feel them lose themselves in emptiness.[23]

Anomie is thus a crisis of morality, and Durkheim took morality quite seriously. Without a commonly accepted morality, he knew, a society cannot long survive. However, moralities cannot be constant. As societies are changing, moralities must change to fit their new conditions:

Profound changes have been produced in the structures of our societies in a very short time; they have been freed from the segmental type with a rapidity and in proportions such as have never before been seen in history. Accordingly, the morality which corresponds to this social type has regressed, but without another developing quickly enough to fill the ground that the first left vacant in our consciences. Our faith has been troubled; tradition has lost its sway; individual judgment has been freed from collective judgment. But, on the other hand, the functions which have been disrupted in the course of the upheaval have not had the time to adjust themselves to one another; the new life which has emerged so suddenly has not been able to be completely organized, and above all, it has not been organized in a way to satisfy the need for justice which has grown more ardent in our hearts.[24]

Rather than nostalgically calling for a return to a previous morality (which many in his time thought could be reinstated by limiting the exercise of democracy and increasing the authority of the powers that be—a proposal which is again finding favor today), Durkheim pointed out the falsity of attempts to return to earlier conditions of society and morality:

The remedy for the evil is not to seek to resuscitate traditions and practices which, no longer responding to present conditions of society, can only live an artificial, false existence. What we must do to relieve this anomy is to discover the means for making the organs which are still wasting themselves in discordant movements harmoniously concur by introducing into their relations more justice by more and more extenuating the external inequalities which are the source of the evil.[25]

A societal sickness can only be cured, Durkheim pointed out, by curing the society. The cure does not lie in adjusting people's attitudes towards injustice (by reducing their expectations) but in adjusting—attacking—the injustice itself:

> It is not a new philosophical system which will relieve the situation. Because certain of our duties are no longer founded in the reality of things, a breakdown has resulted which will be repaired only insofar as a new discipline is established and consolidated. In short, our first duty is to make a moral code for ourselves.[26]

By "discipline" and "moral code" Durkheim meant far more than a personal regimen of individuals. He was speaking of a social discipline. Societies can only function, Durkheim believed, on the basis of such commonly accepted disciplines. They have as their function the integration of individuals and groups into society and the reduction of their separateness. He referred to this as the control of "egotism." (Robert Nisbet[27] suggests this French word might better be translated today by *alienation* or *isolation*. It is a kind of hyper-individualism which Durkheim saw as the obstacle to social existence.)

> The only power which can serve to moderate individual egotism is the power of the group; the only power which can serve to moderate the egotism of groups is that of some other group which embraces them.[28]

As Ernest Wallwork comments:

> Durkheim denies the widespread assumption in his era, as well as in ours, that discipline is incompatible with self-realization, freedom, and happiness. Discipline, by restraining limitless ambitions and by canalizing limited reserves of psychic energy in pursuit of determinate goals, is the indispensable means without which regular realization of human potentialities would be impossible.[29]

The danger is in overbalancing toward the side of the state, making individuals serve the state rather than vice versa. Still, it is the function of society, Durkheim believed, not to bring individuals to serve it, but to serve the fullest possible existence of the individuals who make it up, to bring about the realization of human potential:

> The fundamental moral duty of the modern state has become the positive promotion, protection, and defense of the rights and

privileges associated with individualism. This responsibility . . . is a collective aim superior to the individual qua individual, for "it is not this or that individual the State seeks to develop, it is the individual *in genere,* who is not to be confused with any single one of us. . . . The cult of the human person, with all that such a cult implies with respect to the protection of individual rights and the promotion of his moral and physical well-being, is thus the fundamental ethical duty of the state, the polestar for moral guidance."[30]

It is bracing, at a time like the present, when many Western "liberals" are tempted to denigrate human freedom and the rights of the individual—and are prone to accept uncritically the Marxist call for the priority of social and material rights over "formal" rights—to hear such a ringing affirmation of the importance of the rights which people have struggled for in the Western world for so many centuries.

But we should not be complacent. When he speaks of the realization of human potential, Durkheim is not speaking of something which we can ever say we have finally achieved. In this context he frequently uses an expression that is crucial for us to grapple with (we shall have reason to refer to it at length in Chapter 8). Society, he says, "obliges us *to surpass ourselves.*" There is, in the way in which he used this expression, something which, as a theologian, I am moved to call "eschatological." Durkheim wrote: "To surpass itself a being must, to some degree, part from its nature—a departure that does not take place without causing more or less painful tensions."[31] There is a sense in which a new type of human existence—perhaps what Paul called "new creation"—is waiting to be revealed, and he looks forward to it with yearning. Durkheim was not, in the usual sense of that word, a religious man (the grandson of a rabbi, he himself was a secular Jew), and yet here—as in other areas—he demonstrates a kind of religious expectancy as he anticipates what humankind will be like in the future. Rather than take an essentialist position which says that everything is already laid out in human nature, he takes an eschatological one, affirming "That which is is nothing compared with that which shall be" (cf. Rom. 8:18-25, I Cor. 15:35-55, II Cor. 3-5, and I John 3:2 for striking parallels).

Durkheim says that what society seeks to do, in promoting the fulfillment of human potential, is to change the human beings who make it up: "The task of education is not limited to developing the individual in accordance with his nature, disclosing whatever hidden capacities lie there only seeking to be revealed. Education creates in man a new being." He said the same thing in another way: "Society seeks to inculcate in its members an ideal image of what they ought to become."[32]

What was exciting to Durkheim, as he studied the ideals of education in societies as diverse as Australian hunting and gathering bands and modern international civilizations, was a common tendency that could be discerned in all such developments—the attitude that the new being would be a universal one:

> As we advance in evolution, we see the ideals men pursue breaking free of the local or ethnic conditions obtaining in a certain region of the world or a certain human group, and rising above all that is particular and so approaching the universal.[33]

Yet Durkheim recognized that this was still future. The universal ideal would have to emerge alongside of and co-exist with more local conceptions. In the modern world, the task of societies, he believed, was to reconcile two forms of patriotism—national patriotism, the fruit of the long development of the nation-state, and world patriotism ("the human ideal"). As long as there are states, Durkheim thought, national pride will continue to exist, but his hope was that societies would find their honor "not in being the greatest or the wealthiest, but in being the most just, the best organized, and in possessing the best moral constitution." By this process, he hoped civic duties would become "only a particular form of the general obligations of humanity."[34]

By now the reader will understand what I meant by saying at the outset that Durkheim is to be clearly differentiated from sociologists of what is. He was clearly a sociologist of that which is coming to be, and what he believed was coming to be in the 20th century, for the first time in world history, was a society with no smaller base than the entire world.

He knew that such a society would not come about painlessly. He had a first-hand experience with ethnic chauvinism in his deep personal involvement in the Dreyfus cause, and he lost a son in World War I. Nevertheless, he was quite sure that, with the increase of contacts and communication between people of formerly discrete nations and civilizations, a new international mental and emotional life was being activated, out of which new worlds would come. The process, he said, could be documented from history many times before, times when passions become more active, sensations stronger, and people feel transformed and begin to transform their environments. He referred to them as "states of effervescence" in which humanity is made anew:[35]

> Such was the great crisis of Christendom, the movement of collective enthusiasm which, in the 12th and 13th centuries, bringing together in Paris the scholars of Europe, gave birth to Scholasticism. Such were the Reformation and the Renaissance, the revolutionary epoch, and the Socialist upheavals of the 19th century. At such moments this higher form of life is lived with such intensity and exclusiveness that it monopolizes all minds to the more or less complete exclusion of egoism and the commonplace. At such times the ideal tends to become one with the real, and for this reason men have the impression that the time is close when the ideal will in fact be realized and the Kingdom of God established on earth.[36]

All well and good, you may say, but Durkheim did not live to see neo-colonialism succeed imperialism, or liberal democracy give way to fascism; he did not witness the scientific development of torture, or the rise of the multi-national corporations; he knew nothing of the use and proliferation of nuclear weapons, and little of the modern despoliation of the environment—to name a few of the developments which concern us. How can anyone, knowing of the history of the 20th century, continue to hold up such dreams?

One can almost hear Durkheim's response:

> You speak of an anomic world. Its *anomie* will not cease in the short-run. You can expect it to continue until such time as the new world society in which you in fact already live has formulated moral codes and disciplines to create world community. But even now, as you listen to the voices which are being raised in protest at injustice, do you not detect a yearning for a kind of justice no existing formula can satisfy, an intense life developing which is seeking ways to come forth?[37]

As I sat in at the meetings of the Seventh Special Session of the United Nations in September, 1975, as that body discussed the proposed New International Economic Order, I couldn't help but sense the sociological (and theological) meaning of what was going on: in place of the unplanned order which had developed by dint of past histories and the accidents of geography and the use of raw power by those who had it, the nations of the world were sitting down and trying to plan a just order of international economic relations. Durkheim would have been ecstatic. As one of his students, I understood well during those days the keenness of his foresight. But as a theologian as well, I considered myself specially blessed to be able to witness what I took to be signs of God's Kingdom. By this I do not mean that I believed that the institutions which were being proposed and the laws which were being propounded were to be equated with the order of God's coming reign, but I sensed that in and through these institutions and laws the Kingdom was bearing witness to its presence in the world.

As speaker after speaker got up and challenged the world community to create an order in which hunger and misery would be abolished and new links of international solidarity would be forged, I perceived some of those "small beginnings" of obedience of which the Heidelberg Catechism speaks.[38] I sensed some of the "prelibations of heaven's glory given upon earth" to which Jonathan Edwards referred in the 18th century.[39]

But, someone is bound to object, does the New Testament not say it is God who brings in the Kingdom? You are just talking about human plans and aspirations!

Such an objection is hard to answer from within our recent Protestant theological understandings. Our understanding of God's activity is according to categories which distinguish sharply between God's action and human action—one indeed wonders what the relationship is between them. The area of theology which should help us here is the doctrine of the Holy Spirit, but we have tended toward a docetic, abstract pneumatology. In Chapter 8 I hope to sketch out what I believe would lead to a more helpful pneumatology. Here let me say only that I do believe it is God who establishes his Kingdom, but that the New Testament says he is doing that right now, and in the historical realm. Eschatology is in process of realizing itself. In doing this God can, certainly, act directly or use either angels or the very stones to declare his glory (as I am sure he is using the environment to announce his judgment on our technology right now), but his normal means of establishing his reign is not through disembodied angels or physical objects—nor by direct intervention—but by the activity of human beings. These include those who are conscious of being his instruments as well as those who are unaware of or even opposed to being that. I'm sure that at the Seventh Special Session all three categories of instruments were to be found!

Furthermore, it was obvious at that meeting that the devil and his angels had not been dispersed. Wherever God's Kingdom is being established the "power of lawlessness" (II Thess. 2:3ff.) is also seeking to do its work. The "developed" nations—most notably my own—were quite reluctant to tread many of the paths on which the others beckoned them, and their reluctance has been made more patent at other meetings since. No one can contend that the Year of Jubilee is just around the corner. There will continue to be poor debtor nations and starving peoples alongside affluent nations and overfed people for a long time to come. The oppression of the powerless will not be done away with by a few meetings, nor will the powerful disband their empires in response to a few well-drafted appeals. Until such time as humans show greater love of justice, God's judgment will continue to fall upon us. The age in which we live, anyone with eyes and ears open knows, is marked much more by the sign of the cross than by the sign of the resurrection. And yet we live, the Bible tells us, in the time of promise (Mark 1:14f., II Cor. 6:2), in the age of the resurrection, in the time between Christ's resurrection and ascension and his coming to reign in glory. To read the signs of such a time is to read of God's judgment, but also to read of his grace.

During this period history moves forward. It moves not steadily but in a series of crises. For every advance of the promise of God—every new sign of life and hope, partial and under judgment though it is—there is an attempt by the principalities and powers to resist the extension of God's reign. There is no steady development of the Kingdom of God on earth. But a process is nevertheless underway.

How can we describe it? It is the process of the work of the Spirit, bringing the power and signs of the Kingdom to create history. This presence of the Kingdom is not the presence which we shall experience at the End, but it already affects all reality. Developments like those of which I have spoken become indications of the End. We should not limit our expectations of what the

Spirit will do. Not only will the gospel be preached and hearts be touched, but the orders and structures of society will be affected—they have been already. It is the role of the church to read the signs of the times and declare their meaning to the world.[40] This is no easy task. As H. Berkhof writes:

> In view of the ambiguity of our history, every interpretation will always remain debatable. But it is unavoidable. It is an act of grateful obedience and as such is never meaningless and without blessing.[41]

*   *   *

In this sub-chapter I have sought to describe a comparative historical sociological way of looking at developments in today's world, and to suggest that this way has much in common with a Biblical eschatological vision of world history. Perhaps this vision can save us from cynicism and free us once again to hope as we attempt to work out our obedience in the darkness.

Before I conclude, however, it would be appropriate to refer more specifically to the three analyses which I outlined in the preceding sub-chapter and indicate how a comparative historical sociology such as I have presented will lead us to respond to them. It is obvious that I do not propose this analysis as an alternative to the three analyses outlined earlier, but as a way of putting them in a different context. Certain elements of those analyses, it will now be clear, will seem more worthy of consideration than others. Nothing of the seriousness of the Marxist economic analysis of exploitation, for example, will be taken away by such an approach. As sociologically and theologically aware people, we must recognize the fact of widespread and brutal oppression in our days, and of the systemic abuse of power by those who hold it. But, at the same time, it will be apparent that culture is not a mere epiphenomenon of economics and that dialectical materialism is not an adequate total vehicle for understanding or bringing about revolutionary social and cultural change. Leszek Kolakowski, the Polish Marxist philosopher, criticizes the tendency of Marxist systematicians to have an "obsession with monism," a "stubborn desire to arrange the world according to some universal principle," a "search for a single magic spell to make reality transparent and decipherable." He counters,

> We know of no completely flexible final method invulnerable to history's threat of petrification. We know only methods that maintain durable vitality because they have succeeded in creating tools of self-criticism, even though they may originally have included certain dogmatic premises or a belief in certain absolutes.

Then, in a searching analogy he concludes,

> In all the universe man cannot find a well so deep that, leaning over it, he does not discover at the bottom his own face.

Thus liberated by a vision of Marxism's finitude, he can advocate a liberated Marxism—not "a doctrine that must be accepted or rejected as a whole," not

> a universal system, but a vital philosophical inspiration affecting our whole outlook on the world, a constant stimulus to the social intelligence and social memory of mankind.[42]

Therefore, while we can benefit from Marxist analysis, we need not accept it as a total system.

Similarly the Ellulian critique of technology as a self-directing and self-augmenting Leviathan will not be ruled out by a Durkheimean analysis. We will have to be alert to every possible loss of freedom which commitment to present types of technology brings in its train, and consider with fresh vigor the whole question of "appropriate technology," as advocated by E. F. Schumacher and his group, but we will recognize that—even in the perspective of the 22 years since Ellul wrote *La Technique,* some victories have been won against the technological machine, and that, although anomic technological activities continue, the voices of protest have been more effective with each passing year.

When it comes to considering the "managerial" analysis of our present crisis, we will recognize from a Durkheimean perspective the importance of the problem of scale which these analysts raise, as well as the need, which Durkheim often emphasized, for intermediary associations at levels between the state and the individual which serve to organize society at these levels and thus knit the whole more tightly together. We will question, however, the assumption behind this analysis that the organizational and managerial problem is the only major problem society confronts today.

People find ways to abuse institutions so as to maximize personal profit. They often mask their desire to continue such profitable activities under the guise of a love of unchanging institutions. This is, however, not true conservatism, but mystification. The true conservative recognizes that new institutional arrangements need to be made, and new codes of law devised, to serve such ancient purposes as the fulfillment of human potential. The history of a people is a constantly developing history.

But what will appear to a student of socio-cultural process to be the most insidious element of the managerial analysis is the growing tendency of those who espouse such analysis to claim that today's problems are "too technical" to allow popular participation in their resolution, and thus to argue for increasing reliance on "experts." Whether this takes a "conservative" form (the "experts" are in the corporations and we should deregulate the economy so they can do their thing) or a "liberal" one (we need a government bureaucracy of "experts" to run our economy), its manifestly anti-democratic animus is cause for suspicion that free servant institutions are becoming less free and will be less efficient servants than they were created to be. We will be aware of the possibility that the institutions of our society are coming to serve different people than they once did. What is crucial is that such institutions and organizations—and the "experts" who run them—should remain accountable to society.

*   *   *

The darkness, we all recognize, has deepened. This is not an age for easy confidence. As Christians we ought to know that we shall continue to dwell in the darkness until God's morning has broken. But it is in the darkness that we are called to repent and to exercise our discipleship. We do it knowing that in many places God's light is already dispersing the darkness, and we should remember that he has told us to keep our lamps burning. We remember that it will not be when the morning has broken that the Bridegroom will appear, but during the night, while it is still dark. It is during the night that the marriage-feast will begin. Therefore, in the spirit of the Dutch Reformed document *Foundations and Perspectives of Confession* (1950), let us not be weary of well-doing, but let us continue to procure oil so that we can go in to the feast:

When we consider the victory of Jesus Christ, we do not despair of this earth, but remain faithfully within it and, aware of all that still resists God's reign, the Spirit constrains us to hasten patiently, to sigh joyfully, and wait actively for the complete revealing of God's glory over all creation.[43]

5: THE ANNOUNCEMENT

> Commitment to Jesus Christ is inescapably a personal, social, community, and public historical event which affects the world and the human beings in it for whom Christ died.
> —Policy Statement on Evangelism, National Council of the Churches of Christ, March 3, 1976

HE COULD HAVE WAITED TILL A MORE OPPORTUNE TIME. WE hadn't gotten the ghettos cleaned up. We hadn't established good relations between the races. We hadn't gotten international food reserves set up, nor even improved the terms of trade for the poor nations. Sexism was still a problem, and the church was far from renewed, when the announcement was made, "He has come!"

* * *

It is at night that the Bridegroom comes. The marriage feast begins at night. The time of waiting is over. The future has become present.

* * *

The trouble with doing evangelism is that when you get involved in it—the real thing, that is—you're inevitably tinkering with eschatology. As Jose Miranda writes, "Evangelizing is really efficacious by virtue of the faith which it arouses. The *proclamation* that the kingdom *is arriving* has to *make* the kingdom *arrive*. . . . There is no more penetrating imperative than the indicative, 'The kingdom has arrived'. . . . When one is convinced that the moment of justice has arrived for the whole earth, this conviction (which is New Testament faith-hope) causes the *eschaton* effectively and really to come."[1]

Now this is certainly not our normal understanding of evangelism. Evangelism has been misunderstood for a long time as being the call to people to assent to the historicity of certain facts about the past and to relate to a community whose life is focused on the past. While celebrating the past in an eternal cult, this community expects nothing from the present—and its primary hope for the future is for a dissolution of the present in a "spiritual" kingdom beyond history.

To understand evangelism biblically, however, is to see that in evangelism we are called to invite people to participate in a present reality, to respond to God's present working as well to his past acts, and to hope for the fulfillment of this present history in the future. Biblical evangelism is calling people to active repentance and faith, calling them into solidarity with a community which knows itself commissioned to participate in God's present activity as he creates history.

Stephen Knapp puts it sharply:

> Evangelization is the process of proclaiming the past and present liberating work of Christ in such a way that people are led into the ongoing process of conversion and into communities of faith demonstrating and proclaiming the Lordship of Christ, communities which incarnate in their life-style the transformation of values that accompanies salvation . . . and engaging in prophetic/evangelistic action and proclamation to individuals and structures in the world.[2]

To make the announcement, "He has come," is thus to unmask the false, spiritualizing eschatology which Jesus unmasked in his ministry and reveal the entrance of the Kingdom into history, of the future into the present. The call of the evangelist is the word of the angels to the disciples at the time of the ascension, "Why do you stand there looking up at the sky? This Jesus, who was taken up from you into heaven, will come back in the same way that you saw him go to heaven" (Acts 1:11, TEV). It is to call people to go back to Jerusalem and prepare to be part of God's eschatological activity.

The disciples obeyed the call of the angels. They returned to engage in what the Dutch *Foundations and Perspectives of Con-*

fession referred to as "active waiting." Shortly thereafter the Holy Spirit fell upon them and they became an eschatological community enacting and proclaiming the new age.

If we examine their evangelism, we see that it was never just a testimony to past events. The Jesus to whom they testified was alive and working in their fellowship. When they proclaimed his salvation, people could see that salvation taking place among them. Theirs was not an idle or dead testimony. And, interestingly enough, they did not need to say, "Join us." Those who, through their testimony, related to Christ knew that to relate to him meant to relate to his body. This learning, supporting, worshipping, and witnessing community was in living relationship to him (cf. John 15).

To make the announcement, "He has come," is thus to say to people, "God has begun to gather people in order to set in motion his eschatological work of establishing justice and love on earth. Will you be part of his party?"

In the New Testament accounts, and traditionally, evangelism has been associated with the call, "Repent." This word is often understood in a narrowly religious sense (as in the TEV translation of Acts 2:38, "Turn away from your sins"). Yet its true significance is much greater, as can be seen by observing what people did who followed the call, and as can be seen by recognizing that Jesus used the same word in his standard proclamation (cf. Mark 1:14f.) and noting how its context defines it there. For we see that those who heeded Peter's command to repent (a) became the recipients of a new hope, (b) changed their life-style, (c) became part of the vanguard community of the kingdom, and (d) were active in works of love and healing.

They did, in other words, what the Jesus of Mark's Gospel intended: hearing the proclamation that the right time—the *kairos*—had come, that the kingdom was at hand, they believed the good news and changed their way of life accordingly. They became disciples.

These were not just religious changes. In fact, we don't know that those who became disciples had a "personal experience" or what we call "spiritual rebirth." Their inward experiences, such as they were, were part of a much larger total change—a totally new understanding of themselves as related to God's dawning history.

The call to "repent," they might have said, had awakened them to a realization that the salvation long spoken of as future had begun and that God had called them to be his agents.

Throughout the New Testament, imagery of awakening is used to refer to this change. Perhaps one example gives the flavor. Paul tells the Romans to be active in love because "you know that the time has come for you to wake up from your sleep. For the moment when we will be saved is closer now than it was when we first believed. The night is nearly over, day is almost here" (Rom. 13:11f., TEV). He then goes on to describe the task of Christians as "fighting in the light."

Paul thus understood his apostolate as being more than a religious one. At the beginning of Romans he says his call is "to lead people of all nations to believe and obey" God (Rom. 1:5, TEV). His ministry, in other words, was not to found a religion. It was part of the way in which God was acting to create history. His task was to tell people what God was doing—establishing his justice through Jesus Christ (Rom. 3:21-27), breaking down the middle wall of partition between Jews and Gentiles (Eph. 2:14), combatting the principalities and powers in order to rescue his alienated creation (Col. 1:13 *et al.*), triumphing over the power of death (II Tim. 1:10), overcoming class and caste distinctions (Phlm. 16), etc. Paul was not called to bring people to assent to a particular understanding of the atonement, or to a specific Christology, or to the historicity of certain events. All of this was subservient to people's waking up to what God was about and obeying him. He certainly called people away from immorality (e.g., Rom. 13:13). This was part of his call, but in asking people to leave "the works of darkness" he had a purpose in mind: that they should become fully free to devote themselves to the tasks of the Lord's combat, the works of day.

As a convert to the faith who had a "personal experience," it took me many years to learn to read Paul on his own terms, instead of proof-texting him to buttress a particular evangelical understanding of Christian experience. One of my favorite texts in my early years as a Christian was Galatians 2:20: "It is no longer I who live, but Christ who lives in me; and the life I now live in the flesh I live by faith in the Son of God, who loved me and gave himself for me." This verse expressed perfectly my sense of the meaning of my life by virtue of the fact that I had given myself to Christ—a transformed life in which he was mystically alive.

I discovered the verse while studying Luther's *Commentary on Galatians.* Galatians—or rather those parts of Galatians which spoke of justification by faith, the work of Christ on the cross, the believer's freedom from the law to live by grace, and the new life of faith—became a crucial and dearly beloved letter to me.

I had difficulty, however, understanding the beginning of Galatians, where Paul talked about the events following his own conversion. I didn't understand why he dwelt at such great length on what was to me a problem of Christian "social ethics"—the argument with Peter at Antioch over whether Jewish Christians should eat with Gentile Christians. This section seemed to me unworthy of the sublime heights of the rest of the letter. (I had the same opinion of the "historical sections" in Romans 9-11 and the "ethical sections" starting with chapter 12; I preferred the "theology" of chapters 1-8.)

I also had difficulty understanding the relationship of verse 27 of Galatians 3: "You were baptized into union with Christ, and so have taken upon yourselves the qualities of Christ himself" to verse 28: "So there is no difference between Jews and Gentiles, between slaves and free men, between men and women; you are all one in union with Christ Jesus" (TEV). I could understand the central importance of the former: it spoke of the believer's personal relationship with Christ—a "spiritual" thing. But the latter seemed to me to be "application" rather than "a central spiritual truth"—important, but something that followed *from* what Paul was *really* concerned to talk about rather than being on a level with it.

When, in 1972-73, after a trip to White-ruled Southern Africa, I became more concerned with the importance of incarnating the Christian message in ministries of liberating love, I found little help in Paul. I looked elsewhere in the New Testament for inspiration.

I didn't need to. If I had only understood Paul on his own terms, I would have seen the relevance of his teachings for a Christian's historical involvement in the work of the Kingdom. But I only came to realize this—and to recognize why it had been obscured for me before—when in October, 1975, I read an article by Krister Stendahl on "The Apostle Paul and the Introspective Conscience of the West."[3] In this article, written 12 years earlier, Stendahl examines the question, What was Paul's main concern in writing about the Law?

It has long been the consensus of the Western Church that Paul was obsessed with his guilt before God, based on his understanding of the Law, and that the problem of conscience was uppermost in his mind. Stendahl finds this hard to square with the rather robust conscience Paul displays in many places (e.g., Phil. 3:6). Is it possible, he asks, that we have misinterpreted what Paul wrote about the Law?

He suggests that in his writings about the Law Paul was not trying to convict his readers of guilt; his writings are "part of a theological and theoretical scriptural argument about the relation between Jews and Gentiles"—a problem of history.[4] He had been earmarked by God to become the apostle to the Gentiles, and "it is quite natural that at least one of the centers of gravity in Paul's thought should be how to define the place for Gentiles in the church, according to the plan of God."[5] Paul is concerned to show how the Gentiles are saved without the Law.

After the first century, however, when Christianity no longer had a sizable Jewish constituency, the Jew-Gentile problem was no longer alive. Augustine later re-applied what Paul wrote about the Law and justification to a more general and timeless human problem, that of the introspective conscience. Augustine's argument reached its climax in the penitential struggle of the Augustinian monk Luther.

Following Luther, the Reformers interpreted what Paul says about the Law in terms of a general principle of "legalism" in religious matters. "Where Paul was concerned about the possibility for Gentiles to be included in the messianic community, his statements are now read," Stendahl writes, "as answers to the quest for assurance about man's salvation."[6] Paul's problem was to explain why there was no reason to impose the Law on the Gentiles—who now, through Christ, have become partakers in the fulfillment of the promises to Abraham; but Western Christianity reverses this by saying "The Law is the Tutor *unto* Christ. Nobody can attain a true faith in Christ unless his self-righteousness has been crushed by the Law and he sees his desperate need for a Savior. . . . Paul's distinction between Jews and Gentiles is gone. . . . All men must come to Christ with consciences properly convicted by the Law and its insatiable requirements for righteousness."[7]

We must distinguish, Stendahl writes, between Paul's concern with God's history-making activity and the Western introspective conscience. The Pauline "once for all," he writes, "cannot be translated fully and only into something repeated in the life of every individual believer. For Gentiles the law is *not* the Schoolmaster who leads to Christ. . . . The faith in the Messiah Jesus gives us the right to be called Children of God."[8]

When I read this article, I understood what Galatians was all about, and why it contains such "diverse" elements arranged in such a "strange" order. Paul was writing to the Galatians to call them down for going back on the fundamental gospel he had proclaimed to them: that in Christ God has done away with the distinction between Jews and Gentiles. All people could now relate directly to God by faith in Christ, so the Law could no longer be either a mediator between humankind and God or a dividing wall between Jews and Gentiles. The Galatians, by seeking to follow the Law, were making the same error Peter had made in Antioch: failing to recognize that God's history-making activity in Christ had changed all that. Therefore the climax of the letter comes in 3:28, with the ringing affirmation, "You are all one in Christ."

The center of the letter is, thus, what we might call a "social ethical" concern or a "historical" one, rather than a "theological" matter. Paul didn't make such distinctions. For him theology was in the service of ethics and salvation history.

This is a crucial matter for our interpretation of Paul, and how we interpret Paul will determine, to a great extent, how we pursue evangelism, for Western evangelism has been based largely on our presumptions about Paul. Traditionally, in Western evangelism, we begin with the goodness of God, present the Law as God's righteous will, and show people how they've failed to fulfill it. Then we present Jesus to them as savior from sin and guilt. We tell them to come to Jesus, to join our church, and to live the new life of righteousness, awaiting the coming of the Lord. It is all highly personal and individualistic. Paul's concern—and that of Jesus and much of the New Testament—for God's history-making activity and the call to us to participate in it is absent. Instead of being the vanguard community which God is gathering together to proclaim his wisdom to the principalities and powers (Eph. 3:12) and call the nations to faith and obedience (Rom. 1:5) the church is simply a new religion—"Christianity"—a new principle of division among humankind! No matter how sophisticated our casuistry, we effectively communicate to the world our conviction that it is not by grace, but by becoming adherents of our religion, that people will be saved.

By our evangelism we thus fundamentally misrepresent what God is about. A. A. Van Ruler quite correctly objects to this: "A person is not human in order that he or she might become Christian. A person is Christian in order to become human."[9]

How then can we phrase the message we have in evangelism? I would like, in the remainder of this chapter, to deal with that question. A good starting point is in the summary of the evangelistic message proposed a few years ago by Hans Küng. The message of the gospel, he says, is that:

> In the light and power of Jesus we are able, in the world of today, to live, to act, to suffer and to die in a truly human way, because we are totally dependent on God and totally committed to our fellow human beings.[10]

I think Küng catches the essential dynamic of evangelism well—we are offering our hearers something, it is a new type of human existence, it is centered on a new relationship to God which is at the same time a new solidarity with our fellow human beings, it is powered by God and it is inseparably related to God's self-revelation in Jesus Christ.

I would like to demonstrate how Küng has caught the essential spirit of the New Testament message. I've spoken earlier in this chapter of Paul and the Synoptic Gospels. Let me take my illustrations now from the Gospel of John.

In his description of Jesus' encounter with the Samaritan woman at the well (ch. 4), the Fourth Evangelist portrays some of the misunderstandings we are likely to have with regard to our relationship with God. The Samaritan woman regards religion as something cultic: one worships either on Mt. Gerizim or in Jerusalem. Jesus replies that it is not in any particular location that one relates to God, but in spirit and in truth. The woman regards relating to Jesus as something objective: "Give me this water that I may not . . . come here to draw" (v. 15). Jesus says when one accepts the gift he has to offer it becomes an internal spring that feeds a new life for that person—it is not something the person gets but something that happens to him.

Similarly, in the discourse following the sign of the loaves and fishes, Jesus says, "Do not labor for the food which perishes, but for the food which endures to eternal life, which the Son of man will give to you" (John 6:27), and then he identifies this bread with himself, "I am the bread of life; he who comes to me shall not hunger, and he who believes in me shall never thirst" (v. 35).

We are tempted to understand this verse in a traditionally evangelical way: what Jesus is saying is that we should enter into "a personal relationship with him as Lord and Savior." Great caution is needed lest we (a) add things to this idea which are not intended, and (b) fail to appreciate the meaning of coming to Jesus. He is offering believers a share in the divine life which was his; that share will be experienced as we live as he did; he is not just offering a "spiritual high," nor—in verse 40—just "life after death," but a distinctively different quality of life beginning right now. The way to that life is to do as Jesus did, to make life-giving the central characteristic of one's life. The way to "enter into a personal relationship with Jesus Christ" is to follow him. His words *are* spirit and life (John 6:64). The life he showed was a life for the other, an exocentric as opposed to an egocentric life.

I do not mean by this that Jesus' life was merely an example for us. The Fourth Evangelist clearly presents Jesus as the one who, through his life, death, and resurrection, works salvation for those who believe in him. But his life and death are at the same time exemplary for the believer.

This comes out clearly in chapter 12, when Jesus tells his Greek visitors:

> Unless a grain of wheat falls into the earth and dies, it remains alone, but if it dies, it bears much fruit. He who loves his life loses it, and he who hates his life in this world will keep it for eternal life. If anyone serves me, he must follow me (John 12:24ff.).

There is certainly a unique sense to these words which applies to Jesus and his self-sacrifice on the cross alone; but there is a prescriptive sense as well, for we cannot relate to Jesus' self-sacrificial offering, the Fourth Evangelist is saying, unless we ourselves are transformed into persons who offer themselves for others. (As Isaac Watts put it beautifully: "Love so amazing, so divine, demands my soul, my life, my all"—see also Rom. 12:1.)

Evangelism becomes a completely new and exhilarating thing when conceived of in this way. I no longer feel guilt for "laying my trip on somebody else," for I am not witnessing because I want anyone to join my organization or because I want people to worship according to my liturgy or because I want them to qualify to pass my spiritual test (and get into the kind of heaven I imagine). As John V. Taylor has written:

> We can leave the eternal destiny of men in the hands of him who was slain before the foundation of the world. And yet, unless we are to be guilty of the ultimate arrogance and paternalism, we must covet for all men what, in our moments of highest aspiration, we covet for ourselves: the privilege of walking consciously in the steps and in the power of the Crucified.[11]

Hans Küng's summary of the Christian message has, I believe, much to commend it. I have adapted it slightly, however, to make it somewhat less existential and more historical and to strengthen its communal character. You will recognize in this adapted form some of the concerns shared in the last chapter:

> In the light and power which Jesus provides and the hope which he inspires, we are able, in the community into which he calls us, to live in the world, to suffer and to die with our fellow human beings in a newly human way, as citizens of the new humanity which God is bringing into being: totally dependent upon God, and awaiting from him the fullness of the kingdom, we are freed from the need to find justification elsewhere, freed to become totally committed to our fellow human beings, as we seek to serve his dawning kingdom.[12]

This is a life-centered concept of faith, not a soul-centered one. It does not follow the tradition of the Western introspective conscience by encouraging a lot of navel-gazing, but seeks instead to encourage Kingdom-expectation and Kingdom-participation. Its central message is not "Come to us," but "Let us follow after him."

Evangelism is thus the announcement of a distinctively new

social understanding of human existence in Christ. Far from being merely the attempt to get people to say, "Yes, I believe that," it is the attempt to bring them to the joy of being able to affirm with others, "Christ has shown us the new way of God's Kingdom" and, in that sense, to say, "We have been crucified with Christ. It is no longer we who live, but Christ who lives in us, and the life which we live in the flesh we live by faith in the Son of God, who loved us and gave himself for us."

D. T. Niles put what I am trying to say in his characteristically pungent way:

> To be evangelists is not an undertaking to spread Christianity. It is rather to be caught within the explosion of the Gospel. Christ is at work . . . and in his working we are caught, impelled, given until *we become part of the lives of those to whom we are sent* (emphasis mine).[13]

Niles differentiates this type of evangelism, in which the evangelist learns more about Christ from the people to whom he is sent and from the context of his mission, from "propagating Christianity."

There is thus an openness to the process, which means that the evangelist will herself or himself be surprised by the outcome. It is not all previously laid out. Evangelism becomes, like a U-Haul truck, "an adventure in moving." What the poet Wallace Stevens advised for walkers in the woods of life is applicable to evangelism:

> Throw away the lights, the definitions and say of what you see in the dark that it is this or it is that, but do not use rotted names. . . . Nothing must stand between you and the shapes you take when the crust of shape has been destroyed.[14]

The orthodox theologian Nikos Nissiotis puts it in more theological language:

> The gospel does not offer an easy, unilateral or identical solution to be applied everywhere in exactly the same way. The churches are obliged to present it and link it to the given and changing social and cultural situations in which they live. . . . The essential thing about the universal nature of the gospel message, which proclaims faith in Christ, is that it is rooted in particularity.[15]

Nissiotis does not mean by this that the "essence" of the gospel can be separated from its "accidents" (and then be designated "universal" whereas the "accidents" are "local"):

> Universal and local are two parts of the same essential reality. . . . Without the local and particular, the universal dimension of the Gospel is unthinkable, indeed could not exist. Without the universal dimension, the local is sectarian, separatist, and therefore not truly Christian and evangelical. There is a continuous tension here *which belongs to the essence of the gospel message* (emphasis mine).[16]

Nissiotis means that we need a more dynamic understanding of the relationship between the gospel as handed down to the apostles and canonized in the New Testament and the gospel we proclaim. It is not enough to regard the New Testament as a source book from which we draw, for in the New Testament canon itself we have many versions of the gospel as it was proclaimed in many highly specific cultural and social settings. Similarly, the people in the church have received the gospel in highly specific and diversified ways. When we seek to homogenize this, we falsify it and, as the church, we lose our authenticity. Nissiotis explains the reason in this way:

> The Gospel message is not defined within itself or by its very nature but in its encounter with and in its announcement to the world. The Church as the carrier of the message to the World is herself the World in process of transformation into a new world.[17]

The last point is a crucial one. It is far from academic. If the church regards the gospel as an object to be possessed, rather than as a word under the grace and judgment of which it stands, it will not be open to the world. The church, in being under the authority of the scripture, must be under the authority of the Lord of the scriptures. The New Testament canon is normative for her life, self-understanding, and witness. But the canon is not an objective norm which can be held at arm's length and measured and defined. That is to understand scriptural authority falsely. The true authority of the scriptures is more dynamic, for the Lord of the scriptures is still alive and speaking. What is mediated to us in scripture is inspired—it has a trans-historical character. But it is mediated to us dynamically: through questions posed by our immediate situation in history, not objectively, as from a handbook.[18]

We cannot pretend to have more direct access to transcendence than that, for we are part of the world to which the gospel is spoken.

This has a further consequence, that we cannot separate our activity in evangelism from the total obedience we offer to the Lord in our historical context. The "Declaration of Evangelical Social Concern," issued in Chicago in November, 1973, put it well:

> As evangelical Christians committed to the Lord Jesus Christ and the fundamental authority of the Word of God, we affirm that God lays total claim upon the lives of his people. We cannot, therefore, separate our lives in Christ from the situation in which God has placed us in the U.S. and the world.[19]

We are called not just to orthodoxy, it has been said by many recently, but to orthopraxis. Our praise of God will not just be doxological in character, but praxiological, as we seek to express our devotion to God in obedience. Richard Mouw describes how, in the '60s, he felt compelled to offer more to God on the altar than his church expected:

> I was committed to various political causes, the most important having to do with my decision to refuse induction into the military. . . . It seemed to me that my concerns were a proper extension of my evangelical experiences. I remembered lines from songs that we had sung with endless monotony at "evangelistic meetings": "I Surrender All," "Is Your All on the Altar?", "Nothing Between My Soul and the Savior," "Break Down Every Idol, Cast Out Every Foe."
>
> Wasn't it proper at least to raise the question of whether my draft card should be surrendered to the lordship of Christ? Shouldn't nationalism be offered on the altar of sacrifice? Doesn't racism stand between the soul and the Savior? Shouldn't we be constantly on guard against political idols and economic foes? I could not understand why evangelicals did not want even to hear such questions.[20]

The reason evangelicals didn't want to hear such questions is, as we saw earlier, that they had learned to read scripture in such a way as to dichotomize between the personal and the social, between the private and the historical.

Even though great attempts were made to overcome this, this dichotomization is still present in the latest semi-official statement of world evangelicalism, the Lausanne Covenant (1974). Article V reads in part:

> Although reconciliation with man is not reconciliation with God, nor is social action evangelism, nor is political liberation salvation, nevertheless we affirm that evangelism and socio-political involvement are both part of our Christian duty. For both are necessary expressions of our doctrines of God and man, our love for our neighbor, and our obedience to Jesus Christ.[21]

Once one has distinguished between evangelism and social action as Lausanne did, or between "the transcendent" and the historical as the Hartford Appeal did—in such a way that the former is clearly primary, while the latter is secondary—one will not be surprised if a certain hesitancy enters into our Christian social action.

That is clearly the case in the reaction of Lewis Smedes, one of the signers of the Hartford Appeal (who was also present at Lausanne) to the Boston Affirmations.[22] A dedicated "evangelical for social action" himself, and signer of the Chicago "Declaration of Evangelical Social Concern," Smedes illustrates the bind even the best motivated person can get into when theology creates false divisions. He joins issue with the Boston Affirmers at four points:

(1) He accuses them of identifying the Kingdom of God "with useful efforts to improve the quality of human life"; they "rightly reject," he says, "the notions that God's Kingdom is only future or only inward or never touches down anywhere in human life as we live it now." But he thinks they too simplistically identify God's Kingdom on a one-for-one basis with particular human efforts to make the world a better place in which to live. As opposed to this Smedes suggests:

> History should be clear enough for us, if the Bible is not, that whatever snippets of the kingdom order are present in human affairs, they are mixed up with human ignorance, pretension, and sin. Only God himself, sometime, not now, not in the most promising human action, will make the earthly order identical with his heavenly kingdom.[23]

(2) He accuses Boston of saying we can *know* where the Kingdom is, check off the places, make a list, point to movements

and struggles, and say, "Lo, here," or "Not there." "But," Smedes objects, "how do we really know for sure? What prevents another group of people from making another list. . . . What infallible yardstick have we got for measuring kingdom quotients?"

He admits that Boston doesn't pinpoint precisely—they point to general endeavors and aims, not necessarily to every program. But that is not enough tentativeness for Smedes. "Do we not, in fact, have to say," he asks,

> that *it seems to us* that this or that struggle embodies sufficient kingdom goals and *seems* to use means that are at least consistent enough with kingdom norms to deserve our involvement? And do we not always have to accept the reservation that we might be wrong? And even where we may be right, is there not always enough human obfuscation and human duplicity in all our efforts that they deny even as they signal the promise of God's kingdom?

(3) He finds fault with Boston for "leveling the Bible's witness to God's unique acts for redemption through Israel's history and the ministry of Jesus Christ" to the level of the human struggles of our times. The Biblical accounts thus become mere "metaphors", and "models."

(4) He accuses Boston of saying the only theology worth affirming is natural theology, by which he means a theology in which *we* discern in history what God is doing kingdom-wise and we interpret what we should do in response. He opposes this to a "theology of the Word." He calls for a theology which is "an affirmation of transcendence, of transcendent norm, and transcendent expectation . . . in the Biblical, Judaeo-Christian manner."

By the end of Smedes' critique one has lost the sense that he meant what he wrote at the beginning, that theology should "summon us to social action with vigor and intensity." He so limits what we can affirm of what God is doing here and now—as contrasted with what he did there and then—that the nerve of social action is cut.

Certainly there is a uniqueness to God's choice of Israel, to his incarnation in Christ, to the events of Christ's passion and resurrection, but—and this is the crucial point—it is not a uniqueness which separates those events from God's other activities in history, but a uniqueness which discloses what God is doing elsewhere. Those events are particularly transparent to our understanding and they make other events more visible and comprehensible to us. They do not lessen the significance of these other events but make them appear more significant because God's purpose is more clearly perceived.

Smedes' position has uncomfortable similarities with that of the Sanhedrin in the Book of Acts when it sought to oppose Peter and the apostles. So sure were they that God's past dealings were normative and fixed that they could not perceive how, in the ministry of Jesus and the witness of the apostles, he was acting in a new way. What Peter was saying must have seemed like "natural theology" to them rather than "a theology of the Word." So the Sanhedrin forbade them to preach.

But Gamaliel had a concept of the Word which incorporated a considerably greater degree of mystery and transcendence than the Sanhedrin's concept, and he therefore advised them, "Keep away from these men and let them alone; for if this plan or this undertaking is of men, it will fail; but if it is of God, you will not be able to overthrow them. You might even be found opposing God!" (Acts 5:38-39).

Smedes is certainly right in resisting what he takes to be a one-to-one identification of movements in history with the establishment of God's Kingdom. He is correct in reminding us to be aware of our need to maintain a certain tentativeness in our enthusiasm for given movements or programs (a point many of the Boston Affirmers would second).

Where I have difficulty accepting his critique is not in his questioning of the movements the Affirmers endorse, but in the theological criteria he sets up to guide us in assessing social movements. The crux of the matter is his distinction between "natural theology" and a "theology of the Word," in his introduction of a "transcendent" realm existing somehow apart from the historical realm.

In his own intention, to be sure, the transcendent is to function as a "norm"—a norm for judging the historical. He leaves the door open, however, for a principial separation of the transcendent from the historical. And there is in his critique of Boston a strong indication that he has walked some distance through that door. In other words, the transcendent functions in his understanding as more than just a norm—as a realm separate from the historical.

We are all too familiar with what this can lead to in minds less sophisticated than Smedes': to non-involvement in the historical, to religiously based passivity, to resignation. An example of this aberration is found in a recently published answer by Billy Graham to a person who asked him about his historical expectation.[24] The reader asked whether Graham really believed, as had been reported to him, that the world was getting worse all the time. He himself thought it might be getting better.

Graham replied by citing the Parable of the Wheat and the Tares. He interpreted it in the following way:

"The wheat," Graham wrote, might refer to "the thousands and thousands of Bible study groups that have appeared in recent years," to the "many thousands in our nation who have found Christ," and even to the "many Christians who have developed a concern for the social problems that affect us."

The tares, on the other hand, might refer to the growth of pornography, he answered, to the increase in divorce and abortion rates, to sexual permissiveness.

Note the difference: the wheat refers only to Christians, whereas the tares refer to social phenomena. Graham did note positively that many Christians have a new social concern, but he described them as the wheat, rather than refer to what they were doing as a sign of the Kingdom, or to new Christian social movements as a leaven within history.

Graham then went on to draw the lesson: "The Bible says society will never be perfect until Christ comes again and brings judgment." (The reader didn't, however, ask about perfection— he only asked about improvement!) "As long as people seek to serve themselves instead of Christ, there will always be evil in this world." (True, to be sure, but the reader didn't claim it would be otherwise.) "But we know that some day Christ will come, and we 'look for new heavens and a new earth, wherein dwelleth righteousness' (II Pet. 3:13)." (In other words, don't bank on this world—the "historical" world. Look for the next—the "transcendent.")

Christians traditionally seem to be caught between an idealized past world and a remote future. Graham gives his reader no guidance for the present. The future hope Graham seeks to inculcate is, therefore, alienating, because it separates the believer from the historical. Such a future hope encourages us to be passive in the face of injustice today.

At its worst, however, the separation between present and future hope leads to positive support by the church for reactionary and repressive regimes. The most notorious American example today is the support Campus Crusade's Bill Bright gives the Park regime in Korea. But such misapplied support is not new. It is a familiar phenomenon in church history: in exchange for permission to carry out "religious" and "evangelistic" activities, the church lends its full support to a given government. It can do this because it believes the kingdom it seeks is "not of this world," because it is concerned with "men's ultimate welfare," not "passing conditions." It thus applies "Gospel values" only to the "Kingdom order" and feels it is the Law, rather than the Gospel, which applies to this present order.

Where Boston erred, in the eyes of some, was in reducing the distance between the Kingdom and the world, between Christian hope and contemporary realities. Yet this is exactly what we saw earlier that Jesus did, and it was the reason for much of the offense he caused in his day.

Humanity does not seem comfortable with a religion that refers to the present. It is of the nature of religion to deal, Mircaea Eliade tells us, with what happened *in illo tempore,* there and then.[25] It is of the nature of biblical faith to deal with the here and now—seen in the light of remembered history celebrated eucharistically, having a fundamentally positive attitude toward God's present activity because it knows that the one who came will come again, that the one who rose rules, that the one remembered from the past comes to us now, not from the past, but from the future. His transcendence is not that of a less historical realm, but of a world that is in the process of becoming, of a Kingdom not yet fully realized. Toward that Kingdom he is working right now. Sacred history is not in suspension! To that Kingdom—and to his activity in establishing it—we must in evangelism bear witness, while—in proclamation and in action—we work toward its coming, calling others to be part of its realization.

We cannot expect this to happen if we put everything under the rubric "maybe." The church has spoken that word, given that non-signal, too often. As Daniel Berrigan writes,

> We Christians swing in the winds, impaled on the sharp pivot of "maybe". From the point of view of any acceptable or understandable tradition, we are captive and dying. . . . Most of us have given . . . the big "maybe" as people take . . . the Fifth Amendment (which is its political translation). The church, for example, lived in this moral fog of "maybe" in the Viet Nam decade. The church seldom delivered the Big Lie. . . . What it said was, "maybe, maybe, maybe. . . ." But when the word *no* is needed, "maybe" simply will not do.[26]

The Christian doctrine of the forgiveness of sins gives us the courage to be daring, to say "yes" even when we are not able to publish a thesis explaining why we interpret the situation as we do. Like Melanchthon, advised by Luther, we can "sin boldly," leaving the role of the spectator, the critic, the analyst, and becoming committed and engaged.

For this reason *A Response to Lausanne* will be a better guide to us than the Lausanne Covenant itself. It holds revelation and experience, kingdom and history, the past and the present much more closely together than does the Covenant. It does not separate between two realms or orders of being, between a "pure" realm of the gospel in and of itself and another realm of "application of the gospel." It says instead:

> We affirm that the evangel is God's Good News in Jesus Christ. . . . It is Good News of the reign he proclaimed and embodies; of God's mission of love to restore the world to wholeness through the Cross of Christ and him alone; of his victory over the demonic powers of destruction and death; of his Lordship over the entire universe; it is Good News of a new creation, of a new humanity, a new birth through him by his life-giving Spirit; of the gifts of the messianic reign contained in Jesus and mediated through him by his Spirit; of the charismatic community empowered to embody his reign of shalom here and now before the whole creation and make his Good News seen and known. It is Good News of liberation, of restoration, of wholeness, and of salvation that is personal, social, global, and cosmic.[27]

How then is this evangel to be communicated? The communication of a holistic gospel must itself be holistic:

The communication of the evangel in its wholeness to every person worldwide is a mandate of the Lord Jesus to his community. There is no biblical dichotomy between the Word spoken and the Word made visible in the lives of God's people. Men will look as they listen and what they see must be at one with what they hear. The Christian community must chatter, discuss and proclaim the gospel; it must express the Gospel in its life as the new society, in its sacrificial service of others as a genuine expression of God's love, in its prophetic exposing and opposing of all demonic forces that deny the Lordship of Christ and keep men less than fully human; in its pursuit of real justice for all men; in its responsible and caring trusteeship of God's creation and its resources.

There are times when our communication may be by attitude and action alone, and times when the spoken word will stand alone; but we must repudiate as demonic the attempt to drive a wedge between evangelism and social action.[28]

How, then, will people respond to the gospel? Will we expect a "religious" response? To expect a dichotomized response to the gospel would be to deny its wholeness; as is the gospel, so must be the response:

The response demanded by the evangel is that men and women repent of their sins and every other lordship than that of Jesus Christ and commit themselves to him to serve him in the world. . . . Men must experience a change of understanding, attitude, and orientation. . . . But the new birth is not merely a subjective experience of forgiveness. It is a placement within the messianic community, God's new order which exists as a sign of God's reign to be consummated at the end of the age. . . . We must allow God to make visible in the new humanity the quality of life that reflects Christ and demonstrates his reign.[29]

Perhaps that is enough to say about evangelism in general, for evangelism is time- and location-specific. The kind of evangelism we need is a contextual evangelism—an evangelism alert to the current historical and cultural moment in each place where the church is called to witness.

The Evangelical Methodist Church in Bolivia, which produced a manifesto on "Evangelism in Latin America Today," stated that "the historical moment in which we are living requires that our priorities, expectations and tasks influence our evangelism." Referring to "the anguish and tensions of a continent caught between liberation and captivity" where "a minority enjoy the power and privileges of a consumer society (while) millions struggle in hunger and poverty, weakness and frustration, oppression and repression," the document states that "evangelism helps us to endure suffering and also to fight against the sources of unjust suffering and to change what can be changed."[30]

The Bolivians referred at the same time to the "climate of expectancy" of "a new society" and the emergence of a "new man" on the Latin American continent today, and said that evangelism responds to this climate with the word of resurrection—"the pledge and guarantee that make working for the new man and the new society worthwhile."

They defined evangelism therefore not only as holistic, biblical, and incarnate, but also as conscientizing:

> True evangelism is *conscientizing*: it leads man to become aware of himself and of his circumstances, before God and man, and to assume his historical responsibility. Evangelism calls man to be what he already is in God's purpose: a creature in his image and likeness, a steward and collaborator in creation, a brother to all men, a son adopted in love. But it also reveals his condition as sinner, as bad steward, as rebellious son, as irresponsible brother. Evangelism thus makes possible for men to move from a naive and guilty conscience to a critical conscience, beginning the process of abandoning the idols, myths, and habits which prevent him from being an authentically free, responsible and active agent of history. We therefore reject all evangelism which reinforces an escapist attitude toward life, an alienation from reality, an irresponsible stance toward society.[31]

As North Americans we cannot simply import from Latin America definitions or programs of evangelism. They would not be authentic in the context of White middle-class North America (though there is a similarity between manifestos coming from Latin America and the Pastoral Letter of the Catholic Bishops of Appalachia[32] as there also is, to some extent, a similarity between Black theology and Latin American liberation theology). Nor would Latin American programs speak to needs and concerns present here but not yet present in the same way on that continent—such as the concerns related to feminism. Our task for the immediate future is to develop a culture-specific evangelism for *our* society at this time in its history.[33]

This is what the next chapters—and particularly the following chapter and the final chapter—will seek to do.

*   *   *

It is at night that the Bridegroom comes. The light of the nuptial procession pierces the darkness. The call goes out, "Jesus has come!" Rise and trim your lamps.

6: TRIMMING OUR WICKS

> We acknowledge that God requires justice. But we have not proclaimed or demonstrated his justice to an unjust American society.
>
> —A Declaration of Evangelical
> Social Concern (1973)

> We have tried to bring about a more just society . . . (but) we have not sufficiently shown this determination to be rooted in Christ's Gospel. Though sometimes denounced as "radical," we have not been nearly as genuinely radical as the Gospel calls us to be. . . . We have not proclaimed the full truth of Christ.
>
> —A Response to "A Declaration of
> Evangelical Social Concern" by the
> National Council of Churches (1974)

JANET COMSTOCK, ELISE SULLIVAN, JEANNE ANNE SINGER, AND Carol Miller hear the announcement, "He has come." They rise and trim their wicks.

Note this: All of the ten young women in Jesus' allegory trim their wicks, not just the five wise ones. Just as all of them had been sleeping—not just the foolish ones—so all of them trim their wicks.

There is a point beyond which an allegory ought not to be stretched, and I sense that I am close to that point here, but let at least this much be said: on the basis of our foundation allegory, we have no reason to view the meaning of evangelism in America today in two separate ways, the one for Christians, the other for non-Christians. When we consider how the announcement "He has come" will strike American ears, we are—as Christians and non-Christians—one people.

Just as Isaiah did not separate himself from his people but said, when he saw the glory of God, "I am a man of unclean lips and I dwell in the midst of a people of unclean lips" (Isa. 6:5), so must we as Christians affirm our solidarity with the people of our land. It may be hard to affirm this theologically—the mystique of individualism tends to deprive us of awareness of corporate responsibility. It ought to be easier, after over half a century of American sociology, to affirm sociologically that there is such a thing as American society and that we all belong to it and are shaped by it.

In this chapter I will carry forward the description of what that society is like—not, in this case, in order to describe the darkness which has descended upon America and the Western world, but in order to consider the meaning for America of the message, "He has come."

*   *   *

I sense that the message comes to America differently in the late '70s than it would have a decade or even less ago. But I don't want to exaggerate this difference. Social worlds change slowly. America's sense of self (Durkheim would have spoken of our "collective representations") has changed in the last few years—though our position in the world and our internal life have remained more constant than we would like to think.

In 1954, I was an American Field Service exchangee in Germany, and I also traveled through the Netherlands and France that summer. I remember having a tremendous sense of euphoria in being an American. I came from the country of Franklin Delano Roosevelt, Dwight D. Eisenhower and the Marshall Plan. Boulevards were named after FDR, and monuments of Marshall Plan munificence were everywhere. European styles—from pop music and jeans to chewing gum—were being set by American youth. The relaxed "American way of life," with its commercial enterprise, affluence, technological "know-how," and its broad smile and open hand, was winning converts from Europe's more traditional, less commercial, less relaxed ways.

Seven years later, going as a teacher to Ghana, I was warmly received by faculty and students, because, unlike the British, I, as an American, had no colonial past. They believed Americans were the "non-imperialist Westerners," that we weren't as "stuffy" as the British, and that we had no evil designs on their nation. Our ways were informal, our academic style was non-traditional and refreshing; we were "open to the future." At least so our mystique went, and people believed it.

In both instances these perceptions of what America represented came to me from outside. They were something of a shock, for I was that kind of American of whom Ralph Waldo Emerson had such a horror, the "man with soul so dead who never to himself hath said, 'This is my own, my native land!' " I tended to be an Anglophile, and it shocked me to see how positively others perceived the country I valued so little.

I relate these experiences because I believe millions of Americans had similar experiences and shared them with others, and that such reports contributed to a national sense that we were a warm, friendly, well-loved, beneficent country, and that Americans were welcome anywhere (except perhaps in France!).

It is a tremendous shock to me nowadays to listen to the travel ads on the air and find that the ad agencies think what is keeping Americans from traveling abroad is a perception that we're not loved. Now we're told, "Yes, this country is, even in these days, a place where Americans are welcome, a place where you don't have to fear race riots, an anti-tourist animus, or a hatred of Americans." Or we're told, "Yes, your American Express credit card is still welcome in Scandinavia," or "In the Netherlands we all speak English."

As I listen to these ads, I say to myself, "Then the change has reached the level of the way we collectively understand ourselves." And I think, "How the mighty have fallen!"

Frankly, this change in self-perception made the celebrations of the Bicentennial much more tolerable for me than I had anticipated. I was keyed up to expect jingoism, national chauvinism, and expressions of overweening pride, but—after listening to the speeches and reading and hearing the propaganda—I concluded that perhaps Nixon had taken much of it away with him to San Clemente after his farewell speech (in which he repeated, as you'll remember, some of the banalities about our "generosity as a people").

So I'm inclined to think this says something about the way in which the evangelistic announcement, "He has come," ought to be made in America today. Fewer people than there would have been a decade ago will be moved to respond to that announcement, "Well, of course he has! And it's about time! After all, we've been pretty good disciples all these years. We knew he'd stop here first." There will still be some who will thus presume upon the grace of God. But I sense that many will now respond to the announcement with a sigh of relief, "You mean he didn't cross us off his list?" A third group will be pleased that the Lord confirmed the good opinion they personally had of the nation's righteousness but weren't mouthing as loudly as before.

If it is the task of the church in its mission, as Niebuhr said, "to comfort the afflicted and afflict the comfortable," an evangelistic approach ought to be sensitive to such changes of nuance in a national mood. If some such change in our national self-perception has indeed come about, I believe we need a different evangelistic approach, but how different it will be and in what way are questions I will be able to answer only after we have taken a deeper look at the change and examined what it represents.

*   *   *

If you asked any ten suburban Americans how they would account for our change in self-perception, I expect at least six would answer with one word: "Vietnam."

I wish I could interpret that profoundly, and say that, as a nation, we have come to appreciate the dangers of what Senator Fulbright called "the arrogance of power," that we have learned that it is not our role to set morality or determine political, economic, or social systems for the world. I think some have come to appreciate this view, and many are at least wary of new attempts to get "mixed up in the affairs of other countries." For some, however, it seems to be simply a matter of hurt pride: no repentance or second thoughts on our past wisdom are involved.

For most what it comes down to is that we lost. There is something in our national ethos that says, "Better not play the

game than be a loser." Had the Thieu-Ky government been able
to subdue the Vietcong and send the North back beyond her
borders, I suggest we would still be engaged in large-scale adven-
turism overseas today and that the rhetoric of our Bicentennial
would have been intolerable. As it is, we didn't go into Angola or
Lebanon and I question whether we would, as a nation, be able to
come to a common mind today about the advisability of coming
to the aid of even our closest allies in an hour of crisis, if it involved
sending "our boys" in. The negative wisdom of George
Washington's Farewell Address is having its day.

In the collective mind, in the aftermath of Vietnam, we have
become non-interventionists—our hands are clean. Covert intervention by the CIA or other agencies—even if it involves murder
and subversion—troubles our national conscience much less. Intervention through domesticated foreign nationals—paid by us,
bribed by us, trained by us in methods of counter-insurgency
(including the systematic, scientific use of torture)—seems not to
be a matter of morality. Intervention through encouraging the
purchase of arms may even be a plus (it provides jobs for Americans and helps us keep our international balance of payments in
the black). Intervention through American-based transnational
corporations is "a private matter" (and if everybody else bribes,
our companies have to do it, too). Intervention through others—
particularly other "third world" nations, like Brazil—is not American intervention.

Yet, through all these ways America is intervening today as
efficiently as before—or perhaps more efficiently*—in the interests of maintaining the world in its present state—a state favorable
to us, to our allies, and to our standard of living, "a world friendly
to democracy."

This is a serious accusation. It is not made lightly. The reader
will recognize that it has much in common with the Marxist
analysis of the present world crisis in Chapter 4. It also has much
in common with Ellul's critique of technology as the master of
those who employ it, particularly as Bellah and Heilbroner refine
that critique by relating it to the economic system in which
technology operates.

---

*The best example of greater relative efficiency is the field of arms sales. Whereas,
at the height of the Vietnam War, we spent $30 billion annually to keep Thieu's

There is a difference—at least of *élan*—between these two critiques, in a way which bears on my interpretation: whereas the Marxist analysis stresses the class struggle and the will of the bourgeoisie (that is, of international capitalism) to dominate, Ellul's analysis requires a much smaller quotient of human will to operate—humans are in the power of forces greater than themselves. To Ellul class domination is subordinate to the domination of society (of all classes) by technology. To most Marxists it is the capitalist, who controls technology and uses it to continue and extend his domination, who is the villain, not technology itself, which most Marxists regard positively.

I do not find it necessary, sociologically or theologically, to choose between these two critiques as if they were alternatives which exclude each other. To take one example, I would argue that the nature of technology in the automotive industry and the nature of international economics is such that Ford did not have absolute freedom of choice with respect to increasing its investment in the Philippines when martial law was introduced by President Marcos. In that instance, the market required expansion, and the mode of production required diversification both of centers of production and sales. If Ford were not to expand in the Philippines, it would have had to expand elsewhere. It could not stand pat. But the number of places where it could expand on such highly favorable economic terms has become increasingly limited.

At the same time that Ford made what was to it (I assume) a purely economic decision, however, it was buttressing the

government in power, we now help keep 51 repressive regimes in power at a cost in 1975 of less than $9.5 billion—most of which was in credits, not giveaways. The authors of "The Commerce in Death: Foreign Military Sales," a Corporate Information Center brief published in June, 1976, comment that "Defenders of foreign military sales both within the Department of Defense and within industry claim that such sales are the answer to basic economic and political problems. Foreign military sales will ease unemployment, improve the U.S. balance of payments, cut production costs by sharing them with other countries, protect the U.S. lead in technological know-how, and extend American influence abroad, because sales are accompanied by technicians, training and advisory personnel who create dependencies on these services. In short, foreign military sales are a foreign policy tool." For some of the ten corporations with the largest sales in 1975 "foreign military sales have now become crucial for their continued success as economic institutions; their survival is now entwined with the proliferation of weapons around the world."[1]

political/economic/military policy of the U.S. Government. That policy is to forge links with right-wing regimes, increase the dependence of those regimes on U.S. capital and technology, provide jobs for some of the masses of unemployed in such nations, provide industrial plants throughout the "free world" capable of producing military technology, and improve the U.S. balance of payments.

Marcos, in his turn, could offer Ford something it can't get everywhere: a strike-free economy, a docile labor force, lack of effective political opposition, freedom from the fear of nationalization, and the opportunity to repatriate a large proportion of profits.

In an industry with a more gentle image, the makers of infant feeding formula are engaged in the same type of intervention with other, but equally deleterious results. Finding the markets of the developed countries glutted with their products, Bristol-Myers and other firms began in the mid '60s to develop markets in developing countries, where breast-feeding—the method of infant feeding medical experts in those countries recommended as best—was common. Sophisticated advertising campaigns spread the values of artificial feeding as—supposedly—more hygienic and more "modern." A "need" was created, and the companies' products have sold. U.S. dairy farmers have a new outlet for dehydrated milk. Bristol-Myers has a new outlet for vitamin additives, and a fantastic source of profit. A dependency on the U.S. economy is created. At the same time new health problems are created by bottle-feeding in places with impure water to mix formula, low standards of hygiene, and usually no refrigeration for keeping the once mixed formula safe. The desire of U.S. and other companies for profit over-rules all other considerations.

Many in our country would be shocked if they heard and understood this story. Many, hearing it, have been moved to horror and even action. Others respond callously, "Well, they don't have to buy it, do they?" Still others would want to distinguish between what private companies do and government policy.

If a definite answer is sought to the question, "Is there a determinate effort by the people of the United States to dominate and oppress other peoples?" what is our answer?

The first part of the answer would seem to be that, owing to the

Vietnam debacle and the Watergate scandal and the ensuing investigations, the government is less inclined to interfere directly and overtly in the affairs of other nations. This is in response to the expressed will of the people. Our direct, overt involvement is now more closely in the range of what other major powers do—we are not clearly "the world's policeman" at present.

Secondly, no one can say what the extent of covert activity by the government is. And here the people—and their representatives—have been more apathetic. Certainly there has been no disavowal by the CIA or the Department of State or the Pentagon of such activity in principle. It can safely be said that our tax dollars, with our compliance, are being used for this purpose, though no one can say to what extent. The purpose of such activity would be easier to define: the maintenance of regimes "friendly to us" and friendly to overall world "stability" (the continuance of present patterns of distribution of wealth and resources) and the weakening or overthrow of hostile regimes, and those that challenge the status quo.

Intervention through foreign nationals—either in our employ, or of their own accord—in sympathy with our national goals continues. Such intervention has as its goals those defined above but as its special "track" working within the electoral process (through supporting one party or individual in an electoral campaign against others) or within the decision-making processes of the government (as in the case of bribes by U.S.-based transnationals). Here again, we as a people are either lethargic about this issue or in agreement with the policy. There has been little public outcry concerning it, even when the issue has been that of U.S. aid to foreign government officials engaged in the suppression of domestic unrest through the use of torture, and the training of them in scientific torture techniques.

Intervention through arms sales—"letting them fight their own battles"—has grown immensely and has contributed to (a) building up costly regional arms races, thus diverting needed funds from development; (b) bolstering military and one-party regimes and the role of the military as a political/social force within such countries; and (c) warfare and destruction. Such intervention also ties these countries to the U.S. military-industrial-scientific complex and is thus a form of colonialism. There is little sign that the

American public disapproves of something so beneficial to its financial well-being.

Intervention through American-based transnational corporations grows apace. Critics differ in their assessment of the effects, which are not, in any case, uniform, since different governments receive transnationals differently, some restricting their activities and others giving them practically free rein. Nevertheless, my estimate would be that, in the main, transnational activity does constitute a form of intervention in the determination of the economic future of many nations. The transnationals operate on a scale so great that only large national corporations or state capitalistic ventures can compete with them; they tend to monopolize markets and inhibit labor-intensive competition (with intermediate technology) from developing, thus biasing the country's future development toward a capital- and energy-intensive mode of production. Furthermore, the corporations frequently engage in "need-creation," turning the economy away from that which all people need toward the production and consumption of unnecessary or prestigious goods, encouraging the formation of a cultural elite and contributing to the development of the values of Western consumerism. The American people participate directly in this activity through the corporations which they as individuals and as members of pension plans and other institutions own.

Through our cinema, our books, and our magazines, and lately through the sale of our TV programs to foreign networks, we further contribute to the "value revolution"—a very real and insidious form of intervention. The contribution of present styles of tourism should also be included in such an analysis, as should the effect of labor migrations to the U.S.

Finally, the choice of various regional "vicegerents"—such as Brazil and Iran—to act essentially on our behalf without the besmirching of our name will have long-term and significant geopolitical effects. Yet this has taken place without ever raising the policy to the level of national debate.

What conclusion will we, then, draw? Is there a determinate effort on the part of the people of the United States to dominate other peoples? It seems that any hesitancy must rest mainly on the interpretation of the word "determinate." There is no doubt but that the people of the United States are, in many subtle and not so subtle ways, engaged in the activity of domination of other peoples. There are different levels of public awareness of what we are doing, and there are different levels of concern with the ways we are doing it. Some of what we do takes place semi-automatically, through the operation of the technology to which we are committed. Some takes place through conscious decision of a Metternichean sort, the determined effort to suppress revolutionary change throughout the world. Could we hope that a considered effort at "consciousness-raising" might change all this?

It is clear, at least in my mind, that we have no reason to be more optimistic about awakening the conscience of Americans to their involvement in oppression than the Christian Institute of South Africa has to believe that it can awaken the conscience of White South Africans to what they are doing to Blacks. The Christian Institute is quite realistic about the difficulties involved in bringing about change. They recognize that "People hold their opinions to justify, maintain or protect their vested interests—wealth, safety, reputation, advancement, health and families."[2] But at the same time

> The reasons people give for maintaining their attitudes are usually inaccurate. They attest their high idealism, their historical indebtedness, or their desire to maintain justice, truth or freedom. Whites will give many reasons for the support of the apartheid policies such as "maintaining Christian civilization," "our great traditions," "permitting the Bantu to develop in his own way," but the real reason is that they desire to maintain their superior position and fear that they will not. They believe that their vested interests are protected by the apartheid system and therefore they will not change. There's money in it.[3]

And it comes down to some pretty ugly things, like the multiplication of squalid slums, the perpetuation of malnutrition for generations of children, the development—in many countries for the first time—of an urban proletariat, the alienation of land from the people of the country, the imprisonment and detention of some of the most creative minds many countries have produced, the death of thousands by torture, and so forth. Even if Americans could learn to understand the connections between the U.S. and these results of oppression, it is unlikely they would be willing to pay the price of significant change. That price would involve contentment with a smaller share of the world's resources, more reliance on public transportation, satisfaction with fewer luxury goods, fewer vacation trips, less energy use, the necessity of doing for ourselves what foreign migrants now do (the least attractive jobs within our society), paying more for our coffee and chocolate, eliminating domestic industry which could not compete on a truly free world market (and the retraining of our labor force and the reshaping of industry accordingly), a willingness to see proportionately more Tanzanias and fewer Brazils develop, and the acceptance of a world controlled not by the rich and powerful nations, but by international law and international institutions. As the Christian Institute comments: "People change when it is demonstrated that it is in their interest to change. When they themselves see it that way, they will do something about it. Such change cannot be imposed but must arise in their own experience."[4]

Until such a time—if it comes—we shall continue to live in a world marked by oppression, repression, and the domination of the weak by the strong. Durkheim would call it an anomic world. The Bible—and Marxism, for that has biblical roots—calls it an alienated world. The Marxist says that alienation exists because the rich exploit the poor and alienate from them what is rightfully theirs, and that our entire mode of production is an expression of such alienation. The New Testament says that alienation exists because humanity is in a state of disobedience to God and that, through human sin, forces have entered into this world which exert power over humanity, both visibly and invisibly.

The Bible's generic name for such forces is "the principalities and powers," but it would be a shallow reading of scripture which did not recognize that these demonic powers have other names as well. What Marxism calls "capitalist domination" and what Ellul calls "technology" could constitute specific names for such demonic forces, as could "racism," "militarism," and "national pride." Kolakowski would encourage us to add "Stalinist monism." It is characteristic of the Bible to take these forces seriously—realistically—as existing in their own right, apart from the human individuals who are under their sway. Just as Durkheim would say a society is greater than the sum of its parts, for it has a social reality transcending the reality of the individuals who make it up, so the Bible would say that the principalities and powers are at loose in the world, wreaking havoc, and people come under their sway.

All this must, then, be considered, as we consider how to frame our evangelistic approach. If we believe that human beings operate with total freedom, we will assume that, with intelligence and will, they can overcome the alienation which at present exists, and we will tend to take a confrontational approach. Our "good news" will come off sounding pretty much like bad news.

If, on the other hand, we recognize that human freedom operates only within a circumscribed realm, and that people are often under the sway of forces beyond their control, our message will have to be proclaimed differently. Our gospel to powerful North America will be, in a certain sense, a "gospel of liberation"! At the very least, it will be a pastoral—as opposed to a confrontational—approach. It will not exclude judgment and confrontation, but it will operate out of an over-all perspective of grace, out of a conviction of the sovereignty of God over all principalities and powers, out of faith in the risen and ascended Christ, and out of a profound hope that, through the Spirit, he is now working to establish his Kingdom.

I find such an approach in Isaiah the Prophet. He anticipated by 28 centuries the wisdom of the Christian Institute when it lays down this principle of social change:

> If it is desired to change a person's attitude we must first discover a motivation for this in the place where he believes his personal interests to be vested. He must discover that it is in his own interest to change. This is not cynicism; it is the realism of dealing with sinful man.[5]

Isaiah knew how to deal with sinful humanity. He did not presume to think he could scare the people of Judah into changing from their sinful ways by confrontational preaching. Isaiah could get confrontational, but—like Hosea—it was within the context of God's covenant compassion.

There is a certain kind of "prophecy" which differentiates itself from the real thing by the lack of compassion the "prophet" has for the people to whom—or rather against whom—he prophesies. It is a sadistic kind of "prophecy" which derives pleasure from seeing people squirm, which does not really desire that people repent and be healed. Such was the attitude of Jonah at the repentance of Nineveh, intended by the author of that book to shame Israel for its hardness of heart vis-à-vis the Gentile world and distinguish that attitude from God's love and concern (Jonah 3:10-4:11).

Isaiah had plenty of reason to condemn Judah. The Lord had revealed to him his dissatisfaction with the people's failure to live in covenant faithfulness with him. Judah had shown its unfaithfulness in its foreign and military policy, in its corrupt leadership and the corruption of its economic life, in the oppression of its poor and powerless by the rich, in the lack of justice in the land, in its religious idolatry, in its insincere religious cultus.

Isaiah was out taking a stroll at sundown and he saw the oxen and the asses returning unguided from grazing to their masters' pens, and he took notice of how each knew its own master's pen. "How unlike God's people Judah!" he thought:

> The ox knows its owner,
> and the ass its master's crib;
> but Israel does not know,
> my people does not understand.

He knew that the nation, despite its having been chosen and reared by God, had rebelled against him (Isa. 1:2-4).

But notice how he approaches them: rather than excoriate them for their sin, he seeks to convince them that their present way of life is bringing them grief. It is like the insight of the Christian Institute document that *Change needs dissatisfaction:* "A prerequisite of change is a dissatisfaction with life as it is; satisfied people do not want to change."[6] Isaiah asks the people to consider their present military condition, at war with Samaria and Syria, and to understand how much they have suffered:

> The whole head is sick,
> and the whole heart faint.
> From the sole of the foot even to the head,
> there is no soundness in it,
> but bruises and sores,
> and bleeding wounds. . . .
>
> Your country lies desolate,
> your cities are burnt with fire;
> in your very presence aliens devour your land;

it is desolate . . .
the daughter of Zion is left like a booth in a vineyard,
like a lodge in a cucumber field. . . .

If the Lord of hosts had not left us a few survivors,
we should have been like Sodom (Isa. 1:5-9).

He asks them to consider their domestic situation, and how justice
is not to be found in their land:

How the faithful city
has become a harlot,
she that was full of justice!
Righteousness lodged in her,
but now murderers.
Your silver has become dross,
your wine mixed with water.
Your princes are rebels
and companions of thieves.
Every one loves a bribe
and runs after gifts.
They do not defend the fatherless,
and the widow's cause does not come to them (Isa. 1:21-23).

The basic thrust of his argument is, "They have brought evil upon
themselves" (Isa. 3:9). It is their failure to live by the knowledge of
the Lord which is responsible for their shortage of food and the
carrying of many of the people away into exile (Isa. 5:13). The
punishment has come from the Lord, certainly, but it has been
meant to lead them to repent so that they might be healed. And so
Isaiah addresses the people, in the second person, in the words of
the Lord:

"Come now, let us reason together,
says the Lord:
though your sins are like scarlet,
they shall be as white as snow;
though they are red like crimson,
they shall become like wool.
If you are willing and obedient,
you shall eat the good of the land;
but if you refuse and rebel,
you shall be devoured by the sword;
for the mouth of the Lord has spoken" (Isa. 1:18-20).

He addresses his appeal to two levels: first and, it would seem,
foremost in his strategy, addressing King Ahaz, a hard-hearted,

unbelieving man, the one person most responsible for the tragedies; but also, as a complementary strategy, addressing the people directly, over the heads of their rulers.

Even with Ahaz, Isaiah's style is not confrontational but evangelical: he offers Ahaz the Lord's every assurance that he is still with his people, and that if Ahaz will only trust the Lord, all will go well, the threats of Samaria and Syria will come to nothing (Isa. 7:1-10). He offers to demonstrate this with a sign, but Ahaz refuses. Isaiah says then the Lord will himself give him a sign of his faithfulness, that he is Emmanuel, God-with-us, a sign that within a short time the threat from Samaria and Syria will be gone (Isa. 7:11-17).

Although Ahaz refuses to believe, Isaiah feels called by the Lord to continue to proclaim the promise. He goes in to his wife and she conceives a son and he names the child "The spoil speeds, the prey hastens," a prophecy of the defeat and despoiling of Samaria and Syria by Assyria. The Lord will be faithful to Judah, and the nation need not fear those of whom they now stand in dread (Isa. 8:1-15).

Isaiah's guidance is rejected by the leaders again and again. He turns to the people and warns them:

> O, my people, your leaders mislead you
> and confuse the course of your paths (Isa. 3:12).

He announces that the Lord has begun the judgment of the leaders and of the upper economic class (Isa. 3:13-4:1). He predicts that evil will indeed befall Judah, but that the Lord's promise to the nation, collectively, will not fail, because "A remnant shall return" (Isa. 7:3). After the darkness will come a time of great light, a period of messianic peace (Isa. 9:2-7).

We could go on, reconstructing other elements of Isaiah's ministry, particularly how he ministered in the year 722 when Assyria, having destroyed the northern kingdom of Samaria, turned against Judah, and we could, in that context, further develop the themes already presented, but what is more germane to our discussion is a consideration of what accounted for Isaiah's "evangelical" style of prophecy.

I find the origin of this evangelical mode in his vision of the glory of the Lord in chapter 6. Several points bear noting:

(1) His vision is of the holiness of God, and of a world filled with God's glory. This is an eschatological vision, of the future of the world. God's glory, in the Old Testament, is his reputation for being holy, for holiness is an internal characteristic of God—pertaining to God as he is in himself; glory is the external manifestation of this character. But, as all Judeans were only too painfully aware, the whole earth was *not* full of God's glory. Judah lived in the midst of nations which did not give to Yahweh the glory due him. Isaiah's vision is significant, therefore, in that it was an eschatological vision of a world that had come to the fullness of Yahweh's plan for it. From that vision came his conviction that one day such a world would come to pass—he saw the future as already present.

(2) When he has had the vision, he goes on to say, "My eyes have seen the King," giving Yahweh that name for—if not the first—then one of the first times in Old Testament literature, affirming Yahweh's reign as mysteriously present in the midst of historical reality.

(3) When he sees the holiness of God and hears the heavenly choirs sing Yahweh's praise, he wants to join in the antiphonal chorus, but he cannot, for he feels convicted of sin. "Woe is me!" he cries out, "for I must remain silent"—Ernst Jenni's suggested translation of a word translators have long pondered over—"for I am a man of unclean lips and I dwell in the midst of a people of unclean lips." Isaiah considers himself one with his people in sin. He is not "holier than thou." Even though he is one to whom the vision has been granted, he knows he is part of the world which God needs to transform in the establishment of his Kingdom.

(4) But then he has an unexpected experience of cleansing, and learns that his people will experience a cleansing as well. They also will be purged by fire, but in the end God's grace will save a remnant. The stump which is burned over and over again when the tree has been felled is "the holy seed" of God's eschatological people.

Therefore, although Isaiah's message is for the nation, he proceeds at the same time to gather a group of disciples to bear witness to the testimony of God's grace through the deep "distress and darkness, the gloom and anguish" of Judah's immediate future, until the day that the same people who walked through the darkness will "see a great light" (Isa. 8:16-9:2).

It hardly needs saying how similar all this is to the New Testament conception of history and to Jesus' apocalyptic and eschatological proclamation, and particularly to our foundation allegory. There is the imagery of darkness and light, the prediction of a division among the people, the affirmation that God is working in present events toward the consumation of his reign, the sense that history moves forward through a series of crises, and the image of God as the covenant-faithful one whose will it is that his people should come to salvation. The difference between the two prophecies is Jesus, God's anointed, and the foreshortening of the time till the eschaton which occurs in his ministry. But that is the subject of our next chapter.

Before we leave this chapter, let us try to draw the necessary links between the evangelical prophecy of Isaiah and our practice of evangelism among the middle-class people of the Western world—and particularly America—today.

The Christian Institute of South Africa considers the most effective means of social change today to be helping people to recognize their own need for change, and to realize it is in their own interest to change. The message, to be effective, will be neither an appeal to charity nor an appeal to reason or even theology:

> The purpose of reasoning is to make a path in people's minds for them to walk on when they are ready; or to knock the props from an untenable attitude, or to provide a theoretical background for an emotional response that is taking place. . . . When men know what they ought to do or be, they have a reasonable ground to move on when the pressures prove it is in their interests to do so.[7]

But our primary effort should be to help them see that the present situation is not in their interests and that the desired change would be. (I will speak of ways in which the church can most effectively do that in the last chapter.)

It is not at all difficult to adapt Isaiah's preaching to our own situation. We can point out to present-day America that it has become like Isaiah's shed erected in the midst of a farm—our country has lost friends in the world; racial strife is dividing our cities; a profit-above-all type of technology has ravaged our environment and lowered the quality of our lives; current residential patterns are failing to give us satisfaction or community; consumerism is linked up with the drug culture, alcoholism and shattering loneliness; senior citizens feel unwanted and estranged; we have no real security even in our suburbs; divorce and suicide rates have been climbing; there is alienation between young people and their parents; and, even with our affluence, financial security seems elusive to us.

If the dominant message of our society seems to be that of Burger King—"Have it your way"—the reality of its consequences seems to be desolation (I think of Durkheim's perception of the necessity of a moral discipline in society). We can say to America what Isaiah said to Judah: "You have brought this evil upon yourselves" (Isa. 3:9). At the same time, though, we can relate it, as Isaiah does, to the judgment of God: "The Lord of hosts has a day against all that is proud and lofty" (Isa. 2:12). But what is important in this is that our proclamation not fall into the trap of the law, but always be proclamation of God's gracious will. Geiko Müller-Fahrenholz hits the nail on the head when he examines the bulk of Christian exhortation in our day:

> The form in which the appeals for a swift change of attitude and a radical reorientation of all values reach us is the form of the law. But from the New Testament we know that the law "kills." It judges man, it oppresses him, it even cripples his conscience. It does not set free.[8]

What we are concerned to do is to set free, to liberate, and only the gospel is liberating.

But, someone asks, what about declaring straightforth to people that they are bringing on ecological and international doom? Can that not be part of our preaching? Müller-Fahrenholz, though he believes in the essential accuracy of such prophecies, doubts it:

> Descriptions which forecast total catastrophe in terms of apocalyptic inevitability overstrain the capacity for hope in the scope for constructive action and merely engender apathy. . . . Nothing will be gained if people are paralysed by shock at the appalling enormity of the crisis. On the contrary, it is essential that they should not remain stunned by the shock of discovering the future but should be free to act in a courageous and imaginative way.[9]

Fahrenholz pleads for a clear, simple, graspable presentation of the essential facts, with the avoidance of both over-information and apocalyptic language. But he recognizes that "apathy is more than just a consequence of intellectual and spiritual lassitude." He suspects that, even if we explained everything clearly and avoided paralyzing people with apocalyptic or confusing them with over-information, people still might not respond. He speaks of "an inability to grieve"; he asks:

> Have we perhaps banished the crisis and its appalling magnitude from our conscious minds in order to avoid squarely facing the fact that it has been engendered by our own errors and our own in-adequacy? Are we perhaps denying ourselves the release of freely expressing our grief over creation laid waste by our idolatry of the principle of growth, and the inequality between rich and poor created by our acquisitiveness? Shall we perhaps fail to master the crisis simply because we cannot and will not weep over the despoil-ment of the future? . . . The idea that we lead our comfortable lives not only at the cost of millions of our fellow human beings in the Third World but also at the cost of our own children and grandchil-dren, is an extremely hard one to accept. . . . We seem unable to grasp that this global crisis is largely the result of the very virtues we have constantly been exhorted to practice—efficiency, industrious-ness, thrift, to name but a few. Admissions of this sort mean uproot-ing all our habitual concepts of values and accepting all the uncer-tainty and disorientation this entails, but the spiritual anguish in-volved is such that we almost instinctively recoil from it or else cast about for ways of evading it.[10]

The knowledge of our culpability creates such a great psychologi-cal turmoil within us that we try various ways of evasion. It is not just that we do not understand the connections between the current world crisis and the way our society functions, nor just that the dimensions of the problem are so great and its apocalyptic character so frightening that we are paralyzed into apathetic resignation—if not cynicism. No, here Müller-Fahrenholz strikes deeper: it is a *spiritual* problem involving a deep, inner perception of *guilt*, which creates such fundamental anxiety that—in order for us to be evangelized—we must be *liberated* from its terrible bonds and *reconciled* to God.

Part of the way in which this can happen, Müller-Fahrenholz thinks, is by the congregation being restored to its place "as the centre and agent of mutual support and caring." He does not mean the congregation in the parochial sense necessarily, but house churches, discussion and fellowship groups, and the like, which can become close healing fellowships which help their members become "advocates of life oriented toward the future," by helping us assume pastoral responsibility for one another so as to overcome our common resignation, apathy, and exhaustion.[11]

But, he goes on, if guilt is a large part of the problem, and inner defense mechanisms need to be overcome before the quest for new values can succeed,

> the Church's task of creating freedom and reconciliation gains fresh importance. The Church cannot stand by and accept the vicious circle of apathy, resignation and evasion, because it lives in the knowledge that forgiveness and new beginnings are always possible.[12]

And then he becomes quite specific about what elements of the Christian evangel speak to this need:

> The death of Jesus on the cross is the guarantee that all human life can be redeemed and renewed, despite all its demonic distortion, its frailty, its violence, and its apocalyptic misery. (The Church) accepts all the uprooting and uncertainty because the promise says that the coming Kingdom of God will be a real home and a real country for the whole of creation.[13]

Müller-Fahrenholz calls for the church to "bear true witness" by working against fatalism on the one hand and refusal to take things seriously enough on the other. It can give people the courage to repent, not, he says, by preaching "blind optimism" but "trust in the Lord of the future." This, he says, "can help us to take upon ourselves the immense effort of rethinking that is needed and do all that is humanly possible."[14]

My only criticism of Müller-Fahrenholz's essay would be that the word *rethinking* does not express the fullness of what he had been speaking about, for the church is called to be much more than a center of thought. He is calling for it to combine in its ministry a type of existence—living for each other—with a courage to face reality. I would add the necessity for the church to incarnate in *works* of liberation the *gospel* of liberation which, as a *liberated community,* it proclaims. Evangelism is a matter of speaking, but also of doing and being.

*   *   *

The announcement is made: "He has come!" The time for sleep has ended. Rise and trim your wicks. The wedding-procession is already dispersing the darkness with its light.

7: THE BRIDEGROOM

(1) The Crucified and Risen Lord

> Jesus means discovering Jesus. It is never a static
> concept, something or someone pinned onto a
> theological collector's board, dissected, labelled and
> very dead. Rather he is our journey, with surprises
> round most corners.
> —John Poulton, *Jesus in Focus*

KALAGORA SUBBA RAO IS A HINDU FROM ANDHRA PRADESH IN
India. A vision of Christ he had when a school teacher several
decades ago profoundly transformed his life. Now a committed
follower of Christ, he has gathered together a community of tens
of thousands of Hindus who, like him, are devoted to Christ's
service but have not been baptized into formal membership in any
church. M.M. Thomas refers to Subba Rao's community as "a
Christ-centered fellowship within Hinduism."[1]

Subba Rao regards organized religion as the jail of Christ, from
which Christ seeks constantly to be liberated. What Christ desires,
he believes, is not that people should form a religion but that they
should serve him by renouncing self and living for others.

Subba Rao describes how, through a vision, he became a
disciple of Christ. In this dramatic testimony he describes Christ as
the one perpetually searching after his lost people, undeterred by
their sin.

> Who are you that are rousing me from my sound midnight sleep
> and showing me your clean way with great care? How could you
> open the door which was closed and strongly bolted? Tell me why
> you came here at all to this horrible sinner?

Do you know me? Have you ever seen me? You call me by name. Is it that we both were one without "You" and "I" in some distant past? Tell me. Otherwise, how is it that my heart is upset with joy by your very presence?

Don't you know that I am a hard-hearted sinner who never cares to know who you are? In some unknown past I forgot myself in "Maya" [illusion] . . . and clung to this body, and happily worshipping it, willfully ignored the Eternal Truth.

Seeing you made me forget myself; seeing you after forgetting myself, I have recognized you. Now there is no more "Agnana" [ignorance] which had misled me to think in terms of "I" and "mine". Now I am quite free from the bondage and hence can freely walk in your footsteps.

The experience of being found by Christ is thus, for Subba Rao, a personal liberation. It is parallel to—though different from—Christ's own liberation, as he conceives of it: In order to be able to meet his lost people, he had to become liberated from religious "hirelings." Subba Rao learns at what great cost he did this.

Yes, I heard that you were the God of a Religion. I also saw several churches beautifully built for you. I also heard that very many worship you there. Then what made you come here to me without gladly receiving their services?

Have the very fanatics that destroyed you in the name of Religion now made you an article of merchandise? Unable to tolerate them bartering you in the market of Religion for their livelihood, have you come to me, this fallen atheist, as your refuge?

Above all, how could you slip out of that impregnable fortress of Religion? Could not the closely-guarding hirelings detect you? What hazards and agonies you must have suffered all through the unbeaten paths! Your tender feet are blistered and bleeding. My heart breaks at that very sight.

Seeing his visitor suffering so, Subba Rao's heart is broken. He yields himself to Christ's service:

Oh, Brother, let me not see you in awful tears. Don't be worried that you have no shelter. All you need is a body through which you can complete the remaining service to humanity, is it? Then, here is my body. It is no more mine. No more "Maya." Dwell in it forever and ever.[3]

Subba Rao is a Hindu. He expresses his experience in terms of Hindu religious perception (there are similarities to Isaiah's call,

but also real differences). Yet one aspect in Hinduism is transformed completely: instead of suffering being regarded as something to be delivered from, as one seeks *Moksha* (deliverance
from the body, bodily suffering, and even human existence)—
suffering is seen positively. Voluntary suffering on behalf of others
is what makes Christ who he is, and it is that to which he calls
those who would be his followers.

It is not only to Hinduism that the concept of redemption
through suffering love seems nonsensical. We have a similar
phenomenon in our own "Christian West"* in every form of
triumphalism which denies the way of the cross, and it is on the
horror of suffering as God's chosen way to salvation that Rev.
Moon is basing his triumphalistic appeal. The way of the cross has
never been popular. As Paul said to the Corinthians, "Jews want
miracles for proof, and Greeks look for wisdom. As for us, we
proclaim the crucified Christ, a message that is offensive to the
Jews and nonsense to the Gentiles" (I Cor. 1:23, TEV).

The way of the cross is the way of the lamb that before its
shearers is dumb (Isa. 53). What Subba Rao reminds us is that,
when in this chapter we consider the Bridegroom, we have to
begin with the affirmation: *the Bridegroom is the Lamb.* In terms
of the wedding imagery of this book, that affirmation is where our
Christology must begin.

We have spoken of God as the wedding-maker, of different
attitudes people can take toward invitations to weddings, of the

---

*A good example is found in the furor created by the inclusion in the Armed Forces
Worship Book of Sydney Carter's hymn "It was on a Friday Morning." The hymn
articulates the bitterness of one of the thieves crucified with Jesus. A number of
groups have taken exception to the refrain in which the thief, in his dying anguish,
says "It's God they ought to crucify/Instead of you and me/I said to the
carpenter/A-hanging on the tree."

The very irony of the hymn is that it *was* God who was crucified. He was the
carpenter. But the Veterans' Authority Chief of Chaplains demanded that the
hymn be "removed from all new Books of Worship within 24 hours," because
"we do not think it the proper hymn to be sung in a hospital where there are sick
people." He further called it "sacrilegious." He called instead for "a positive
creative spirit."

In order to cut the hymn out of the books, parts or all of four other passion hymns
had to be removed, including "There Is A Green Hill Far Away." Those hymns
somehow had not upset people, perhaps because the death of Christ is hidden in
them behind archaic language, and they contain a certain theistic apologetic
which puts God himself beyond suffering and limits suffering to his incarnation.

difficulties of waiting, of the night-time in which both the waiting and the marriage supper take place, of what it means to make the announcement that the Bridegroom has come, and of what might be involved in trimming our wicks. Now we come to consider the meaning of the allegory's central figure: the Bridegroom.

Presenting Christ in images appropriate to a given age and cultural context is a permanent task of the church—part of its apologetic as well as its liturgical responsibility. There is only one Jesus Christ—as the writer to the Hebrews says, "the same yesterday, today, and forever" (Heb. 13:8)—and yet that Christ is a living Christ, risen from the dead and ascended, whose Spirit is abroad today. We must note that the Spirit *is* the Spirit of Jesus. We don't start from scratch: God is one. We must not confuse creative Christology with license, for on that way lies idolatry. Such radical freedom has developed in recent years in the Western world with regard to the Christian tradition that there are more contenders for the person and office of Christ today than at any previous time in church history. The Council of Nicaea, we might say, had to decide between two understandings of Christ— that of Arius and that of Athanasius. The Council of Chalcedon had to choose between four. On the other hand, we have, to take just a sampling, the following options:

—the idealistic, but deluded, would-be Messiah of *Jesus Christ Superstar;*

—the lovable, innocent teacher of *Godspell;*

—the secular Jesus of radical theology (smell his armpits);

—the abstract "Christ of God" of neo-orthodoxy (read about him);

—the harmless Jesus of liberalism (now yoked, it seems, to the human potential movement or the message, "You're OK!");

—the docetic Christ of evangelicalism—he *seemed to be* human, but he really was always God;

—the abstruse "christic principle" of much contemporary theologizing;

—the close and personal Jesus of the charismatic movement (often *so* close and *so* personal!);

—the commercial Jesus of religious hucksterism;

—the Jesus of Rev. Sun Myung Moon, a failure whose ministry points us to the need for a new messiah today.

There are so many to choose between—and who would dare say he had listed them all? Yet to each I feel like saying what Mary Magdalene said to the "gardener" on Easter morn: "Sir, if you have carried him away, tell me where you have laid him, and I will take him away" (John 20:15).

It is true that we have the responsibility to be creative *in interpreting Christ*—but to *invent* new Christs is to engage in idolatry. That is why the writer to the Hebrews followed up his affirmation that Christ is "the same yesterday, today, and forever" with the warning, "Do not let all kinds of strange teachings lead you from the right way" (Heb. 13:9, TEV).

It is the task of the church, in its teaching ministry, to do Christology not just with an apologetic intent—in order to communicate more effectively—but also with theological intent: to state who Christ is and mark off who he is over against who he is not.

Some aspect about each of a number of the contemporary candidates is attractive to me, and yet, taken by itself, each is either extremely thin—as is the Jesus of *Godspell*—or is dangerous in the possibilities it gives of one-sided interpretation—a forced choice between the secular Jesus *or* the Christ of faith.

If we believe in a Christ who is Lord of history, then the Christ who speaks to us today—if he is to speak with authority and power—will have to be both grander and more obviously incarnate than any of these images.

The history of which we have been speaking in this book is not something about which we can be facile or optimistic. It is the history of a world in anguish, in the throes of tremendous transformations, the history of a world in which the powerful oppress the weak, in which revolutionary and institutional violence are locked in mortal combat, in which no forward movement is made without pain. It is a world, we have said, of night, in which the principalities and powers are at large—it is the world of Beirut and Belfast, of Soweto and South Boston, of Uruguay and Uganda, of Prague and Panama. A Christ who can speak to such a world may be the Bridegroom of the New Testament, but he will not be a beauty contest king. He is the Christ of Rouault's "Christ

Mocked" rather than that of Sallman's "Head of Christ." He is Second Isaiah's Man of Sorrows, not a soporific "bridge over troubled waters."

And yet his word is not the word to which secular theology, building on a true but partial insight, limits him, a word which is expressed well by the line of the spiritual, "You have to walk it by yourself." Christ does not leave us alone in our aloneness. The theology of the death of God presented us with a Jesus who, recognizing that life was abandonment and aloneness, chose a life of personal commitment and responsibility and showed that path to others. But the responsibility was joyless, lacking in any dimension of transcendence. Without the help of the Almighty—on which the composer of the spiritual mentioned above knew he could count—it could be nothing but stoic.

Secular theology, in its attempt to be "honest," went from its emptying of the doctrine of God to emptying the doctrine of Christ. It told us to forget the good news *about* Jesus in order to appropriate the good news *of* Jesus.

But, as those who unmistakably bear the marks of Christ's suffering amid the suffering of today's world testify, there is a good news *about* Jesus. A Mother Teresa can testify, out of her years of ministering to the dying on Calcutta's streets, "He is the word to be told, the light to be lit, the love to be loved, the life to be lived."[3] You wonder who this Jesus is for Mother Teresa. The language is traditionally evangelical. It might seem that the Christ is the removed and antiseptic Christ of the sanctuary—the Christ of heaven. Far from it. Mother Teresa finds Jesus among the suffering ones to whom she ministers. "The poor," she says, "are very beautiful people. We will be judged by what we have done to the poor. We will be judged as treating Christ in the way we have treated the poor."[4] Others testify similarly.

John J. O'Donnell writes:

> To identify with the passion of Christ today is not to try to conjure up an emotional experience reproducing the sufferings Jesus endured long ago. Rather it is to locate the passion story as it continues in our world. For our history today is still the largely suffering history of God. In the cross of Jesus God once and for all sided with the wretched of this earth—those beyond human hope. To proclaim his cross is to place ourselves with the wretched of the earth today. In this way the symbol of the cross is not so much a symbol for a past

event but rather a summons to our present mission. Jesus is risen from the dead, and with his resurrection has dawned the sure hope of God's final victory over evil. But thus far the victory has appeared in one man only—Jesus of Nazareth. For us and for our world the victory is incomplete—it is not yet. The cross of Jesus reminds us of this fact until he comes again. The symbol of the cross reminds us that as the passion story goes on, we must participate in it, struggling to free men and women from the oppressions that enslave them.[5]

Putting O'Donnell's words in the language we have been using, we might say that to wait for the Bridegroom is to take up the cross of the Lamb. In other words, Christology is known not just in confession but in praxis. In recognizing the radical contemporaneity of the Risen Christ with our history we discover a Christology which is at one time confession and commitment, a statement of faith and a summons to involvement. As the Lausanne Covenant puts it, "A church which proclaims the cross must itself be marked by the cross."[6]

What does it mean to proclaim the cross? It is to say something which is at one and the same time an affirmation about Christ and an affirmation about God.

In the West we have been slow to recognize this fact. In 1946 a Japanese theologian, Kazoh Kitamori, produced a book called *Theology of the Pain of God.*[7] Writing so soon after the defeat of his country, with the recollection of Hiroshima and Nagasaki and the horrors of Japanese militarism still fresh, Kitamori offended a highly traditional Christian world by appearing to resurrect the ancient heresy of patripassianism, the teaching that God the Father, and not just God the Son, suffered. Kitamori himself was careful to distinguish between the suffering of God and the suffering of the Father, but the offense was present, because Western theology was less Trinitarian than he. Following the model of Greek theism, Western theology spoke of God as basically changeless and immutable, beyond suffering and pain. Kitamori challenged this conception of God.

His fundamental affirmation was that, "God in pain is the God who resolves our human pain by his own. Jesus Christ is the Lord who heals our human wounds by his own (I Pet. 2:24)."[8] Kitamori saw far more than an analogic relationship between human suffering and divine suffering. "Human suffering," Kitamori wrote, "is able to serve in comprehending the meaning of God's pain. Human suffering does not have this value within itself; it is only given to man by God's pain." But that does not take away from human suffering. Quite the contrary: "The surpassing grace of God's pain makes human suffering valuable and precious."[9] To Americans, about to be enchanted by "the power of positive thinking," and to many Western theologians as well, this seemed highly "negative thinking" about God.

It was not until the early '70s that Jürgen Moltmann reopened within Western theology itself the question of the suffering of God, in his book *The Crucified God*. Taking within his compass not only Kitamori's contribution to Christian theology, but Jewish theologies developed in the light of the Holocaust, Moltmann made a major contribution not only to christology and eschatology, but to the doctrine of the Trinity as well. To my mind Moltmann's book is the most significant contribution of the decade to Western theology.

Setting himself firmly against that optimism which he calls "the official creed of the Western world," the theologian known as "the founder of the theology of hope" challenges theologians in the Western world to consider the negative more than has been their wont. "Unless it apprehends the pain of the negative," he writes, "Christian hope cannot be realistic and liberating."[10] He understands the cross as the supreme negative. "The cross," he writes, "is the test of everything which deserves to be called Christian. . . . The cross refutes everything."[11] "The deity of God," he goes on, "is revealed in the paradox of the cross."[12]

Moltmann quotes a story by Elie Wiesel, a survivor of Auschwitz:

> The SS hanged two Jewish men and a youth in front of the whole camp. The men died quickly, but the death throes of the youth lasted for half an hour. "Where is God? Where is he?" someone asked behind me. As the youth still hung in torment in the noose for a long time, I heard the man call again, "Where is God now?" And I heard a voice in myself answer: "Where is he? He is here. He is hanging there on the gallows. . . ."[13]

"Orthodox" Christians are bound to be offended at this "minimization of the uniqueness of the sufferings of our Lord." Is this not sentimentality? they ask. Is Christ's passion simply a metaphor for all human suffering?

Moltmann would not wish to imply that it is. There is a tension involved in the formula *Jesus Christ,* he writes, the tension between the historical particularity of Jesus and the universality faith attributes to him as the Christ.

The titles attributed to Jesus, Moltmann writes, are variables, which faith in each age coins to express who he is *for us.* The name *Jesus* is the constant. It "can neither be translated into other languages nor be replaced by other names, or by the names of other people. His history cannot be replaced by other histories, or by the histories of other people." Therefore, "if one wished to say who the Christ, the Son of Man, the Son of God, the Logos, etc. actually is, then one must use the name of Jesus and recount his history."[14]

What is unique in the story of Jesus, Moltmann explains, is that he was the Son of God. What is unique in the cross of Jesus is that the Son of God died. But he can go further. Christian faith, he writes, has always affirmed more than this: it has always affirmed the representative nature of Jesus's death—he died *for us.* Although Moltmann has difficulty with the traditional understanding of Christ's death as expiatory, that Christ died as our substitute—a difficulty I do not share—I am stimulated by the following positive interpretation of the representative significance of Christ's death:

> Christ experiences a hell of rejection and loneliness on the cross which no longer need be suffered by believers in this way. . . . Christ experiences death and hell in solitude. His followers experience them in his company. As an eschatological forerunner he paves a way for men through judgment and godforsakenness, which is only passable for men in his company.[15]

As our representative (or, taking up an early Christian title, "Pioneer"), Christ does not, Moltmann says, make himself superfluous—"like an employment agency—but so to speak founds a new firm." He makes the way ready for us, Moltmann writes (John 14:3). This is "creative action." "His representation is not just mediation for a while but also the basis for the new being."[16]

Traditionally Christian theologians have, despite the best intentions, maintained a certain separation between the passion and the resurrection. Moltmann, following Barth, sees the two as a single moment. In his understanding of the passion as creative action, Moltmann has begun to speak of the resurrection. He has made the transition from the cross to Easter Sunday not cheaply or in a facile manner but in a way which affirms their essential unity. The one who rises, he writes, is the one who is crucified. The one who cried out, "My God, my God, why hast thou forsaken me?" is the one who sits at the right hand of the Father. "The confession of faith (in the Lamb)," Moltmann writes, "takes the form of an anticipatory doxology. . . . The confession of faith in Jesus concludes with the future hope, 'Amen. Come, Lord Jesus!' " Therefore he can say the history of Jesus, the crucified one, "is open to the new creation."[17]

Moltmann's earlier theology of hope is thus not canceled out by his theology of the crucified God, but is, as he said at the outset, its "reverse side":

> For me . . . this [book] is not a step back from the trumpets of Easter to the lamentations of Good Friday. . . . The theology of the cross is none other than the reverse side of the Christian theology of hope, if the starting point of the latter lies in the resurrection of the *crucified* Christ. . . . The dominant theme then was that of *anticipations* of the future of God in the form of promises and hopes; here it is the understanding of the *incarnation* of that future, by way of the sufferings of Christ, in the world's sufferings.[18]

To relate this to our previous language: the Bridegroom who is affianced to the church (and thus, in an anticipatory way, to humanity) is the Lamb slain by humankind, who is at one and the same time "our Passover feast." The one slain and utterly forsaken, abandoned by God, is our way to God, for he is God among us and for us. Crucified *by* us, he rises *before* us.

The resurrection of the crucified Christ means that humanity no longer lives in the unredeemed world of death. Christian faith operates with a new eschatological understanding of time.[19] The difference, Moltmann writes, can be seen in the shift which occurs between the preaching of Jesus, which is still in harmony with Jewish apocalyptic, and that of Paul. The preaching of both is eschatological—Jesus preaches the Kingdom of God, Paul "the righteousness" or "justice" of God, but

> The difference between them is not the superficial one of changed ideas, but is determined by their different theological situation. For Paul, that which for Jesus was the future is the present or the future of God inaugurated in the history of Jesus. . . .
>
> The difference in their theological situations is determined by a shift in the *eschaton* itself, from that of a future which is just beginning to a future which has already begun.[20]

Jesus and Paul stand on opposite sides of the decisive *novum* in history, the resurrection. The resurrection of the crucified Christ discloses the meaning of the crucifixion: it was for us. A historical happening to Jesus has become an eschatological event.

We cannot affirm faith in the resurrection without coming into solidarity with the crucified Christ (as Paul affirmed in Galatians 2:20) and—as Subba Rao recognized—if one would be united with Christ in his sufferings, one must unite with those with whom he united by his suffering, the poor and oppressed of the world. In other words, one cannot simply hold Christ at arm's length and make affirmations—or ask questions—of him. *The question of who Christ is must be asked from a position of being questioned by Christ.* Christ will not agree to become simply the object of our questioning. He is himself the subject. And therefore he asks us not just "Who do men say that I am?" but "Who do you say that I am?" (Matt. 16:13ff.).

Thus Moltmann believes that he cannot write an "objective study" of Christology. That would be a contradiction in terms. A book of Christology—a book concerning the suffering of God—must pose the following question: "What does it mean to recall the God who was crucified in a society whose official creed is optimism, and which is knee-deep in blood?"[21]

Let us pose that question in the language we have been using: what does it mean to wait for the Bridegroom in the dead of night? What does it mean to go to a marriage-feast in a world where fornication and adultery are the norm? It is to base our lives on a different wisdom from the wisdom of the world. It is to choose to follow the suffering one and take the path of suffering. It is to anticipate crucifixion—the Bridegroom is the Lamb. But it is to hope for resurrection—the Lamb is the Bridegroom, and "Blessed are those who are invited to the marriage supper of the Lamb" (Rev. 19:9). It is to give account to this world of the hope that motivates us (I Pet. 3:15).

The world will ask for an answer from those who question its wisdom, for this world has clear objectives and, it is convinced, it knows how to organize with maximum technological efficiency to achieve them. It will ask us to account for our failure to accept its wisdom, and our accounting must be a strong questioning of the world's own "wisdom." As Kosuke Koyama, a Japanese Christian and former missionary to Thailand, observes, this world is convinced that—to take an example—by substituting supersonic airplanes for the ox-cart, it can bring about a reign of universal *shalom*. It may admit to "kinks" in its system, but it does not doubt the efficiency of the system itself. But Koyama was impelled to raise questions even more loudly, for he had come to believe that the steady increase of science and technology is threatening to destroy humanity. So Koyama had to raise questions about the world's "efficiency."

> In order to vanquish the enemy "efficiently," the world engages in this astronomically "inefficient" enterprise. $200 billion wasted in the face of a poverty-stricken world will not eliminate our enemies: hunger, disease, illiteracy, and war. Man must become "spiritually inefficient" (blessed are the poor in spirit) in order to see what kind of apocalyptic conduct of "inefficiency" he's in!

> Man spends all his savings, and cannot achieve his objective. In this immense frustration God stands as an efficient God. Going through a most inefficient process, he proved himself to be the most efficient One. He has achieved his objective. His efficiency is not, however, an ordinary efficiency. It is the efficiency in a great paradox, the efficiency of the Crucified One! "Crucified efficiency" is the message which must be given to both the "ox-cart" and the "supersonic" people. In this "crucified efficiency" is hidden new life for the great issues we face within the framework of technological civilization, the problems of development, social justice, crisis of faith and search for the meaning of life. "Crucified efficiency" teaches us ... that technological efficiency needs to be enlightened by the sense of the "efficiency" of the Crucified One. Technological *shalom* (peace, salvation) must sit in the *shalom* feast of the Messiah.[22]

To come to the marriage feast of the Lamb is to opt for "the efficiency of the crucified one." It is to anticipate a wedding by the light of five lanterns, while it is still night. It is to know that the one you marry is the Lamb that was slain—one who was oppressed and afflicted, yet he opened not his mouth, wounded, bruised, stricken, and oppressed, yet for our transgressions. It is to marry one whose "grave was made with the wicked," to marry him in the faith that "the will of the Lord shall prosper in his hand" and we shall "see the fruit of the travail" of our soul and "be satisfied" (Isa. 53:4-10). It is to bet on one who is committed to being a loser, convinced that his losing is the path to victory. (Those who believe in "technological efficiency" would do better to marry Rev. Moon's "bridegroom," for he is committed to winning.)

The alternatives are posed sharply, and, I believe, biblically, in Thomas Klise's futuristic novel *The Last Western*.[23] This is a modern parable describing an American Christ-figure, a quadri-racial youth who comes to his twenties toward the end of the century in a society whose technological efficiency—a logical extension of today's—can only be described as awesome. The U.S. is run by a military/scientific/industrial regime which, through the manipulation of the world's economy and its own people's minds, rules with an iron hand and a heart of stone. Willie grows up unable to comprehend the logic of such a dehumanized world and Christians' accommodation to it. His downfall is that he continues to ask questions.

When, after having achieved unprecedented financial success as a major league baseball pitcher, he learns that the whole sport/commercial complex is built on inhumanity, he gives up all his rewards. He goes back to Houston, where he grew up, only to find that it has been destroyed in riots and bombings and that all his loved ones have been killed. He has a complete mental breakdown.

He is taken to a hospice by a bizarre, neo-monastic order— which, he later learns, is known by the name of the Silent Servants of the Used, Abused, and Utterly Screwed-Up. On regaining his health, he joins the order. One of its chief marks is that its members do not take themselves very seriously. One of their chief missions is offering themselves as substitutes for those condemned to die. The world considers them not only subversive, but—and this is a stronger criticism—useless, for they never achieve anything—and the world is based on achievement.

But the Servants understand their mission in the following way:

> The Servants will always choose the way of serving the poor, the lonely, the despised, the outcast, the miserable and the misfit. The mission of the Servants is to prove to the unloved they are not

> abandoned, not finally left alone. Hence, the natural home of the
> Servants is strife, misfortune, crisis, and falling apart of things. The
> society cherishes failure for it is in failure, in trouble, in the general
> breaking up of classes, stations, usual conditions, normal routines
> that human hearts are opened to the light of God's mercy.[24]

To make a long story short, Willie goes to seminary, becomes a
very untraditional but widely loved priest, is made a very untraditional but, in the best sense of the word, evangelical bishop, and
then becomes a highly untraditional and highly unsuccessful
pope. He is killed by one of his former fellow monks at the height
of a universal celebration of love he proposed.

Everything that happens is easily predictable to anyone who
knows either the story of Christ or the nature of our civilization.
Furthermore, everything is a kind of unfolding in Willie's life of a
story which his Native American grandmother Cool Dawn told
him when, as a young boy, he could not understand his catechism
lessons about the death of Jesus. Cool Dawn's story is the most
creative re-telling of the Christ story I have seen in contemporary
literature. I believe it is so germane to our understanding of who
the Bridegroom is that I would like to recount it in fairly great
detail.[25]

> Once upon a time the Great Spirit said, "Now men have everything
> they want—trees, beautiful flowers, animals, rocks, waterfalls, moun-
> tains. Still they are unhappy. They do not love. They do not share
> with one another. So I will show them how to love."
>
> Then the Great Spirit made a special man—a beautiful noble
> man—and sent him into the world with a great secret. No one knew
> what this secret meant, not even the special man who carried it in his
> heart.
>
> Now when the special man came into the world, there was great
> suffering everywhere.
>
> The babies did not have enough food.
>
> The tribes were at war.

Two tribes have been living in perpetual hostility for decades.
One of the tribes has the tradition that the brave who can perform
the most heroic jump into the river from the cliffs which overarch it
will rule the tribe for a year. In addition, that person is given the
right, on the night of his installation, to make one new law.

The man with the secret in his heart astounds the tribe by jumping from a height never attempted before. He becomes king, and is given the name the Eagle King. When asked what new law he would like to make, he proposes that there shall be no more laws except the law, "We must try to love each other." He is ridiculed and threatened with revolt. The brave recognizes that he has gone too far too fast. He retracts the stipulation that there will be no laws and makes as his new law that each year at the feast the king must take a goblet of wine, hold it up above all the people, and say, "We must try to love each other." The people then must repeat the words after him. Then all shall drink from the cup.

No one takes the Eagle King seriously. "What kind of law is this?" they sneer. "It is the easiest law any king has ever passed," they say. "He must be a weak king." But they agree to do as he requests, to make the toast with the king once a year and say, "We must try to love each other."

The following day the Eagle King is apprised that the enemy tribe is camped in a place where it can easily be overwhelmed. The general proposes an immediate attack. The Eagle King responds, to the dismay of all the warriors,"This is the day I shall make peace with the enemy." He goes with gifts on a mission of peace. He overcomes the enemy tribe's suspicions and asks that they in turn return to his tribe four warriors they have been holding prisoner. The war council refuses. The Eagle King says, "Let the four men go and keep me in their stead." The four who had been condemned to die embrace the Eagle and he tells them, "Remember, you must try to love other people as your brothers and sisters." They return to the tribe. The Eagle King remains imprisoned in their wooden cage.

The next day scouts of the enemy tribe find ten bushels of golden apples on the river bank. "This is the king's ransom," they conclude. One scout takes a bite of an apple and falls down dead. The tribe demands that the Eagle be executed. Their chief asks instead for a large ransom. Word is sent to the Eagle's tribe, but they refuse to give the ransom.

The amount is reduced to one colt. This offer is still refused.

The amount is reduced to one bushel of grain and one cask of wine. Again the Eagle's tribe rejects it.

The king of the other tribe is in a quandary. He knows that the

Eagle is innocent, that he sincerely wanted to make peace. He desires to release him, but the Eagle's tribe has not responded. The Eagle King will have to be bound and hurled from the cliffs to his death, or else the other king will lose face. But the other king cannot bring himself to execute him. He contrives to let the Eagle King escape from the cage in which he is being kept.

But, when the other king gets back, he finds that the Eagle King is still in the cage, for he had obeyed the word which he heard from his heart which instructed him, "Stay here and destroy the cage for others."

There is no longer any way out. So the Eagle King is bound and thrown into the river. His body dashes onto the hardest rocks and vanishes below the foam. The people go away. But a great whirling and purling noise brings them back to the river. They see a great, golden bird emerge from the water and lift itself out of the river past the cliffs into the sky.

Those who have believed in the Eagle King's mission—the warriors he had ransomed, the enemy king, and the guard who saw his agony—continue to meet together and say the words of the toast, "We must try to love each other." And, Cool Dawn tells Willie, "they formed a special tribe, which is scattered across the face of the earth." Willie asks if she is a member. She says she is. Willie says he wants to become one, too. And he does—his whole life is modeled on the wisdom of the Eagle King, and it is an affront to the wisdom of the world, which crucifies him.

What is attractive to me in Klise's parable of the Eagle King is that it holds soteriology—the teaching of the church concerning how Christ saves—and Christology—the understanding of the person of Christ—closely together, and it holds them both together with discipleship. Since the Eagle King stayed in the cage, it has been destroyed for others; it can never be an object of terror again. Similarly the resurrection has taken place, but the death and resurrection of the Eagle need continual outworking in the mission of the new tribe, as more and more people are introduced to and practice the new life of love.

Putting this in Christian theological terms, Christ's death on the cross is past, but there is much more dying that needs to be done, much more suffering that needs to be entered into, voluntarily. Christ has risen so that we might come to newness of life and hope, in anticipation of the ultimate resurrection of all flesh. The church exists to practice and proclaim the way of the cross and resurrection, and it does this in a world still marked by enmity and oppression. Humankind is still under "the curse of the law," and yet the beachhead of reconciliation is there, in the "new tribe" whose only law is love, which does not require success or achievement in order to find joy.

As I write this, I am forced to re-think my mental image of the marriage supper of the Lamb. Until now I think I have been imagining the marriage feast as a rather grandiose affair. Perhaps until now I have been interpreting it as a Christian version of the triumphal procession of the lion. But, as I read Moltmann and Kitamori, Koyama and Klise, and as I meditate on Subba Rao's vision, I think that the marriage feast of the Lamb will be a rather "homey" affair—five lanterns, a jug of wine, a table, a couple of rough benches—and a lot of love.

This book has been addressed to the danger that we will fail to recognize that the invitations to that marriage supper are going out—and are to be responded to—right now. The danger resides either in our being so mesmerized by the far future eschatological feast (when "people will come from East and West and sit down at table with Abraham, Isaac, and Jacob in the kingdom of God," cf. Matt. 8:11) that we will fail to recognize that the call of Jesus is for us to come right now, or that we will fail to take the whole idea of an eschatological feast seriously.

A Jeanne Anne Singer errs on the one side—like the man to whom Jesus spoke the parable of the Great Banquet (who could well exclaim, "How blessed will they be who will eat bread in the kingdom of God!" Luke 14:15)—for she separates the eschatological feast from current eschatology. A Carol Miller—and, to a certain extent, a Janet Peterson Comstock—errs on the other side in not taking the eschatological feast seriously.

But Jesus' preaching, even prior to the resurrection, is clear. For us who live after the resurrection it ought to be doubly clear that God's intention is serious: he will establish his Kingdom—he is inaugurating it now—a new time has begun.

In a moment we will look at what it means for us to preach the resurrection. First let us take a closer look at Jesus' own eschatological preaching. Here I will rely closely on the thoughts of

C.H. Dodd, particularly as he expressed them in compact form toward the end of his career in a book called *The Founder of Christianity*.[26] Dodd's understanding of Jesus here in many respects parallels the discoveries of the Bultmann School and those involved in the "new quest for the historical Jesus" in the '60s, when the excesses of skepticism about the historical Jesus had been overcome.

Jesus' preaching was not a timeless, general religious teaching, but it was rooted specifically in a concrete historical moment, a moment which he understood as crucial in God's dealings with Israel and humanity, the time of the in-breaking of the Kingdom of God. Jesus believed that "the people he addressed stood in a situation in which decision was urgent and delay dangerous."[27] His declaration that the Kingdom is present meant, "It is no time for the nicely calculated less and more of 'practical morality'."[28]

Dodd emphasizes the strong connection between John the Baptist's conviction that it was time "to prepare a people fit for the Lord" (cf. Luke 3:1ff., Luke 2:67-80) and Jesus' sense of his own mission. But there is this essential difference: Jesus' preaching was more eschatological than John's, because by beginning his ministry Jesus had in fact brought the hoped-for Kingdom close—"You no longer look for the reign of God through a telescope," Dodd writes, "you open your eyes to see."[29]

> His master aim was to make people aware of the presence of God as an urgent reality, and to induce them to give the appropriate response, so that they might become effectively members of the new people of God which was coming into being.[30]

In gathering such a new people through his proclamation of the Kingdom, Jesus had in fact initiated the Kingdom. In other words, as Moltmann puts it: *what* Jesus said was given its peculiar urgency by the fact that *he* said it. Because he said it, people should know that the *kairos* had come.[31]

Here the offense comes for the modern liberal mind. What a Janet Peterson Comstock—and she is here symbolic of theological liberals—does not recognize is that the call to commit oneself to God's reign is a call to identify with the one who proclaimed it. The new people Jesus calls into being is mysteriously not separate from but closely united with him. The message concerns not only those to whom it is proclaimed, but the proclaimer, and the two are united in the church, which was—and we cannot over-emphasize this—central to Jesus' message. Dodd comments that Jesus' "aim was to constitute a community worthy of the name of a people of God."[32] That people, the church, must be understood as part of Jesus' intention: he would, by his proclamation, awaken in people such a response that they would identify with the Kingdom of God by relating to him and, through their common ties to him, to one another. A new people would thus be formed, which would become a force in history for the achievement of God's purposes.

> In an historical view, the one evident outcome of the whole life and work of Jesus was the emergence of the church, a society which regarded itself as carrying on the distinct vocation of Israel as the "people of God," and yet was quite clear that it was a *new* Israel, constituted by a "new covenant." It had taken shape, not about a platform or a creed, but about a personal attachment to Jesus himself.[33]

The Bridegroom is central to the wedding feast. The feast is the supper of his community with him. It is appropriate to expect that those who believe they have heard and received Jesus' message have a personal relationship with Jesus as their Lord and Savior. This is biblical to the core. It is not an evangelical "invasion of privacy" to be concerned about this. Nor need it be a maudlin thing involving the kind of mawkish sentimentality about Jesus that is quite unworthy both of his conception of his ministry and of his call to discipleship. Frequently that kind of Christology is an excuse for the kind of cop-out which Jeanne Anne Singer was created to represent. Jesus is *not* to be reduced to "a bridge over troubled waters" or the one who "walks with me and he talks with me and he tells me I am his own."

We will only understand the meaning of personal attachment to Jesus when we recognize how he conceived of himself. As Dodd effectively brings out, "He undertook his mission . . . as Messiah, as Son of God, *as the Servant of the Lord*" (my italics).[34] It was—and this is crucial—in terms of II Isaiah's vision of the Suffering Servant that Jesus understood the meaning of his divine sonship and how we must understand the meaning of personal relationship to Jesus.

Let us recall II Isaiah for a moment. Interpreters have always been puzzled by the mysterious alternation in the Servant Songs between a conception of the Servant as a person and a conception of the Servant as a community. That is the key to what we are after: Jesus maintained that alternation—he did not dissolve it![35] The mystery of how Christ relates to the church as his "body" is nothing but the continuation of the mystery of the Servant of Isaiah.

To be personally attached to Jesus is thus to understand oneself as called to the same servant ministry as he was. Such discipleship will be costly, not sentimental. Jesus is not just the supreme example of such servanthood, whom we might seek to follow; much more than that, we seek to be united with him, as branches are to a vine (John 15). He is the Messiah; we are the messianic people. As the branches of a vine are part of a total vine, so we understand our servant ministry only in the context of that total servant people, the community of the cross. To be part of the church is to be part of a servant community. To quote the Lausanne Covenant again, "A church which proclaims the cross must itself be marked by the cross."[36] Jesus' preaching thus leads to a radical reorientation of our lives away from individualism to community, for community is part of the grace which Jesus offers. Athol Gill comments that the call of the first disciples (Mark 1:16-20) is a symbolic portrayal of how our lives are radically reoriented by Jesus' proclamation toward community (Mark 3:13-25). Such a call is itself "an act of grace," Gill comments, "the beginning of a new community of God's people and a preparation for the mission of the disciples in which this grace is to be extended to others (Matt. 10:8)."[37]

So, in place of the usual Evangelical progression from Jesus to individuals to the church—which is also, in essence, the liberal progression—we have a much less schematized time-frame. The church is Jesus' body. Individuals find meaning for their lives in its community. The community is thus part of the grace of the proclamation and in a real way precedes the kerygma.

Jesus' own message brought into one God's Kingdom, his own messianic role, and that of his community in a way that has too long eluded our individualistic Western minds. Because of our individualism, we have had difficulty seeing the continuity between Jesus' message and that of Paul. Preaching the resurrection has seemed to be a totally new thing, added after Jesus' own ministry, and not integrally related to Jesus' proclamation of the Kingdom.

But, with the background that we now have of Jesus' own ministry and proclamation, it should be easier for us to understand the continuities which exist between Jesus' preaching of the Kingdom and the New Testament kerygma concerning the resurrection.

Central to the kerygma is an affirmation of the resurrection and of its significance for the church. It is a theological affirmation, with an immediate ethical consequence: Christ *has been* raised; we therefore "walk in newness of life" (Rom. 6:4).

Just as Jesus called the disciples to new life in community with him, so the community of the church is a community of new life in fellowship with the risen Christ.

It has sometimes seemed as if the fellowship Jesus had with his disciples is something we are not meant to experience till the *eschaton,* and as if new life is only partially open to us today. But, if we look more closely at what Paul is saying in Romans 6, we see that his conception of the in-breaking of God's future into the present is as radical as that of Jesus: rather than following a strict parallelism in speaking about death and resurrection, Paul changes the time focus. "We were buried therefore with him by baptism into death"—that is the first part of the affirmation—and then he goes on, "so that as Christ was raised from the dead by the glory of the Father"—he does not then say what would be most natural: "so we might also be raised with him at the last day"—but rather "we too might walk in newness of life" (Rom. 6:4).[38] The concomitant of our union with Christ's death in baptism is our union with him *now* in his resurrection. Being united with Christ mysteriously in his death, we are mysteriously united with him *already* in his resurrection. The hope that the Christian tradition in its mainstream forms has reserved for the far future is for Paul a living contemporary hope. To realize this is crucial for our witness. A postponement of resurrection hope will lead to quietism, to accommodation to the orders of the world, to a reduction in our expectation of what the Christian community can do and how history can be transformed.

To accept the radical contemporaneity of Jesus' and Paul's

understanding of God's eschatological activity is to be able, as William Carey put it, to "attempt great things for God" because we "expect great things from God."

Roger Garaudy, once the leading theoretician of the French Communist Party, reaffirmed the Christian faith he had earlier abjured when he came to understand—through his participation in the Christian-Marxist dialogue—that the resurrection meant that history was to be transformed. As one working for the transformation of history, he came to see that the resurrection was in fact a spur to such efforts:

> So that the good news could be proclaimed to the full, it was necessary for (Jesus) to tell the world, through his resurrection, that every frontier, even the ultimate frontier of death itself, had been overcome. . . .
>
> Until then, all the wise men had meditated on destiny, on necessity confused with reason. He showed them their folly. He, who was the reverse of destiny, who was liberty, creation, life—he took the inevitability out of history.[39]

In another place he says:

> The resurrection is not a "fact" in the positivist sense of the term. It is a creative act, an affirmation of the impossible through which history opens the future to all possibilities. It means that our future cannot just be one more fact, something that flows from the data of the past.[40]

Garaudy is thinking historically—not just existentially—about the resurrection. We in the mainstream of the Christian faith must learn from him what that means:

> It does not mean inserting the resurrection into the perspective of history, but rather perceiving history through the perspective of the resurrection.[41]

The resurrection is thus a creative event which transforms history. It is existentialized, or pietized, only at the cost of dehistoricizing it. It is "modernized" (because of its affront to our "liberal" and "enlightened" secular minds) only at the cost of de-radicalizing it. But this need not happen. The resurrection can be taken on its own terms, in its own context, as an affirmation about history—the new era has dawned. Then we understand why there is no longer Jew nor Greek, slave nor free, male nor female (Gal. 3:28); why the principalities and powers need to be addressed right now (Eph. 3:9); why the church must understand itself as God's eschatological people (I Pet. 2:9f.). There is, despite Garaudy's legitimate fears of positivism, something objective about this affirmation. He would agree that it is not just a matter of the believer's own inner disposition (a matter of viewing the world *as if* it were already a different world)—it *is* already a different world. This is what makes the good news so good—and what makes sin so horrible. Christ has risen, and he reigns, and we are his people; the power of the resurrection is behind our ministry, and every power that withstands his reign is resisting a power that has already been legitimized.[42]

To express this in the language we have previously been using, we may summarize by saying that the Lamb that was slain is none other than the Lord who rises, and he rises with the marks of the crucifixion still on his hands. The Bridegroom who comes in the middle of the night is the one who once supped with his followers on the night before his death. The community which gathers with him to eat the nuptial meal is a community gathered by the power of his resurrection, which knows itself called to be marked with the blood of the Lamb.

They join in singing the eternal song:

> "You are worthy to take the scroll
>   and to break open its seals.
> For you were killed, and by your death
>   you bought for God,
>   people from every tribe, language, nation, and race.
> You have made them a kingdom of
>   priests to serve our God,
> and they shall rule on earth" (Rev. 5:9-10, TEV).

Knowing themselves called to be a kingdom of priests, their whole life is dominated by the praise of the Lamb, and they sing:

> "The Lamb who was killed is worthy
>   to receive power, wealth, wisdom, and strength,
>   honor, glory, and praise!" (Rev. 5:12, TEV).

And their hope is that one day "every creature in heaven, on earth, and in the world below" will join in singing:

> "To him who sits on the throne and to the Lamb,
> be praise and honor, glory and might, forever and ever!"(Rev. 5:13, TEV).

(2) The Ascended King

> In Jesus Christ the Kingship of God is among us. In
> Him, God reaches out to seize and liberate a guilty
> and lost world. In Him God's Kingdom breaks
> through decisively into the dominion of the ruler of
> this world, and so he is the foretoken and pledge of
> the future complete realization of this Kingdom.
> —*Foundations and Perspectives of
> Confession,* Article 4[43]

A CHRISTOLOGY WHICH STOPS AT GOOD FRIDAY AND EASTER
Sunday cannot be complete. A Christology which fails to speak of
the ascended Christ cannot be complete. Furthermore, a Christology will not be contemporary unless it deals with the kingship of
Christ. Not only will a Christology based only on Christ's ministry,
passion, and resurrection be less than fully biblical, it will speak to
our contemporary situation less than a Christology ought to.

This is a perspective on Christology which, in the Western
world, has been maintained consistently by the Reformed tradition, emanating from the theology of John Calvin. It is not mere
theological nit-picking which makes the Reformed tradition insist
so strongly on the need for an extension of Christology into a full
consideration of the ascension, but a deep theological insight. I
believe this insight has been finding its fulfillment only in the last
few decades. Calvin himself did not develop it as far as he might
have, in terms of a Christian understanding of history—he was
too much bound by the individualistic eschatology of the Western
Middle Ages.[44] He put the germs of such a further development
forward. In some respects he did this with unnecessary timidity,
but the foundations and beginning of the later development are
clearly there, in Calvin's own writing; he laid the foundations of a
Reformed perspective on history which is only in our present day
being developed to the fullness of its potential. These foundations
are in Calvin's theology (1) in his treatment of Christ's acension
itself; (2) in his understanding of civil authority; and (3) in his

"third use of the Law." I wish at this point to go a little more deeply into each of these.

(1) If Roman Catholic social thought has generally tended toward a creationist perspective, based on natural law, and Lutheran thought has been characterized by a bifurcation between church and state based on its emphasis on the cross, and Anabaptist thought has taken a disjunctive veiw of the present world order and the Kingdom, based on a radical eschatology, then Calvin plotted a new path by his decision to focus his understanding of the present stage of God's work on the ascension. The present, he believed, needs to be understood not only as a time between the two comings of Christ, but as a time significant in itself, during which Christ already sits at the right hand of God. This is, for Calvin, the age of the *regnum Christi,* the reign of Christ. "All things are now subject to Christ," he wrote. "This subjection will, nevertheless, not be complete until the day of resurrection, because that which is now only begun will then be completed."[45]

With the affirmation that Christ's reign has already begun, the die of Reformed theology was cast: "Calvin thinks of the Kingdom of God or the Kingdom of Christ," Thomas Torrance specifically states, "as operating in history and on earth."[46] For Calvin this does not entail a naive denial of the power of evil or of the reality of corruption on earth. He was well aware of these. We live in a time of overlap between two world-orders, he said. But, Torrance comments, "Calvin takes this overlapping of the ages so realistically that he speaks of the world as *already in a manner renovated by the coming of Christ.*"[47] Calvin writes: "He is . . . the Heir of the whole world, so that all things ought to be subject to Him and to acknowledge His authority" (Commentary on Matt. 27:25).[48] This is a world-historical affirmation. Calvin will not settle for less. In a sermon on II Timothy 2:5f. Calvin says, "The Lord Jesus did not come to reconcile a few individuals only to God the Father, but to extend His grace over all the world."[49] When it comes to explaining what this means, Calvin's primary and most consistent answer is that "the Church of God will be expanded throughout the entire world." That, he says, is the supreme purpose of the ascension, to fill all creation with the *regnum Christi.*[50]

Here the church-centered thinking and the spiritual/secular

dichotomy of the Middle Ages kept Calvin from stating the full, world-historical implications of the *regnum Christi*. His own understanding of the ascension could have led him further. He tends, however, to see the church as mediating between the risen Christ and the secular order. He speaks of the church as the earthly counterpart of the risen Christ. But the church, Calvin believed, has a mission to the whole world: "The *regnum Christi*," Torrance writes, "presses through the Church, in its obedience to the risen Christ, to bring all mankind under its sway in the Gospel."[51] This sounds, to our ears, a little like triumphalism. Nor would I want to imply that a Calvin more liberated from medievalism would have reduced the strength of that affirmation, for Calvin really believed that the church "already bears the new order of the Kingdom." He even spoke of the church as the Kingdom or of the Kingdom as "the renovation of the Church."[52] Nevertheless, this is kept from being triumphalism by Calvin's insistence that the church has such a status only in its call to servant ministry; this role was not given it for its own glorification, but for the advancement of Christ's Kingdom in the world.

Had Calvin been free of the Hellenic distinctions between time and eternity, and of the medieval dichotomy between the sacred and the secular, he would have drawn out more fully the implications of the ascension for the secular order and been able to see the church more as the midwife of a new order than as the mother, or even as the baby.

The promise of Calvin's insight into the meaning of the ascension was thus kept from fulfillment. His affirmations about the reign of Christ are mainly confined to what we call *Heilsgeschichte*, the history of salvation, and not given free reign in world history.

(2) Under the overarching Kingdom of God, however, there is another kingdom besides the spiritual Kingdom (the church) according to Calvin, namely, the political kingdom. It is to what he wrote about the political kingdom that we look, secondly, for a germ of modern Reformed approaches to the meaning of history.

If the Anabaptists of his day insisted on the necessity of Christians separating themselves from the "wicked" and "abominable" orders of the world, and if the Lutherans made too easy an accommodation to the world through their Doctrine of the Two Kingdoms, then Calvin's unique perspective was that, although the political kingdom was distinct from the spiritual Kingdom, it was not adverse to it but complementary. Calvin could neither divinize the political order nor understand it as the Beast. Neither could he see it in any other light than that of God's overarching purpose. The civil kingdom, he affirmed, wore something of the glory of God just as did the spiritual. God had endowed it with *imperium* (whereas he has endowed the church with *ministerium*). He then goes on to explain why God has given it its authority. The aim of the *imperium* of the political kingdom is "that a public form of religion may exist among Christians and humanity among men."[53] This is a unique formulation. It does not subordinate the political kingdom to the spiritual, or separate them totally, but shows their tasks to be complementary and overlapping. As Torrance writes, "While Calvin will not allow the political kingdom to invade the spiritual, he will not allow the spiritual to abrogate the political kingdom as the fanatics wanted to do."[54]

It offends our American ears, attuned to a rigid separation of church and state, to hear Calvin say that part of the task of the political kingdom is to make possible a "public form of religion among Christians." But let us not fail to see the second part of the sentence as well, that political government exists to promote "humanity among men."

Modern readers may be surprised to see such a Renaissance concept as *humanitas* mentioned by Calvin, but Calvin was in many ways a Renaissance man. In words that would have fallen naturally from the pen of Cicero or Erasmus, he claimed that the task of civil government is to bring about the conditions of humanity on earth. Just as the church participates in the new humanity through communion with Christ, so the civil realm must—if it is faithful to God's intention—promote the condition of *humanitas.* The church has its task ("to begin the heavenly Kingdom in us, even now upon earth"), and, in a similar way, God has given the political kingdom its task:

> To the latter it is assigned, so long as we live among men, to foster and maintain the external worship of God, to defend sound doctrine and the condition of the Church, to adapt our conduct to human society, to form our manners to civil justice, to reconcile us to each

> other, to cherish common peace and tranquility. All these I confess to be superfluous, if the Kingdom of God, as it now exists within us, extinguishes the present life. But it is the will of God that while we aspire to true piety we are pilgrims on the earth, and if such pilgrimage stands in need of such aids, those who take them away from man rob him of his humanity.[55]

Much to our surprise, we discover in Calvin one who would not frown on the current theme of "humanization," but who would see our present concern in mission for a more humanized world as in accordance with God's providence.

There is here, nevertheless, just as we have seen earlier, a dichotomy in Calvin's thinking, between the "spiritual" and the "political." Calvin gives the same priority to the "spiritual" over the "material" which medieval theologians did. In other words, we do not find in Calvin the radical foreshortening of eschatology which we saw in Jesus' own proclamation, nor the strong sense of *Deus incarnatus* which enabled the early Christians to bridge the gap between the sacred and the secular, the spiritual and the material. Yet Calvin's positive valuation of the role of civil authority in the plan of God was an important step toward the freeing of the political from the church's sacralizing influence and toward a recognition of the contribution it would make to history in its own right.

Building on Calvin's positive attitude toward the civil realm, people in the Reformed tradition have made great contributions to the advancement of justice and humanity in the political realm, not least of all in the founding of the United States.

Another question worthy of research would be whether Calvin expected to see growth in *humanity* over time through the contributions of civil government, as he expected to see growth in grace and numbers in the church. He did not, to my knowledge, express any hope for what later thinkers called "progress" in human affairs. Though he expected the church to grow and expand and to bring ever greater blessings to humanity, he seems to have held to a more static view of what the political kingdom would accomplish. His political thinking remains, therefore, less than fully historical, belonging more to the essentialist traditions of the Middle Ages than to the dynamic conceptions of history which followed him.

(3) The third germ of contemporary Reformed thinking is in Calvin's "third use of the Law."* Whereas in Lutheranism a strong distinction has always been made between Law and gospel (emerging out of Luther's own existential experience of the Law in terms of "the introspective conscience" we discussed in Chapter 5), and the Law is seen as having only an outmoded function (it was Israel's tutor until Christ, but "it ceased after the blessed seed came into the world") or a negative one (it is a "hammer that bruises and beats down," a "glass that shows a man . . . that he is guilty of God's everlasting wrath"), for Calvin the Law had three uses, two of which are positive:

(a) The first use of the Law is similar to Luther's second use, to "render us inexcusable and drive us to despair, moving us to seek grace.[56] But Calvin says this use of the Law is "accidental to its true purpose."[57]

(b) The second use deals with civil society: "to restrain certain men, by fear, from doing evil, and thus protect the community." The Law is a deterrent to those not yet regenerate, from committing anti-social acts. It makes communal life possible.[58]

(c) The third use, which Calvin calls "the principal use," is the one which chiefly concerns us: this use, according to Calvin, "pertains to believers in whose hearts the Spirit of God already lives and reigns." Through the Law they can "learn more thoroughly each day the nature of the Lord's will to which they aspire." It will not only teach them this, but move them toward it: "Like a whip to an idle and balky ass," the Law "exhorts to obedience and, through threats as well as promises, leads people to greater righteousness." As they read his Law, "the Lord instructs those whom he inwardly instills with a readiness to obey."[59]

Although this "third use" seems to pertain only to individuals, it is highly germane to our concern with the community of the church. To understand this, we must look at how Calvin understood history. As believers we live in the time between the ascension and the Second Coming. Our history has a past, in the whole history of mankind; it also has a future, in God's total renewal of creation. The present is related to and in continuity with both past and future. Calvin can thus make positive use of the Mosaic Law

*I am indebted to Prof. James Gustafson for this insight.

of the Old Covenant in the time of the New Covenant.

For Calvin there is, in a real sense, only one covenant, between God and creation, extending from the beginning of creation to the end of time. "The form the covenant takes varies," Torrance explains, "but its substance is essentially the same."[60]

Why does Calvin see things in such a strikingly different way? Because to him the risen and ascended Christ is the pre-existent Christ by whom the world was created. There is only one covenant because there is only one Christ, and because Christ is pre-existent, we can know that God has predestined his people from eternity for salvation. This is truly a unique perspective on history. The past is seen in the light of the present and future. The future is seen in the light of God's eternal decree. Calvin escapes the naive linearity of time which so tends to box us in during the 20th century. If for Calvin we are to speak of eschatology, this really is for him the twin doctrine of predestination. Torrance suggests it ought to be called "post-destination"![61] Eschatology is nothing but the working out in history of God's eternal election of his people.

What does this mean? And what is its significance for us? It means that history can be trusted. It is the field of God's working. It means, furthermore, that we should much more expect to see in it continuities than radical disjunctions.

The second reason I have brought in the third use of the Law is that it illustrates how Calvin saw God as concerned *in a positive way* with the establishment of order in the world. According to Calvin, the Law—and this includes the laws of society—is not antithetical to the gospel, grace is not opposed to nature, nor is the church at enmity with Israel. Israel, the natural order, and the Law are rather to be seen in the light of God's promise.

This has important consequences for our present discipleship. One is that, under normal circumstances, Christians are not obligated to set up an alternative society with institutions alternative to those of civil society, if by that attempt they are expressing a hopelessness with regard to civil society and its institutions or a sense that God's promise cannot be fulfilled through them. To model alternative institutions and alternative styles could be part of the church's witness to the world, but for Christians to opt out of civil society and set up evangelical islands, unless civil society is guilty of gross injustice and idolatry, is to confess to a truncated and disjunctive understanding of God's workings. It is to arrogate God to the church much more than God himself has chosen to do. It is the newest form of triumphalism.

Believers can, according to Calvin, live positively in this world while on pilgrimage, witnessing to others of the gospel they have received, knowing that it is God's will to transform creation into the Kingdom of Christ, and that Christ already sits at the right hand of God. Their positive use of the Old Testament Law, and of the moral law known to natural reason and secular philosophers, and of civil codes, is to Calvin one of the ways God intends to bring about that tranformation. Christians share many goals with those who are not yet aware of that promise of God for creation. They can work together with them in civil society for the achievement of these goals. That task is every bit as related to God's work as is their verbal witness to others.

To sum up, then: Calvin laid the groundwork for a Christian approach to history which would be characterized by positive expectation of God's working in that realm and collaborative appreciation of the efforts of people in the secular realm. Because of his essentially medieval eschatology, his thinking was more individualistic than either the cosmic eschatology of the New Testament or the social philosophy of modern times, but, in his understanding of the resurrection and ascension of Christ, in his appreciation of the contribution of civil authority to humanity, and in his third use of the Law, he established a hermeneutic on which recent Reformed theologians have built. Thomas Torrance is right in saying that if Luther's eschatology can be described as "the eschatology of faith," Calvin's eschatology ought to be called "the eschatology of hope."[62] Those who live under the sign of the risen and ascended Lord, awaiting his complete glorification, have, according to Calvin, great reason to hope.

In recent decades Reformed theologians, especially in the Netherlands, have taken Calvin's christological approach to contemporary history several steps further and brought out what I take to be the full significance of Calvin's ascension-centered Christology.

In this case, as we often see in history, the theologians may have lagged behind the people of action,* finally finding ways to rethink intellectually what practical activists had long since seen to be necessary. If one examines, as Max Weber did, what a Reformed understanding of religion and the world has led to in different places, one finds that the sense of "inner-worldly vocation" of the Calvinists and their cousin Puritans has expressed itself constantly in both melioristic and revolutionary ways. Yet a consciously-articulated theological rationale for such endeavors to remake the world has been lacking until recently—although perhaps Jonathan Edwards is an exception.[63]

Nevertheless, the Calvinistic tradition has instilled in generations of believers the spirit of the Heidelberg Catechism, which maintains Calvin's fundamental insight about the third or present use of the Law.[64] In the Heidelberg Catechism, the Law is placed in the section on thankfulness, not on creation and fall, and the question (#115) "Why does God have the Ten Commandments preached so strictly since no one can keep them in this life?" is answered:

> That we may constantly and diligently pray to God for the grace of the Holy Spirit, so that more and more we may be renewed in the image of God, until we attain the goal of full perfection after this life.

Although renewal in the image of God is interpreted here in an individualistic way and not socially† and the Catechism does not encourage believers to look for the progress of God's reign in secular world history, the basis for conceiving of God's activity in socio-historical ways is nevertheless maintained: believers are to understand themselves as those who live in the time of the ascension. The work of the church today is to witness to the reigning Christ over against all false lordships.

That conviction, as Weber and so many others have made clear, has had a remarkable secularizing influence: history is desacralized—"the myth of the eternal return" (Eliade) (in its Christian and non-Christian forms) is challenged, divine right

---

*For an understanding of why Reformed orthodoxy failed to break out of its intellectual prison, see J.P. Martin, *The Last Judgment: from Orthodoxy to Ritschl,* Eerdmans, Grand Rapids, 1966.

†This is seen also in Questions 123 and 124, where "Thy kingdom come" and "Thy will be done" are interpreted in terms (a) of individuals submitting to God and (b) the increase of the church.

kingship is rejected, and a remarkable impetus toward con-
stitutionalism develops, based on the Calvinistic tradition's respect
for the role of law in human affairs.

At various points in the history of the Reformed world, from
Calvin to the early 20th century, attempts were made to overcome individualism and ecclesiocentrism in eschatology. One
thinks of the seminal work of Abraham Kuyper in the Netherlands,
for example. I will not attempt to chronicle them here, nor would
my knowledge of the history of those centuries permit me to do so
authoritatively, but I wonder if scholars of the earlier period would
not agree that not until our century did a fundamental breakthrough come.

It was when Nazism presented a fundamental challenge to all
that the Reformed tradition held dear that—as W.A. Visser 't Hooft
explained to an American audience after World War II[65]—the
theological breakthrough occurred. With the Barmen Declaration
of 1933 the gauntlet was thrown down. As Visser 't Hooft puts it:

> In the light of the doctrine of the Kingship of Christ it is a priori to be
> explained that the state stands under the Lordship of Christ, all
> power has been given to him.[66]

Reformed theologians had been tempted to operate with a "history of salvation" separate from the natural order, but they discovered under pressure that, "the New Testment does not know a
general providence apart from the history of salvation."[67] When
Hitler emerged as a "natural" ruler and unmasked the supposed
neutrality of that sphere through his neo-pagan assertion of violence and racial destiny, the church realized that it had been
deluded in thinking that the principalities and powers were just in
the heavens. They were incarnate on earth, and the church had a
word to speak to them, that—in the light of the ascension—these
powers are subject to Jesus Christ (I Pet. 3:22).

The church cannot allow the state to think it exists in an autonomous or neutral realm:

> A church which knows that its Law is the Law of the state cannot
> accept a fundamental dualism between the spiritual and the political
> realm or a complete separation between the life in the sphere of the
> church and the Christian life in the sphere of the state. A church
> which believes in the actual Kingship of Christ will therefore protest

against any and every attempt of the state to conceive politics as an autonomous realm or to absolutize its own life.[68]

He quotes De Quervain: the church's task is "to understand the state better than it understands itself." He also refers to a prayer of the Dutch church, "that government may be so directed that the King of kings may rule over both rulers and subjects."

The church began thus to express negatively what it had to learn to express positively, that the state had a function to perform in God's providence:

Whether the rulers are aware of it or not, they perform a function within the Reign of Christ. ... The rulers are intended to be the servants of God and of his ultimately gracious purpose. ... If the state revolts against God it is no longer the servant; it becomes the Beast which makes war on the saints.[69]

But God has another purpose in mind for the state:

In the provisional order which exists during the Reign of Christ, the state has the positive function to make life on earth possible and it is, therefore, in spite of its forbidding appearance, an instrument of God's mercy.[70]

When Hitler sought to turn the course of world history against what the church knew was God's plan, the church was pushed to exercise its proper, positive prophetic vocation, to speak out on behalf of all efforts contributing to the intra-historical realization of God's promises.

The church had neglected, in previous centuries, its task of interpreting history. As the authors of *Foundations and Perspectives of Confession,* a document published by the Netherlands Reformed Church in 1950 and 1954,[71] comment:

An article concerning history, concerning the course of events in time and the direction they take, was not known in the older confessions, even though God's revelation is historical through and through, and the Scripture constantly occupies itself with profane history. ... Only recently have we learned to understand more fully the comfort and meaning of this emphasis, after having lived so long in one-sided subjective piety.

But in that document there is an article precisely on history. It reads, in part:

> Because of our faith in the Christ who has come, and in the future
> consummation of the Kingdom of God, we look upon the events in
> time, not as the arbitrary play of free forces, nor as the unbreakable
> decree of fate, but as the arena of God's blessed rule, as the history
> which extends to the destiny determined by Him. . . . The dominion
> of God . . . is the earth's ineluctable end. . . .

The article goes on to affirm:

> We can take our place in history without fear. History is the total
> event, directed from Christ's first coming toward his second coming.
> . . . History manifests itself in a series of crises. There is no evolution,
> but a continuing advance of Christ's work and consequently an
> increasing raging of anti-Christian forces.

But it is not only in the article on history that a historical perspective predominates. In the article on "Jesus, the King," Christ's "sitting at the right hand of the Father" is interpreted as much more than just sitting: "As Lord and King," the article states, Christ "shares God's rule of the world." Describing Christ's kingship as a still concealed one, the document goes on to say,

> The Kingship of Christ is nevertheless an all-inclusive kingship. All
> that exists and all that happens is at the service of this kingdom of
> grace.

Previous Reformed confessions generally restricted Christ's kingship much more. As the notes state:

> The Kingship of Christ is commonly referred to chiefly in relation to
> His Church. Paragraph 5 emphasizes that Christ's kingship is recog-
> nized only through faith and is celebrated and proclaimed by the
> congregation. . . . But paragraph 6 makes it evident that in Christ's
> kingship the whole world is concerned. World events are thus seen
> in their true light. Everything is directed to the future of the
> Kingdom.

The basis for this faith lies in the resurrection of Christ. As Article 8 explains,

> The resurrection of Christ is the proof that God purposes and
> accomplishes not the rejection of man but his exaltation, not the
> destruction of the world but its renewal. The resurrection of Christ is
> the pledge and prophecy that God's mercy wins out over sin and
> death, that the whole creation both in its spiritual and material
> aspects is snatched from the Evil One, and that God's kingly rule
> ultimately carries away the victory.

This is still *in via,* not yet fulfilled, but one day it will find its fulfillment. In Article 18 ("Consummation") the theologians explain the character of God's rule when it shall have come in its fullness:

> The Lord will be an everlasting light over all his creation. Then nature will be glorified and history consummated. Then God's Kingdom will be present on this earth in all its perfection; the nations will walk in it and kings bring their riches therein. Then God will wipe away all tears from their eyes and His glory will be seen and shared in eternal praise and service of Him.

Now nothing is unique about such an affirmation as a final affirmation of a Christian confession. Nothing is unique about it when it refers to the ultimate end-time. What is different about that affirmation in this confession is that prior to the article in which it is contained the theologians have laid a foundation for it by relating ultimate eschatology to contemporary eschatology, by relating this final eschatological hope to contemporary historical realities—by means of the concept of the reign of Christ. What is affirmed about the *eschaton* has already been affirmed provisionally concerning current eschatological activity. There is thus "a continuing advance of Christ's work" from the document's point of view. It does not come completely out of the blue at some future date. The authors are careful, however, lest what they say be interpreted to imply that there is a steady evolution in the development of this world into the Kingdom of God. No generalized evolutionary optimism is meant by what they say. They do not mean to claim that "the world is getting better and better every day in every way," or "we are building the kingdom." The renewal of the earth, they clearly state, "will not be the slowly ripening fruit of man's toil," but it will be "the surprising gift of God's recreative action." But nevertheless that gift need neither be sudden nor come only at the end of time:

> The Kingdom is in a hidden way already present and the consummation does not drop like a bombshell into an existence to which it is essentially unrelated.

The document in other words maintains exactly the balance which Visser 't Hooft commended in his American lectures referred to earlier,[72] when he said:

The Gospel is equally far away from a Manichaean dualism which rejects the world *in toto* and from an optimistic faith in the gradual penetration of the world by divine forces.

This has an important consequence for our Christian obedience. We are called not just to wait for the consummation but to "wait actively." We are called, as Christians, to enter the conflict of the Kingdom of God with all alien powers, in the sure and certain hope that the future belongs to the Kingdom of God because Christ has already been enthroned. To make such an affirmation in the face of the massive injustices of the present world order seems paradoxical. And it is true that throughout this discussion almost every statement we have made has had its "nevertheless." But in this area we cannot be less than paradoxical. What we need are images which help us get beyond pragmatism and positivism, images which express and feed upon the mystery of God's dealings with humankind and lead us to heightened endeavor, increased power to hope, and to affirmation in the face of negation.

One of the theologians who produced the *Foundations* document specialized in such images. This was A.A. Van Ruler of Utrecht. "The Kingdom of God," he wrote, "unfolds in the world as a fan in a lady's hand." There always remains discontinuity, freedom, unpredictability, dialectical interchange and pulsation in whatever we say about the Kingdom, he writes, "because the reality of the Kingdom is ever transcendent—it never becomes identical with its historical-cultural forms."[73]

Van Ruler found the ± symbol of the mathematicians useful.[74] The reign of God is both present and hidden. The church is a sign of its presence, but not as an end in itself, only as a kind of "eschatological intermezzo":

On Sunday morning at the altar the vision of the Kingdom lights up as an eschatological intermezzo, pointing away from itself to the family at home, the commonwealth of man—the Kingdom which is not of this world seeks its realization in the world.[75]

The church is essentially called to mission outward, for it is of the nature of the Kingdom to seek its fulfillment outward. For Van Ruler, as Isaac Rottenberg writes, "The apostolate of the church in all its aspects is a sign of the power of the Kingdom, a historical embodiment of the reality of the new creation." But there is another side to it: the very presence of the Kingdom also arouses the "anti-forces." But they, in their very negativity, become signs of the approaching end. This is the drama that constitutes the stuff of history.[76]

I. John Hesselink explains that, for Van Ruler:

> These last days are the age of an "intermezzo" in which the Kingdom of God is both hidden and revealed: hidden in its completeness at the right hand of God, and yet eschatologically present as the first fruits of the Spirit.[77]

There are already signs that God is bringing his Kingdom, that the Kingdom is present, affecting all reality. Such signs become indications of the end. "The Gospel is preached, and hearts are touched. Lives are affected and so are the orders and structures of society." The signs, though extending far beyond the church, are related to the activity of the church. And yet the negative forces are there as well. Van Ruler believes the church must learn to tolerate and appreciate such paradox, for it is the key to the understanding of how God is saving the world:

> It is a remarkable thing that we, at fifty, are the same persons as we were when youngsters of eight. Everything is changed, inwardly and outwardly. Yet we are the same being. . . . This paradox of identity amidst change is one that we cannot fathom. But it is a fact that both elements exist. We express the fact with the word *continuity*.[78]

The point of the whole matter is that when we say the Bible affirms continuity, we are expressing hope for this world: "God will not create a wholly new world to replace the old. He will recreate this, His old world."[79]

Van Ruler writes also, "God is concerned with life in time . . . in order that it might be sanctified to his service."[80] He is not willing to let this old sinful world go, and that is the source of our hope. "Our destiny . . . lies in seeing the world with God and from God." We can draw no picture of the completed Kingdom of glory—love itself—Van Ruler admits, but "we can let it sink into our hearts":

> In eternity man shall look out over and fathom the entire temporal reality of himself and of the world. All tears shall be wiped from his eyes. . . . He shall see in all things—in the things of this world and of this life—he shall see in them all the glory of God. And he shall repeat after God that they are very good.

"Then we shall apprehend," Van Ruler concludes, "that this incomprehensibly high destiny rests in the eternal good pleasure of God."

Van Ruler's theology has the nature of a doxology, for it is a theology which finds its fulfillment in praise. Such a theology can tolerate paradox. It rejects the counsel of Job's friends and decides that it can do without schematization and with no greater certainty than the promise of God.

A contemporary theologian who worked with the late Van Ruler on the *Foundations* document and in other areas and who carries further similar impetuses is Hendrikus Berkhof. In his book *Christ the Meaning of History*,[81] written in dialogue with Marxists on the one hand and Christian sectarians on the other, Berkhof argues that Christians are "permitted and even commanded to seek and find traces of the resurrected Christ in the events of contemporary history":

> The Church cannot find its place in the world without seeing, or at least the desire to see, these signs. Faith does not depend on vision, but it does lead to vision. For faith, among other things, means the certainty that wherever Christ is glorified in this world and reigns over this world, his resurrection power is active in history, and as such takes on form; i.e., it becomes visible.[82]

Berkhof fights on at least three Christian fronts at once. He challenges the rigidity and "above the battle" position of orthodoxy, which says God will do everything in his own good time. At the same time he challenges the liberalism which expects nothing transcendent and the chiliasm, or dispensationalism, of the sectarians—think of Hal Lindsey—"which wants to know," according to Berkhof, "more than we are able to know." Orthodoxy and liberalism have each, he believes, understood certain truths about the Kingdom, but have failed by their rejection of the truths the others have received. Each was unable to tolerate paradox:

> The Kingdom of God is the work of God himself. This is the truth in the orthodox position. The error is to believe that it must therefore be a sudden event entirely from without. God is active in the world. The Kingdom of God grows. This is the truth in the liberal position. The error is to believe that it is therefore man's labour, and that it is identical with moral and social progress. . . .

> We believe in a God who continues his work victoriously in this dispensation. This is a faith. It is based on the fact that Christ was

raise from the dead in this old world. It is not disturbed by the fact that experience often seems to contradict this faith. It knows that to God the facts are in agreement with this faith. When he looks back into history, looks around in the present, reads his newspaper, and listens to what is happening, the believer expects that he *will* see God's goodness in the land of the living.[83]

Christian faith is marked by an inaugurated eschatology—Christ *is* King, and therefore the Christian looks for signs of his reign here and now. That is why the Christian has every reason to describe Marxism as a *Christian* heresy, since it takes a true affirmation about Christian hope—that it is not just far future hope—and constructs a total system around it, just as dispensationalism takes a fundamental biblical truth—concerning the millennium—and seeks to build its system entirely on that. The Christian does look for signs of Christ's dawning reign now and he looks in many directions. He does not expect all positive change to come about through Christian agency, for God's work is far larger than the bounds of the church:

In the struggle for a genuine human existence, for deliverance of the suffering, for the elevation of the underdeveloped, for redemption of the captives, for the settlement of race and class differences, for opposition to chaos, crime, suffering, sickness, and ignorance—in short, in the struggle for what we call progress—an activity is taking place throughout the world to the honour of Christ. It is sometimes performed by people who know and desire it; it is more often performed by those who have no concern for it, but whose labour proves that Christ truly received—in full objectivity—all power on earth.[84]

Christ is thus really King. All power already legitimately belongs to him, and therefore "Christ's order of life forcefully progresses throughout the world."[85] But be careful! Berkhof does not mean by this that there are no opposition forces to Christ—quite the contrary: "We can see under, beside, and against all this, the growth of the opposition forces. The first should not blind us to the second"—and this is the point—but "the second should not blind us to the first either. . . . The second would not exist without the presence of the first." Berkhof grounds these statements on an exegesis of passages such as II Thessalonians 2. "The growth of the opposition is an indication of the growth of the Kingdom of God."[86]

Berkhof next goes on to relate his interpretation of the meaning of Christ for history to an analysis of the cross and resurrection, in a way similar to that of Moltmann which we examined earlier. He, like Moltmann, speaks of the hope appropriate to those who believe in a crucified God. The cross, he writes with sober, crucified realism, "stands firmly and concretely in the centre of our history. The resurrection stands vaguely at its periphery." Berkhof is not a utopian visionary or a liberal optimist. "In the present dispensation," he writes—and Berkhof means by this until the end-time— "there is no balance between cross and resurrection, let alone an ascendancy of the resurrection. The last and greatest result of the cross is the reign of the antichrist." He goes on, however, to affirm, "But the ultimate result of the resurrection is connected with the new heaven and the new earth. It is beyond the boundaries of this dispensation."[87]

A Christian view of history, based on the ascension of the risen Christ, thus points for Berkhof beyond present history to "the consummation of history":

> Talk about history is talk about consummation. Cross and resurrection are not in balance with each other. The resurrection has the ascendancy and victory over the cross. ... Resurrection is the essence of the consummation.[88]

The final consummation will involve both continuity and break. The world will leave the form of the cross behind and become a new world, but it is the same world which will rise from its broken position. Death will be transformed into resurrection as the old creation is transformed into the new person in the life of the individual believer and of the church:

> We come closest to the secret of history when we see it as a parallel of what Christ does in the life of an individual and of the Church. The believer is and remains a sinner who finds life and justification by grace alone. At the same time he finds a real but contested and often interrupted sanctification of his life. ... Our life is marked by struggle. ...

"But," he adds, "we must not stretch this parallel too far; man is something other than history." The parallel is, however, useful, "when we seek the manner in which the Spirit is present in a sinful world. He is represented in the form of struggle and the small beginning."[89] In the struggle there is both continuity and discontinuity. There will be a break with all the forces which hinder Christ's dominion, at the same time as there will be a continuation of the resurrection forces which are already active in history.

Those forces at present are but "crocuses in the winter of a fallen world"; they are "no more than harbingers of the future for which God has destined the world."[90] There will be a need for a "special intervention from above to set these forces free to reach their full potential." This will happen with the return of the risen Christ. What the world is now experiencing can best be described with the Jewish imagery of "the labour pains of the Messiah."[91] The pains characterize this present world, but point beyond it to the new world which is already coming. The fundamental image is one of the continuity in the process of transition:

> The new world does not fall into the old like a bomb, nor does it take the place of the old which is destroyed, but it is born through the old in which it had been active.[92]

This does not make it any easier to discern what in the present order is the harbinger of the future and what is not. The Kingdom of Christ and the kingdom of the antichrist are still "hidden under the appearance of their opposite" and "everywhere intertwined."[93] But this does not mean that nothing can be known or recognized of them, for "world history is not black or white, but it is not an even grey either. The eye of faith recognizes dark grey and light grey."

We cannot be excused from the need to make choices (as a reading of Smedes earlier might have suggested). We are called to be watchful, and "watchfulness," Berkhof writes, "must lead to choices." What we will be doing as we watch, he is here quite clear, is to interpret, and that is a task we cannot avoid. We must try to interpret what is going on in history, as we seek to recognize our fellow-servants and try to know where the oppressed are in the world:

> He who watches interprets the facts. In view of the ambiguity of our history, every interpretation will always remain debatable. But it is unavoidable. It is an act of grateful obedience and as such is never meaningless and without blessing.[94]

And, although we are all similarly called to watchfulness, the ambiguities involved in the process will preclude the likelihood that there will be a uniformity of interpretation and decision within the church. Our judgments remain relative,[95] but

> We must look around ... in order to discover and support the positive signs of Christ's dominion ... and to discover and oppose the anti-christian tendencies (even in the heart of the Christian Church). For the meaning of our life is fulfilled only when we take part in the meaning of history.[96]

With Berkhof our survey of recent Reformed thinking about the meaning of the ascension for present history ends. We will have occasion to refer to these same theologians again when we deal with the Spirit and with the consummation of history. But that is not our goal in this chapter. Here our concern has been to deal with the ascension, and show how followers of John Calvin have developed further his thinking on it. We have seen that the promise of Calvin's thinking, so long bottled up by Calvinistic orthodoxy, has in this century moved toward its fulfillment as a robust, world-transforming, yet soberly realistic hope, based on the hope mediated to us by the apostles in the New Testament. James P. Martin would say that what has been fulfilled is the teleological element in the Kingship of Christ:

> Orthodoxy did not take teleology into consideration. . . . The goal of the teleology appears to be the sitting at the right hand of God. . . . The difficulty remains of relating to *history* the eternal and spiritual Kingship of Christ now exercised at the right hand of God. The idea of Christ's Kingship is bound to the *sessio ad dextra,* and the trouble seems to be that Orthodoxy interpreted the "sitting" almost literally. The relation of this heavenly rule to the earth, the Church, and history, is tenuous at best. . . . The unity of the New Testament Kingdom of God is lost sight of and its entry *into* history and its "growth" to the Last Day is obscured.[97]

Perhaps, through the work of these recent Dutch theologians, building—many of them—upon Barmen and the impetus Karl Barth there gave, the Reformed tradition has finally begun to speak about the ascension in a seriously historical way. And if the Reformed tradition can provide in the doctrine of the ascension a new theological basis for Christian involvement in the historical, that will have been no small contribution toward overcoming the dualisms of the church in our days.

*   *   *

The Bridegroom has come. The wedding-feast has begun. This small, homey gathering is a foretaste and a paradigm of the world to come.

> Come, all you who thirst,
> Come to the waters;
> And you who have no money
> come, buy, and eat!
> Come, buy wine and milk
> without money and without price. . . .
> Hearken diligently to me, and eat what is good,
> and delight yourselves in fatness. . . .
> And I will make with you an everlasting covenant. . . .
> Behold you shall call nations that you know not,
> and nations that you knew not shall run to you.
> Because of the Lord your God, and of the holy one of Israel,
> for he has glorified you (Isa. 55:1-5).

8: AN EXCURSUS ON FEASTS, or WHEN THE SAINTS GO MARCHING IN

> What remains more appropriate to true religion than
> the belief that it is possible for God to do new things
> such as he never did before?
> —Augustine, *City of God* XII, xx

AND THE FIVE YOUNG WOMEN WHO WERE READY WENT IN TO
the wedding feast.

*   *   *

"When the Jesuits at 16th Street in New York asked me to preach
at the eleven o'clock mass, I seized on the opportunity to give a
sermon on Heaven," the former publisher Frank Sheed writes in
his autobiography, "so that I should not die without ever having
heard one."[1]

I cannot recall that I have ever heard one either, nor have I in
recent years heard a sermon which encouraged me to hope for an
earthly paradise. Yet the outline of this book, based as it is on
Jesus' Allegory of the Ten Young Women, forces me at this point
to write one!

There is no way to deal with the Allegory of the Ten Young
Woman without recognizing that the central event with which it is
concerned is God's eschatological wedding-feast, and without
taking quite seriously the fact that Jesus encouraged his hearers to
hope for the chance to participate in it. God, as we saw in our first
chapter, is a wedding-maker. He doesn't prepare weddings without intending that people shall come to them!

It will by now be clear that I think it is an illegitimate reading of
Jesus' preaching to interpret his eschatology only in a far-future
sense, to say, for example, that the wedding-feast is an event

which takes place only after death or only at the Second Coming. Jesus' preaching was characterized by a foreshortened eschatology, by an affirmation that the Kingdom was already making itself present in history, and by a call to people to participate now, by their discipleship, not only in the cost but also in the joys of the Kingdom. When I write now about the wedding-feast, I shall consider simultaneously his invitation to participate in it within history and his invitation to the feast which transcends the history we know. The "carrot" which I as an evangelist hold out before hearers is, in other words, not just life with the angels in the Kingdom of heaven—it *is* that—but also the joys of life in the Kingdom as it is being realized within our history.

Martin Luther King, Jr. knew that. He was one of the best evangelists of our time. He knew that God had given him a prophet's license, the license to dream. He knew that between reality and the dream there was a big gulf, and that the only way over the gulf was through repentance. He knew it would be costly and painful. But he sought to motivate people not by threat but by promise. He sought to awaken in Americans too given to cynicism about race relations and injustice the capacity to hope. Like his Master, he painted a picture of what the world calls a utopia. He encouraged his hearers to believe that *that* was what God was working to bring about.

At the same time, Martin Luther King did not limit his own vision of the utopia to its fulfillment within the near future in such a way that he would be forced to compromise if it appeared difficult or impossible to achieve. He could, because of his knowledge of its transcendent character, court even death in pursuing the vision, confident that, even if as its prophet he would only see the Promised Land from Pisgah, in God's eternity he would participate in it.

"Would that all the people of the Lord were prophets!" (Num. 11:29).

I believe that it was the Holy Spirit who was active in Martin Luther King's ministry, and that if we understand what the Spirit is doing in the work of such contemporary prophets, much that has been unclear to us about the work of the Spirit will become clear, and the relationship between the Spirit's activity and culture and society today will be better understood.

I have in previous writing[2] expressed my personal sense that we are living in a time of heightened activity of the Spirit. At that time I called the worldwide charismatic renewal a "sign of hope" for the church today. I realize now that until recently I have been looking for signs of the Spirit in too circumscribed an area. My own denomination, the United Church of Christ, does the same in its Statement of Faith, which says that God "bestows upon us His Holy Spirit, creating and renewing the church of Jesus Christ, binding in covenant faithful people of all ages, tongues and races." It says the place to look for signs of the Spirit is in the church.

And certainly this is true. If we examine what the New Testament says about the Spirit, we will find that, with the exception of the Johannine writings, practically every reference is clearly to the Spirit's work in individual believers or in the church.

But still, there are the Johannine writings, with their strong witness to the freedom of the Spirit (a witness which has been particularly developed over history in the Eastern Church, and which has been a strong emphasis recently of the church in Africa), and the unanimous witness of all four gospels that the Spirit "descended" or "came" upon Jesus, in other words that the Spirit was not "born" on Pentecost. What the New Testament seems to claim is that the same Spirit who was once at large came to dwell fully in Jesus during his ministry (see John 3:34—"It is not by measure that God gives the Spirit"—God gave the Spirit totally to Jesus). But that Spirit by whom Jesus was anointed (Luke 4:18ff.) and who gave birth to the church (Acts 2 *et al.*), has a pre-history: we must look to the Old Testament to find it.

There we see that the Spirit was at work in creation (Gen. 1:2, Ps. 33:6), and in the preservation of human life (Job 33:4, Isa. 42:5). It rested on those called to lead God's people (Gen. 41:38, Judg. 3:10), and on the "Servant of the Lord" (Isa. 42:1); wisdom and discernment are the Spirit's gifts (Isa. 11:2, Prov. 1:23), and the Spirit gives to the prophets both energy and divine intelligence (Mic. 3:8, Isa. 61:1), and inspires human culture (agriculture, Isa. 28:26; architecture, Exod. 31:3, 35:31; and jurisdiction, Num. 11:17) as well as political affairs (Cyrus is the Lord's anointed, Isa. 45:1-5). Finally, all human wisdom is the gift of God's Spirit (Job 32:8, Dan. 1:17, 5:11).

But why is this of interest to us? Is it not merely of antiquarian concern, now that we know the Spirit has been given to the church? No, according to Hendrikus Berkhof, that is an illegitimate interpretation of what the New Testament says. The church is not Jesus, and it is the clear intention of the New Testament to present the special operation of the Spirit in the present era "as the restoration and fulfillment of his work in creation." By using words like "vivify," "birth," "regeneration," and "new creation" to describe the Spirit's activity, the New Testament is affirming that, just as the Spirit was once at work in the creation of the world, so is the Spirit today at work in the activity of creation in this world.

> The outpouring of the Spirit is not an incident; as well as the Son, the Spirit "came to his own home." Therefore we are encouraged to discover his traces with joy and gratitude everywhere in our created world. We must even say that only he who knows God's Spirit in re-creation can truly distinguish his signs in creation.[3]

We must therefore beware of speaking as if the Spirit were the "property" of the church. Although, from our perspective, everyone to whom the Spirit speaks or everyone filled by the Spirit in the gospels and Acts is a "Christian," at the time when the Spirit filled them or appeared to them many of them were not (and of certain of them—I think of Zechariah and Elizabeth, Simeon and Anna, for example—we shall never know whether they became members of the New Covenant community).

Perhaps, however, the strongest argument for not drawing the lines too close is to recall that the apostles—and our Lord himself—had to fight most strongly in their time against the idea held by Israel's religious leaders that the activity of the Spirit of God was completely known and predictable. To these leaders it was scandalous to affirm that the Spirit was working freely. And yet Jesus and the apostles dared make that affirmation. It was patently obvious to the early church that the Spirit was acting in new ways in its time.

We therefore need to be wary lest we box the Spirit in anew in our times. There are two ways in which we do this: by limiting *where* the Spirit works—we have seen how we tend to limit that working to the church—and by limiting *how* the Spirit works.

A. A. Van Ruler speaks of a certain "pneumatological docetism" in the church, by which we expect the Spirit to act in "spiritual"— that is, not "earthly"—ways.[4] "If the Spirit is essential for earthly reality," he writes, "so is the earth essential for the work of the Spirit." Through his indwelling the Spirit receives "earthly form" and transforms "creaturely realities" into "salvation realities." The essential activity of the Holy Spirit is his transforming activity.

Look at the verbs applied to the Spirit in the New Testament, he says: filling, indwelling, moving, encouraging, empowering— these all point to the Spirit's ability to change inert things into living things, to bring people from death to life, to empower weak people, to enliven dying communities, to awaken sleeping ones. Van Ruler asks us to demystify words used to describe the Spirit's activity, such as "sanctifying" and "glorifying," and see how they denote that "all existence becomes gripped by the Holy Spirit." He asks us to have more earthly hope for what that means. In Paul Fries's words:

> The relation of peoples, the structures of their society, their culture, the political formation of their lives—all this belongs essentially to God's living in the world. The indwelling Spirit fills creation with salvation.[5]

"Man's corporate, institutional life, his historical existence, is called," Van Ruler writes, "to sing a hymn of praise to God."[6]

So we begin to understand that what Van Ruler means by his critique of "pneumatological docetism" is to call us to biblical realism about the Spirit's activity, not to look for it up in the sky, or just in people's hearts, or church revivals, but in the workaday world, the world of history and culture. He wants us to raise the fundamental eschatological question about the Spirit's activity: in the light of what we know of God's purpose, to what end is the Spirit's activity directed? His own answer is:

> Eschatologically viewed, God's purpose is not to bring Christ to the world, but to transform fallen existence into the Kingdom of God. Christ and his work is the foundation, paradigm, and reality of the Kingdom; there can be no Kingdom, no redemption without him. It is the Spirit, however, that moves in every corridor and corner of history to fill creation with Christian salvation and thus brings the Kingdom to fallen creation.[7]

Van Ruler at this point challenges the "Christomonism" of his earlier mentor Karl Barth, and asks that we become what Protestants have often failed to be: Trinitarian. During this present "intermezzo" the Kingdom is being revealed in the world, as the first fruits of the Spirit are eschatologically manifest. The activity of the Holy Spirit is more comprehensive in scope than the work of the Messiah, in that the redemption accomplished by the Messiah in the fulfillment of the Torah and the Old Testament of Israel now broadens out and takes form in the whole of existence.[8] What once occurred only in Israel is now at work, we are encouraged to believe, in all existence.

At this point Van Ruler finds it helpful to introduce Calvin's distinction between "particular grace" and "common grace."* Already before Van Ruler, at the end of the 19th century, Abraham Kuyper had sought to develop that idea in terms of God's transformation of human cultures through the work of the Spirit. "The stream of particular grace," Kuyper wrote, in a memorable phrase, "breaks all dykes and spills out over all the world."[9] What he meant was that cultures are Christianized by the spilling out into society of the grace Christians have received. Christianity spreads, so does its influence, and the result is an expansion of Christian culture.

According to T. G. Hommes,[10] Van Ruler does not identify the development of Christian civilization and the history of the church as closely as does Kuyper. What Van Ruler says is that common grace is "fertilized" by particular grace and that it needs this fertilization; for him culture retains a greater relative independence. He rejects the idea that secularization is a desirable end, and yet he is wary of the possibility that the church might believe itself called to dominate the culture. Common grace is not, for Van Ruler, supplanted by particular grace. The relationship between Christianity and the world is rather that of an "eschatological dialectic." The church should seek to "christen" culture[11] by "impressing and imprinting the image of Christ in and upon all human existence," but the church must remember that Christ gave it no mandate to establish a sacral, ecclesiastical, or

---

*An exhaustive study of Calvin's teaching on common grace is found in Herman Kuiper, *Calvin on Common Grace,* Goes, Netherlands, 1928.

cultural empire. "Man is not human in order to become Christian," Van Ruler wrote, "but he is Christian in order to become human."[12]

The church's ultimate task is not to Christianize but to "open up the life of society to the perspective of God's Kingdom." The church's mandate to make disciples is an instrumental mandate. People become Christian in order to become consciously part of God's Kingdom-bringing activity. The church, as the community of those who confess faith in God and in Christ, seeks to witness to the Kingdom in all of life and thus to transform culture, but the Kingdom is not to be thought of as a thoroughly Christianized culture. There is no such thing as a *Durchchristung,* Van Ruler said. A "Christian culture"—and Van Ruler believed there was such in the Western world and cherished it—can only remain a "torso"—imperfect, provisional, and proleptic, a foreshadowing or foretaste at most, for only the surface of life is exposed to God's sunlight. Not within human history will sin cease to hold society in its demonic grip.

But there is a danger on the opposite side, the danger that the church will come to think that there is an unbridgeable gulf between its life and common human existence—a danger as present in the "young evangelical" movement as in fundamentalism. It comes to expression today in the sense of some that God's primary call is for those who understand themselves from the Bible to challenge and reject American culture, including its political institutions, and to assert that the Christian has nothing to hope for from them, and that God's work will only properly be done in and through alternative Christian institutions.

Van Ruler would challenge this latent perfectionism by asking those who understand themselves from the Bible to recognize not only the + but also the − in the ± sign of God's work in the world. It is a matter of a different "density of grace" between church and culture, but both partake of grace. There is no ultimate qualitative difference, nor any total separation.[13] The church represents the + sign of believed and proclaimed particular grace; culture represents the − of grace operationalized in the common life of humanity.* Church and culture are dialectically interrelated, not as sepa-

---

*The minus sign is not intended in any pejorative or negative sense.

rate entities, but as the two poles within the same universal scope of God's eschatological acts. The church "is the institution of particular grace *par excellence,* radiating influence upon the surrounding world, and thus fulfilling the potential of common grace deposited in society," but the Kingdom transcends both church and culture. It brings both of them to consummation, and this not merely beyond historical time. As Hommes interprets what Van Ruler is saying here:

> The final fulfilment of the Kingdom will be an historic manifestation, as were, are, and will be the other kairotic moments of its realization. . . . Each time when the Kingdom breaks into the earthly life of man and its structures is a foretaste, an *arrabon* of that future, a moment of "already" in a world which is "not yet" eschatologically transformed.[14]

In history God is readying the world for his Kingdom. Although the judgment will come between this present time and the Kingdom, history will not be nullified by it:

> There will not come another, higher world at the eschaton. This world is the real and only one, and even in the eschaton it is this world that God is about.[15]

Over and over again Van Ruler makes similar assertions of the importance of this world we live in. He does it in his exposition of I Corinthians 13:10 as well ("But when that which is perfect is come, then that which is in part shall be done away"):

> In this verse Paul is speaking of the time when the perfect shall come. He is not speaking of the time when we shall be made perfect. There is a big difference between these two things. To say that perfection itself must still come is typically Biblical. It is a deeper thought than it would be if we were to say that we must yet be made perfect. In the latter instance we assume that perfection already has come, but that we have not yet been made perfect. In this way we construe two worlds: the imperfect world, the earthly, temporal, and material world, and above this world, the perfect world, the heavenly, eternal, and spiritual world. The perfect world already exists, but it exists somewhere else. We do not live in it. This is saddening, but at the same time it provides a profound comfort: we are going to get to the perfect world sometime, in the hour of our death.
>
> The apostle is not able to find such simple comfort in this thought. He suffers much more deeply within the present existence. He says

that the perfect world itself must yet come. It has not yet arrived. . . . The moment shall arrive . . . when the perfect shall come in.

It is not the perfection of another world. Paul does not know anything about two worlds. He knows only this one, this visible and tangible world. It is in this world that the perfect must one day appear. It is the perfection of this one and only, this visible and tangible, and very imperfect world. This is the perfection on which Paul sets his hope.[16]

With this quotation we leave our consideration of Van Ruler's pneumatology. I introduced it to help us draw the necessary links between the present eschatological manifestations of the Kingdom—the present "marriage-supper," to use the language of our foundation allegory—and the ultimate establishment of the Kingdom—the final eschatological banquet. We have seen that Van Ruler takes quite seriously what Paul says about the Spirit being the first fruits, the sign and seal of our ultimate inheritance (cf. Rom. 8:23, Eph. 1:13f., etc.). He sees the final eschatological feast as the consummation of the one appearing in the ± form appropriate to this present "intermezzo." He takes quite seriously the presence of the demonic in today's world, but he refuses to allow us to use that as an excuse for a "pneumatological docetism" which withdraws from this present order.

Van Ruler's eschatology is quite in harmony, I believe, with Jesus' standard preaching, "The right time has come; the Kingdom of God is near! Turn away from your sins and believe the good news!" (Mark 1:14f., TEV) and also with Paul's affirmation, "The time has come for you to wake up from your sleep. . . . The night is nearly over, day is almost here. Let us stop doing the things that belong to the dark, and take up the weapons for fighting in the light" (Rom. 13:11f., TEV). He calls us to recognize that we live in the time of the ascension, and that Christ's Lordship is already being established in a provisional but real way in this world. Just as a provisional revolutionary government is not to be thought of as qualitatively different from that government when it has come into power, so the present small beginnings of the Kingdom are part of the Kingdom. The first fruits are fruits! It is not a matter of collecting Betty Crocker coupons until you've gotten enough to trade them in for some silverware—there's a spoon in the very first box.

Even with our "pneumatological docetism," we have recognized the truth of that in our experiences as Christian individuals and in our experience in the church. We really do experience the forgiveness of sins and new power for our lives when we accept God's call. Similarly we really experience a fellowship that "is like to that above." Now, we need to extend those experiences into the historical and social-structural realm as well. We need not wait till Tennyson's "Parliament of Man" is fulfilled, or till the Peace-able Kingdom comes, before we can experience the first fruits of God's universal *shalom.* The world we live in—a world of which Christ is King—is the scene of many small beginnings which, though small, are nonetheless beginnings.

Beginnings of what? Beginnings of the re-orientation of human community toward God's plan for its future. As the hymn puts it,

> God is working his purpose out,
> As year succeeds to year;
> God is working his purpose out,
> And the time is drawing near.
> Nearer and nearer comes the time,
> The time that shall surely be,
> When the earth shall be filled with the glory of God
> As the waters cover the sea.[17]

We need not look for signs of God's purpose being worked out only through the world mission of the church, as the author of that hymn intended. The stream of particular grace has broken all the dikes, as Kuyper said, and spilled out all over the world. In the lives of nations and civilizations we will find signs of God's working out his purpose. Only in recent times have we become newly aware of some of the cosmic dimensions of God's eschatological activity, which many of the New Testament authors assumed. But as a result of that regained awareness, our eyes are open wide. Thomas Clarke puts it well:

> Contemporary humanity has the opportunity and the challenge of a God-experience in a modality not fully open to it in the past. The world of public structures and institutions, instead of being conceived as a mere neutral setting for the drama of God's search for us and our search for God, now becomes a locus of revelation.[18]

Once we have seen this, we may well say, with Jacob, we have come to Bethel, a place of recognition that God has previously been present in ways we did not understand. "Truly," Jacob said,

"God is in this place and I never knew it! This is none other than the house of God and a gate of heaven!" (Gen. 28:16f.) We will want to say, "God has been active in the world of public affairs and institutions, but we never knew it!"

God has revealed to us, Clarke is saying, the social-structural aspects of his dealings with humankind. His grace, we now become aware, comes to us not only as personal and interpersonal—grace in our lives and in our relationships with others—but as social or public as well. As Calvin said, part of God's grace to us is in his giving us social structures which make life more human. The structures of society are, in other words, not just human-made. God has been acting in the processes of institution-building and the structuring of the relationships among nations:

> Throughout human history . . . God has been giving himself, revealing himself, through the public processes, structures, and institutions of humanity.[19]

Certainly those institutions are corrupted and full of sin. We have learned to analyze this sin, correctly, as not merely the sin of individuals arrogating power to themselves, but as "social sin." We have diagnosed certain structures, correctly, as "oppressive structures."

Clarke says we now need a correlative notion to put alongside social sin, lest we become Manichaean. He suggests the notion of "public" or "societal grace." Just as we recognize that the power of evil often takes structural forms, so we must have a doctrine of grace adequate to cope with the understanding of evil: in the face of structured, societal sin God reveals himself as a God of structured grace. And therefore we look for both grace and sin in our analysis of contemporary reality:

> An insistence on the societal dimension of the human must *simultaneously* seek to attend to the respective embodiments of both grace and sin in public processes, structures, and institutions.[20]

In a private meeting with some of us concerned with evangelism in the United Church of Christ in 1974, Clarke expanded on some of the pastoral dimensions of what he had written. The societal and the environmental, he said, are constitutive of the human, not just extrinsic conditions of being human. By dealing with people's spiritual lives as purely personal or interpersonal we have failed to fulfil our pastoral responsibility. The people to whom we minister are members of society, employees of corporations, citizens of towns and cities. The world in which they live shapes, to a large extent, who they are. We offer them, perhaps, a Christian life apart from the environment in which they live—warning them, it may be, of the need to avoid being conformed to the world and of the presence of evil in the world, but failing to give them handles with which to deal with the world. We provide them with personal grace to deal with social sin. Many of us then complain that the people don't exercise their lay apostolate. But they are wise in not trying to, Clarke avers. They know full well that sin is never approached safely except in the context of grace—otherwise it is destructive. But the understanding of grace which the church has given them is purely personal and interpersonal grace. We have been failing to give them a doctrine of God and of grace large enough to cope with their new understanding of society. As a result they have become demoralized and apathetic. Or else they have sought comfort outside the Christian faith. By helping people to see how God works through the social process, we can free them from their sense of inadequacy to deal with the problems of our day on the basis of Christian faith.

We spoke of Alcoholics Anonymous. Such an institution, Clarke said, is more than just the individuals involved in it. It is a "structure of grace" through which people in need are ministered to. Similarly the federal welfare system and unemployment laws are structures of grace, as are the United Nations peace-keeping forces in the Middle East and the United Nations Conference on Trade and Development. We should learn to look at all these things, Clarke suggested, in the light of Romans 5:20: "Where sin increased, grace abounded all the more." God reveals his gracious presence in and through human societal self-expressions, to the extent that they are truly human and not dehumanizing. Just as he reveals himself through the vehicle of human love in a marriage, so he reveals himself through the vehicles of public processes and institutions.

As the father of a handicapped child, I would want to affirm the presence of God's grace in many of the structures of society which have ministered to him and to us. Life with him has been made possible for us by the ways in which society is structured to share the burdens of families of the handicapped. Now it is not the church which has provided these institutions—indeed, the Protestant churches have a poor record in work with the retarded—but should I therefore conclude that the social institutions which minister to our needs cannot be instances of God's grace? Can I ecclesiasticize God that much? Do I not rather want to praise him that his grace has broken the dikes?

Similarly, now that governments around the world have "taken over" many schools, colleges, and hospitals founded by the churches in their worldwide mission, do we want to conclude that God's work is no longer done in them? Or that it is done only when the churches institute chaplaincy programs for them? Or do we want to rejoice that the principalities and powers have recognized the importance of promoting the health and developing the minds of their citizens?

I would suggest that any Christian who confesses the Lordship of Christ will rejoice to see the promotion of the category of the human, no matter where it occurs. In fact, I would go even farther: any Christian who feels called to evangelism will rejoice more to see a government or an international non-church agency adopt a program which brings health or justice or learning than to see the church undertake such a program. For every such program is a jewel in the crown of the Redeemer, who came that "they might have life and have it abundantly" (John 10:10), and the mission of the church is to proclaim the "infinite riches of Christ and to make the . . . rulers and powers . . . know God's wisdom, in all its different forms" (Eph. 3:8, 10, TEV).

History is strewn, however, with the wrecks of misplaced zeal, with the unfulfilled plans of people who could not or would not carry them out. At present all over Eastern Europe socialist philosophers are asking, What has gone wrong with our utopias? Why has the socialist revolution—which aimed at the overcoming of human alienation—resulted in domination by nameless, faceless bureaucracies? Where, they ask, can we find a socialism with a human face? Why, almost 60 years after the Soviet Revolution, has alienation not been overcome? Why have the very instruments of liberation become new forms of alienation?[21]

As a result some heretical and not so heretical Marxist philosophers are raising anew the question of transcendence (which Marx himself did), but even of transhistorical or metahistorical transcendence.[22] The alteration of oppressive institutions, they are saying, seems to fall short of its goal. When the renovation of life on earth is not ordained to a finality which is even higher, Roger Garaudy asserts, the creative human task is deserted. History must therefore be kept open, he says, to fulfillment partially outside history.[23] A perceptive observer of recent Marxism, Denis Goulet, comments that even though the human race rightly aspires after its own redemption within history—since redemption outside time is alienating —

> Perhaps the human race, like Adam, is summoned by destiny to display a modicum of ontological humility, to recognize its finiteness by admitting that perhaps it may be radically unable to achieve total redemption in time.[24]

M. M. Thomas of India asks, "Should we speak of Christ as the redemption of Prometheus from his curse, releasing him for a creativity which is not self-destructive?"[25]

Both Goulet and Thomas sense that the mood among Marxists today is one of greater openness than there has been heretofore to the contributions Christians might make.

A Marxist like Kolakowski is open to consider what makes for transcendence, to re-examine the role of the human imagination, and of its relationship to creative effort. Willing to forego the dogmatic assertion of the "scientific" nature of the Marxist project, distinguishing between "realism" and "pseudorealism," he puts ideology and human conceptual structures to an examination. True realism, he asserts, admits the importance of the imagination, of fantasy, of vision. Such "distortions" of reality, he says, are "indispensable factors in social progress":

> Ideologies create mirages of distant lands to summon the exertions necessary for the caravan, though in distress, to reach the nearest oasis. If these enticing fata morganas did not loom up, the weary column, depressed by the hopeless situation, would let itself be buried in the desert sands.[26]

Often, he admits, those leading social revolutions have promised more than could be delivered within a short period of time. But the slightest improvement in social conditions requires a fantastic effort; there is a tremendous disproportion between results and effort expended. And such effort must be sustained if a project is ever to become a reality. We err in asking for "the facts": "We should be wise enough not to be deceived by the prospect of a speedy coming of the kingdom of heaven."[27]

Statements leaders make are ideologic in nature. Without ideology we could not function. Ideology encourages people to hope for that which is, at the moment, beyond reasonable expectation; and the only rule that applies is:

> In social life general intentions and slogans must be out of proportion to results so as to be in proportion to the sum of energy required.[28]

Kolakowski has therefore brought Marxism a long way from its original claim to "scientific rationalism." It seems somehow much more like a faith, a systematic expression of a human hope.

But Western Christians in the present day seem to take the opposite tack. Rejecting "utopian visions of the possibility of transformation of human society in this present era into the kingdom of God," they tend nowadays to settle for the mess of pottage of reduced expectation. Giving up ideologies and utopias, they resign themselves to an apathetic acceptance of the status quo, hoping that "someday" there may be a new tomorrow.

Thus, their theology often becomes an apologetic for inaction. The free enterprise system, they say—modern capitalism, with all its limitations—is probably the best system we can hope for. It may perpetuate tremendous injustices and permanently consign large numbers of people and nations to a less than fully human existence, but didn't Jesus say we would always have the poor among us? Anyway, what alternative is there? What other system has proven demonstrably better?

They question the legitimacy of liberation theology—will not one oppression merely give way to another? Is there such a thing as true liberation short of heaven?

One of our denominational leaders, giving the keynote address at a major mission meeting on the theme "Jesus Christ Frees and Unites," said he had to challenge many of the slogans and promises of freedom movements. Freedom, he said, choosing a personalistic rather than a social definition, is "the effort to bring one's desires and achievable goals into harmony," and even such free-dom will only come when, by "rebirth by the grace of our Lord Jesus Christ we cease being natural or fleshly and become spiritual beings."

"The missionary societies of our churches," he said, have, "from real sympathy with the earthly plight of suffering people, given themselves to too many secular causes with results of doubt-ful value." "Great though they are, struggles like those between democracy and totalitarianism, socialism and capitalism, colonial-ism and nationalism, are not," he said, "the main business of the Church. We will never free the world by systems change."

He encouraged the Board to preach the gospel of a uniting and liberating Christ to colonial regimes and budding nations, capitalists and socialists, presidents and generals and ordinary people. He hoped that human selfishness could be "eradicated by floods of Christian love." If people can be converted, he said, things will change. In the meantime we have to recognize that there is a distinction to be made between "God's ultimate long-range goal" and his "immediate business." We ought to expect less than we have been for the immediate future.

In biblical terms, however, what he was calling for was a reduc-tion in hope. When the Bible speaks of hope, it speaks, as Van Ruler said, of hope for this world, for this is what biblical realism is all about. It does not call people away from this present world and efforts to change it. Christians have a role to play in it. Even Che Guevara said Christians were needed for the revolution, and he called them to participate "without the cowardice of hiding their faith in order to assimilate themselves."[29]

Goulet comments:

> One betrays the cause of history by forgetting that what makes human history important is its unrelenting drive towards transcen-dence. . . . Christians must not allow guilt over their past flight from history to beguile them into rejecting that very transcendence which liberated Marxists and critical secularists are now discovering as genuine concerns.[30]

It is for that reason that Goulet finds the thought of L.-J. Lebret, a French Dominican developmentalist, so compelling. I was in-trigued by Goulet's summary of Lebret's Christian analysis of the meaning of development and found reading Lebret one of the most exciting experiences I have ever had. He seemed to "put it all together" for me. I have no need to repeat here the excellent analysis of Lebret which Goulet presents, in brief compass, in his book, *A New Moral Order*.[31]

What I would like to do here is to spend the next section relating Lebret's approach to development to the questions we are asking in this chapter: What is the feast to which the Lord invites us? And how can we unite in a single vision historical and trans-historical hope?

*   *   *

I have always thought that I came from a developed country. As a missionary in Ghana I believed that, as a Westerner and an American, I came from a society which was already developed, and that part of my missionary responsibility was to help the people of Northern Ghana become developed.

My experiences in Northern Ghana made me uncertain about some things. As I confessed in an article I wrote shortly before leaving Ghana,[32] in six years in the North, I discovered that I had much to learn from the "backward" people to whom I had been sent to minister, and that my society had lost much of what they had. I recognized that I would lose much when I returned to America. The fundamental humanity of the simple people among whom I lived, their strong sense of communal solidarity, and their time for people were qualities I would miss when returning to a modern society.

Yet never did I challenge my fundamental assumption—and that of the United Nations, then in its first "Development Decade"—that my society was "developed" and theirs was not.

Lebret made me ask, for the first time, what development really is. Development is not to be confused, he says, with modernization. He refuses to reduce it to merely technological or economic development. As Christians we must view development, he thought, in terms of the total divine-human drama. To use the terms we have been using—we must view development eschatologically, in terms of God's purpose for humanity. What God is concerned to bring about in the world, Lebret says, is a "universal human ascent,"[33] "the greatest revolution in depth that humanity has ever imagined."[34] This will involve the passage of humanity from the less human to the more human, from being less to being more, from lesser to greater worthiness.[35] To live well, Lebret wrote, is for people "to realize to the maximum all their human powers, to lift themselves while elevating others, to utilize all the positive values of society to add still more to their sum, to come to self-fulfillment in the process of giving self entirely in the service of the common good."[36]

"A people is truly great," Lebret wrote, "whose culture, humanism, and spirituality cause its members to grow in their inmost selves."[37] For that reason freedom cannot be regarded as the goal of development; freedom must rather be understood as both an end and a means. "People can use freedom either to fulfill or to demean themselves, either to build community or to oppress others, either to transcend themselves and make history or to become mere consumers of civilization."[38]

The goal of development is not, then, freedom, but humanity's coming to transcend or surpass itself.[39] (This is the same verb, *se dépasser,* which we discovered earlier in Durkheim. I failed, however, to discover any reference to Durkheim in Lebret.) To surpass ourselves (to become "open to metahistorical transcendence," Goulet puts it)—is the goal of development. Waxing rhapsodic, Lebret refers to "the historical grandeur of human destiny as an adventure in possibility":[40]

> When he's really himself, man experiences an intense desire for beauty, a continuous summons to goodness, an aspiration to become ever more himself, in truth; by constantly choosing that which elevates him, by progressively making use of his liberty.[41]

Unfortunately, he goes on, the majority of people aren't free. Economic, political, social, and religious structures "choke in them the possibility of authentic choice." People will only become free and grow, he says, when they become to a greater degree masters of their choices. In the meantime we have to recognize that there is little to be rhapsodic about in the human condition.

Working among fishermen in Brittany in the '30s and in overseas development in Vietnam, Colombia, Brazil, and other places after the Second World War, Lebret was appalled at the poverty he

saw, at the alienation human beings experienced as pawns in a
system beyond either their comprehension or their grasp. In his
early years, seeking a solution to world poverty, he quoted the
Parable of the Good Samaritan. Later on he changed, Thomas
Suavet observes, to the use of the Parable of Dives and Lazarus
("The Evil Rich Man," in French).[42]

Lebret described the problem, on one level, as that of "falla-
cious values," which people—with the intellectual capacity to
question—willfully refuse to question.[43] On another level the
problem is covetousness.[44] A problem in the relationships within
any society, covetousness is also a problem on an international
scale. The "developed" Western nations, Lebret writes:

> are surprised that they are neither loved nor understood, while they
> destroy traditional institutions and values, and the fundamental ethi-
> cal values of friendly human relations.
>
> The Christian order of things is in fact closed to them, and the
> human order is, for them, only that of their own exaltation. The
> tremendous amount of thought and effort they expend on increasing
> their possessions blinds them to the right of all people . . . to at least
> the essentials of life. Their persistent greed has divorced them from
> the higher values of human living.[45]

Covetousness is a spiritual problem. Based on a lack of love, it
results in a denial of justice. Lebret accuses the West of having
gone back on its Christianity, of having rejected, despite its protes-
tations, even the secularized Christian values of human dignity
and justice. The ultimate spiritual poverty of the West is revealed
when, guilt-struck by the gap between the "have" and "have-
not"' nations, it proposes, as the solution for the problems of the
"have-nots," economic growth, and calls it development! Growth,
Lebret responds, is far from development. He goes on to contrast
the two point by point:[46]

Growth is a matter of economic augmentation—whether linear,
geometric, or exponential; development includes growth but development is a humanistic and not an economic concept, having
as its goal "being more," not just "having more."

Growth is a matter of Gross National Product, of the increase of
productivity; humanity is introduced into plans for growth only
secondarily, as when social institutions are proposed in order to

avoid social dislocations (which might reduce productivity!). Development, on the other hand, is the attempt to allow humanity to liberate itself from the sub-human and to aim at human fullness. In development humanity comes first. People may not need to have a fantastically enlarged productivity in order to "exist enough."

Growth is achieved when economic objectives have been reached; development is achieved when human elevation—the elevation of each person in all dimensions of his or her being *("de tout l'homme en tout homme")*—has taken place.

If we use the analogy of a tree, growth is a matter of the increase of the tree's height; development is a matter of the increase and extension, in total harmony, of all parts of the tree: the roots, the trunk, the branches, the leaves. It is a matter of the blossoming of all human capabilities, including the spiritual. "The development of man," Lebret wrote, "is the blossoming of all of him, in a harmony partially determined by his free choices."[47] Such development has a history, for we depend on previous generations; it has a sociology, for we are members of a society with institutions; it has a civilizational context. Harmony in development will not be achieved spontaneously, because not only are the members of societies free individuals, but also the historical institutions of that society have a continued influence on the society, other cultures make their impact, as do other institutions in the contemporary environment. It's necessary, therefore, to "harmonize development."[48] There is no one "recipe" for such a process. What there is—and Lebret and his colleagues in "Economy and Humanism" in Marseilles and later in the Institute for Research and Training in Development worked on this constantly—is "a method of analysis which can be applied generally and a method of coordinating diverse resources according to a country's own internal structures and the degree of international cooperation."[49] In the process great care must be taken not to destroy the values of the particular civilization and to make sure that the process of development is not imposed from above on the people but is an expression of their own dynamism.

To be a midwife of such development is not a task all "development experts" can equally fulfill. One must be consumed by a "burning love for the people" and capable of "self-abnegation."

There is a kind of "monastic order" needed here, with rigid rules and total devotion. (Lebret and his colleagues tried to recruit and train people for such an "order.")[50]

Development, Lebret wrote, is "like a symphony." It requires a written composition, which is the plan. "But the symphony in its execution is the work of an orchestra, with diverse instruments, directed by a conductor."[51] The harmony which the orchestra strives for is a dynamic harmony, developed and maintained in the process of its playing. Whatever plan exists must be regarded solely as the initial plan, part of a "living planning-process"[52] with which the people are constantly associated. As development proceeds, the attempt is made to intensify positive factors and attenuate negative ones:

> It's not a matter anymore of forcing reality to bend to a single style, thought to be universally applicable, but of *promoting a future reality* by constantly improving the process in interaction with all the living elements[53] [emphasis mine].

I deliberately italicized the words "promoting a future reality" because they seem to me to bring out the Christian eschatological basis for all Lebret did in development. He was seeking to promote the Kingdom of God. Many of those with whom he worked were secularists who either had no such conception or would not give it such a name, but they shared with him a burning desire to see humanity transcend itself. Lebret wanted to walk along that part of his journey with such people. He knew that the goal lay farther on than they realized.

Lebret had sympathy for the Marxist/humanist model of nonalienated society, but he knew that, in and of itself, Marxism would not succeed in reaching that goal, for its model of humanism was a truncated one, which considered spiritual and personal excellences only in their bastardized expressions, and "closed the door to genuine transcendence."[54] Lebret doubted the ability of Marxism to found a permanent and authentically human civilization "because it is unaware of the essence of mankind."[55] It is therefore a "spurious humanism." Man, freed from religion, Lebret said, "is more than ever bound to the subhuman."[56]

But Lebret could not find more solace in the West. As long as the West "continues to oppose the humanitarian spirit of Communism with nothing but greedy calculation and a lack of social consciousness," he said, "so long will the Marxist god progressively invade the world."[57] The West has more to offer, and it is failing to do so. Its Christian heritage speaks clearly to the present needs of society.

There are three categories of human needs, Lebret said: subsistence needs (those without which life cannot be maintained); comfort needs, or needs for making life easier; and what he called "the needs of transcendence" *(dépassement)*.[58] For development to occur, the second category is not necessary, but the third is. Yet human economies, East and West, leave the third category to fend for itself (for it doesn't provide economic rewards) and often provide comfort needs for those who already have subsistence needs before providing subsistence needs for all.

If world priorities are to be changed, a revolution will therefore be necessary. Neither major system has the answers. Capitalism is too responsive to the effective purchasing power of those with more than enough, and to the ability of producers to manipulate the desires of potential consumers. State socialism has subscribed to the mass-consumer myth of the West while downgrading the importance of non-economic values and questioning all non-collectivized ones, to the detriment of the spiritual and the artistic and at the cost of stunting personal growth.[59]

It isn't enough, Lebret insisted, to change the distribution of goods—what is more difficult is preparing people to know how to receive them![60]

The world is becoming technologically and scientifically one, he believed, but no new civilization is emerging to help us deal with the new material realities.[61] Without a profound cultural revolution, we won't be able to solve our problems:

> A complete revolution, perhaps man's last and greatest one, has become necessary. It will be more long-drawn-out than others of the past, because it must become universal. It is both a political and an economic revolution, but it can come to its fulfilment only if it is primarily a spiritual revolution—the expression of consideration for others because of their actual or potential value as human beings.[62]

The goal of all our efforts, Lebret maintained, must be the creation of a new international order of global solidarity, in which the human elevation of all humanity *(l'élévation humaine de l'huma-*

nité dans son ensemble) will be possible. The Universal Declaration of Human Rights is just a sketch of the new code of international law, the new ethic of development, which will have to be developed. That ethic in turn will constitute the base for a new system of relations, of cooperation and of aid, that will bring hope to a world in anguish during the tremendous mutation of humanity which we are presently going through. It will demand of the "privileged who are blinded by the obsessive desire of having too much, a radical change in their egocentric, near-sighted perspectives." It will require "the conversion of the satisfied" as much as "the intelligent effort of the less well provided-for."[63]

In the end Lebret doubted whether any other basis than a full Christian view of humanity and history would be sufficient to support such a revolution. He had no doubt that Christianity could provide the needed basis.

If Christians prove themselves committed to the progress of society and to the human sciences, Lebret believed, and accept poverty and suffering, "they can be the most influential and the most effective members of the human race."[64] Without love there can be no solution[65]—and love is the essence of the gospel.

But Lebret recognized that the church must first awake:

> The fact is that Christians, like others, are enmeshed in the deterministic attitudes of their own civilizations. They have always been some distance behind the message, and they will continue to be so. They can however approach closer to it, and . . . this is beginning to happen.[66]

Lebret had great hope for a transformation in the church. He was a *peritus* at Vatican II, and he had a hand in writing *Populorum progressio*. It was an exciting decade in which to be alive. When Lebret died, in 1968, students at the Sorbonne were raising the signs "More power to the imagination" and "Be realistic—demand the impossible." Lebret would have supported both those slogans.

Life in the '70s is a different matter, however. Those who continue to hope for meaningful change in society or church seem to have the burden of proof on their shoulders these days, as the framers of the Boston Affirmations recognized. The pendulum has swung toward historical pessimism, and to a spurious kind of "transcendence" which a man like Lebret never would have recognized—otherworldly, narrowly religious, far removed from the biblical understanding of the Reformed theologians we have been reading and from the inner-worldly hope of a thinker like Lebret.

"We are concerned," the authors of the Boston Affirmations wrote in their opening statement, "about what we discern to be present trends in our churches, in religious thought, and in society. We see struggles in every arena of human life, but in too many parts of the church and theology we find retreat from these struggles." Why should they be disturbed? Because "hopeful participation in these struggles is at once action in faith, the primary occasion for personal spiritual growth, the development of viable structures for the common life, and the vocation of the people of God." And they therefore could not remain silent:

> We can not stand with those secular cynics and religious spiritualizers who see in such witnesses [the "cloud of witnesses" they had listed who "prophetically exemplify or discern the activity of God . . . today"] no theology, no eschatological urgency, and no Godly promise or judgment. In such spiritual blindness . . . the world as God's creation is abandoned, sin rules, liberation is frustrated, covenant is broken, prophecy is stilled, wisdom is betrayed, suffering love is transformed into triviality, and the church is transformed into a club for self- or transcendental awareness.[67]

Strong words! Robert Middleton assigns the Affirmers' zeal to their being "the sons and daughters of the Protestant Ethic," who have applied the ethic this time "not to commercial success but to social reconstruction." He faults them for "falling victim to the American myth that what is needed to accomplish any great purpose is firm resolution and hard work."

It is not that Middleton disagrees with the Affirmers' agenda—it "points the churches in the right direction. By rooting such mandates in the soil of strong theological convictions [Boston] serves the churches well." But he questions the premise on which the authors propose to act—that there is a fundamental reason to hope. "The nub of the problem of Christian action in the near future is this loss of confidence. . . . We now face the problem of sustaining social involvement apart from any hope for real victory." He proposes the old fisherman in Hemingway's *The Old Man and the Sea* as a paradigm of the church involved in necessary but non-rewarding action. He chooses to fall midway between Hartford and Boston, and will one day write a "Bosford Declaration":

> A Bosford Declaration will not retreat from social action of a radical nature; much of the social gospel will be retained. But *it will not expect sweeping victories or wholesale transformations in society; expectations will be moderate* [emphasis mine].

He identifies this position as "Christian realism." This is what it means, he says, "to live by grace," having confidence that God will "complete what is partial."[68]

Middleton's position seems a good compromise between Hartford's call for transcendence and Boston's call for involvement. I was quite attracted to its realism and reasonableness at first. Looking at it again after studying Lebret and Van Ruler and Kolakowski, I recognize that it represents the compromise that will kill the dream. As soon as our hope is compromised—as soon as we stop expecting the "wholesale transformations" the Bible tells us to hope for—that soon do we desert biblical realism for Christian realism, that soon do we confess our doubt that Christ really is King and that God really intends to transform the creation radically, that soon do we begin to assign the transformation to the far future, the eschatological wedding feast to the time of the Second Coming. We then can join with the man in Luke's Gospel who said, "How blessed are those who shall eat bread in the kingdom of God!" (Luke 14:15) and have Jesus need to tell us as well the Parable of the Great Banquet and also wake us up to the fact that the invitations to the banquet are going out right now because now is the time to begin the feast.

Despite Middleton's best intentions, "Christian realism" is as difficult to square with the Jesus of the Gospels as Albert Schweitzer learned it was to find the liberal Jesus in the Gospels a couple of generations ago. Jesus wasn't realistic—he was a prophet, and he proclaimed a vision, the vision of the Kingdom of God. Short of that vision, his death as the Lamb that was slain would not have taken place. "Realists" don't need to be crucified. Much more "reasonable" expectations keep them either from going out on a limb or from offending people.

But Jesus did not call us to be non-offensive. He called us to sow the vision. And how that vision is needed today! As Robert Bellah writes in his bicentennial book, *The Broken Covenant:*

In a period like our own, when we have lost our sense of direction, when we do not know what our goal is, when our myths have lost their meaning and comprehensive reason has been eclipsed by calculating technical reason, there is a need for a rebirth of imaginative vision. In the face of such a situation imagination can sometimes fuse myth and ecstatic reason to render a new vision, a new sense of direction and goal.[69]

It is my conviction that, if we put together Calvin's understanding of the Kingship of Christ, Lebret's concept of the world coming to transcend itself, and Durkheim's social-structural analysis of the emergence of a new world order, we have the kind of vision Bellah is calling for. I think it will have a far more compelling theological basis than the Boston Affirmations (even some of the authors of that statement were unhappy with its low Christology), which will serve as a more adequate launching pad for the rocket of hope Boston correctly felt compelled to send up.

In the end there is nothing complicated about the vision: it is a matter of taking God seriously when he says he is in the process of gathering together an eschatological wedding-feast, and would we please bring our lanterns, and some oil, and our bodies and come?

How will that feast we go to be related to the far-future feast? It will be continuous with it, Lebret would say—the new global solidarity will be the beginning of the new order. The new order of God will be the augmentation of that which is now beginning, its purification and its lifting to a new height, an exponential growth of the hope realized here on earth, a deeper personal communion with God culminating in the beatific vision longed for through the ages.

Lebret operates in a realm of imagery with which I, as a Protestant, am slightly uncomfortable. My tradition doesn't speak of beatific visions—and perhaps it is wrong in that—nor does it reduce the element of discontinuity between the here and the hereafter as much as does Lebret, and much of the Catholic tradition. I'm glad for the vision they offer, but I am more comfortable with the balance between continuity and discontinuity which I find in Berkhof. In an overall perspective of the *consummation* of history, he still finds room to speak about a break:

To talk about consummation is to talk about a *break*. This world will be raised from its brokenness due to guilt and suffering, and will

> leave the *Gestalt* of the cross behind. This means that it will become
> a completely new world. But . . . it is the same world which will rise
> from its broken position. Our expectation of the future includes both
> break and connection, discontinuity and continuity. . . . The con-
> summation will mean a radical break with all the forces which hinder
> [Christ's] dominion. At the same time the consummation will be the
> continuation of the resurrection forces which already are active in
> history. We must be careful with the use of the word "continuation,"
> however. It is completely different from "to continue in the same
> vein." The greatest unfolding of the forces of the resurrection in our
> history is only a small beginning. . . . They are crocuses in the winter
> of a fallen world. Moreover, they are so intertwined with the forces of
> evil that it is difficult for us to imagine what the world will be like
> when these forces are set free and reach their full potential.[70]

Will the consummation occur, then, in time? "Time is the mould of
our created human existence," Berkhof responds. "The consummation as the glorification of existence will not mean that we
are taken out of time and delivered from time, but that time as the
form of our glorified existence will also be fulfilled and glorified.
Consummation means to live again in the succession of past,
present, and future, but in such a way that the past moves along
with us as a blessing and the future radiates through the present so
that we strive without restlessness and rest without idleness, and
so that, though always progressing, we are always at our destina-
tion."[71]

But between now and that fulfillment and glorification of time
not everything will be smooth sailing. Here Berkhof takes the
biblical witness—in its plenitude—much more seriously than has
been the wont of the "mainline" churches, dealing with matters
usually left to the sects. He accepts what the New Testament says
about the antichrist and about the kingdom of peace, or
millennium:

> In the form of the antichrist the power of evil once more receives the
> opportunity to turn against Christ throughout the full breadth of the
> cosmic front.

"God's honor" demands that he give his opponents an opportunity to reveal their power, but his honor also demands that
Christ's resurrection be revealed as far as possible in this
dispensation—in signs such as the restoration of Israel.

> Since sin and death still reign, a brief but fierce setback is unavoid-
> able. But this represents the transition to the union of heaven and
> earth, which is reflected in the kingdom of peace by the abolition of
> their boundaries. . . . The triumph over the antichrist makes it clear
> that redemption is nigh, although there is one more contraction to
> suffer.[72]

We need not reduce the biblical witness to what fits in well with
our liberal evolutionism—there is discontinuity as well as continuity. But we need not make a *sacrificium intellecti* and simply
parrot biblical imagery in simplistic ways, failing to recognize that it
is imagery, that it is a witness, and that it is not prediction in the
crude sense but prophecy in the deepest sense. God expects us to
use thought-forms appropriate to our age to interpret the witness
of scripture, and the intelligence he has given us to understand its
deepest significance. We are not dealing here with a kind of Buck
Rogers adventure, but with fundamental affirmations about the
course of events, about the direction of history.

Perhaps the best way to end this chapter is by using the imagery
of our foundation allegory once more. The Bridegroom comes.
He finds the five young women ready and waiting, with oil in their
lamps. They go in to have supper with him. When they see him,
they are amazed, for they discover that he has marks on his hands
and feet. They recognize that the Bridegroom is none other than
the Lamb that was slain. They are filled with joy as the eternal
doors swing open and they are ushered in to the feast. The doors
are shut, and outside, the world they have come from continues a
kind of existence for a time.

Within the chamber the appointments are humble; the food is
nutritious, but simple; the clothes of the young women are simple,
human clothes. Just as the Lamb still bears the marks of his strife,
so do their bodies remain unglorified.

But the day will come when the walls of the room will be done
away with, when the whole world will become the marriage feast
of the Lamb. Then the women will be transformed. They will still
be the five young faithful women, but they will have new names
and glorified bodies. The world outside will lose its character as
that which stands against Christ's dominion. For all things will be
subject to him, and

When all things have been placed under Christ's rule, then he himself, the Son, will place himself under God, who placed all under him; and God will rule completely over all (I Cor. 15:28, TEV).

And I saw the Holy City, the new Jerusalem, coming down from heaven, prepared and ready like a bride ready to meet her husband. I heard a loud voice saying, "Now the dwelling of God is with humanity. He will live with them, and they shall be his people. God himself will be with them, and he shall be their God. He will wipe away all tears from their eyes. There will be no more death, no more grief, crying, or pain (Rev. 21:2-4).

9: ON NOT GETTING IN TO THE FEAST

> Only the new creation in Christ and through Christ
> will demonstrate the new element in the proclama-
> tion of Jesus and the new element in his anticipated
> resurrection from the dead. . . . The old, unredeemed
> and unchanged world of suffering, guilt and death is
> not capable of demonstrating the new creation.
> —Jürgen Moltmann, *The Crucified God*

FIVE OF THE YOUNG WOMEN, HOWEVER, DID NOT GET IN TO the feast. The door was shut while they went to search, at midnight, for some oil. "Lord, Lord, open to us," they begged, but the Bridegroom only replied, "Truly, I say to you, I do not know you."

It is extremely difficult for me to deal with these verses. The whole attitude of the liberal church to which I have been related since my conversion abhors the thought of eternal punishment. We have been strong on stressing God's grace—to the point, as Richard Niebuhr recognized,[1] of eliminating his justice and wrath as somehow being out of harmony with his character.

It is also that I studied under Karl Barth—who, even if accused unjustly of universalism, still taught us that the accent of the church ought always to be on angels rather than demons, on grace rather than judgment—that accounts in part for my reluctance to write this chapter.

And yet the form of this book, the allegory on which it is modeled, requires that I deal not only with the five young women who got in but also with the five who did not.

I remember how, at Lausanne, I resisted the inclusion in "A Response to Lausanne" of the lines that stated that biblical authority cannot "be found for the false hope of universalism; the reality of the eternal destruction of evil and all who cling to it must be solemnly affirmed, however humbly agnostic the Bible requires us to be about its nature."[2]

I resisted these lines but had to recognize that, on the same principle that had motivated the whole document—that of "wrestling under the authority of God's word"—we had no license to deny that part of the word which spoke of eternal punishment or separation from God. For separation from God, from the eschatological wedding feast, is the essence of the young women's destiny.

I shall always remember the lines spoken by the devil in Shaw's *Don Juan in Hell* which describe the nature of eternal damnation: "To have seen God—and never to be able to see him again—that is damnation." What Shaw has the devil say is in harmony with our allegory. The allegory does not speak of eternal punishment in the sense of burning in hell or suffering excruciating pain. Other New Testament passages do, including some in Matthew (e.g., 5:22, 30; 11:20-24; 13:41; 18:8f.; 25:30). I am not interested in doing neat exegetical tricks to remove these offensive elements. Nor am I interested in dwelling in a ghoulish manner on the sufferings of the damned.

The allegory before us bids us recognize a much simpler, yet equally disturbing idea: that our Lord taught that those who do not respond to the invitation to the wedding feast are excluded from it forever. There is nothing vindictive about it, but it is nevertheless direct and forthright: Jesus is issuing an invitation, now; it requires a response, now. Those who do not respond now have no chance to change their minds later.

To which times do we refer when we say "now" and "later"? The "now" of Jesus' first narration of the allegory was the time of his ministry. He differentiated between that time, as the time when a decision was called for, and the time of the coming of the Bridegroom, when it would be too late to rush out to buy oil.

As presented in the first gospel the allegory was intended, Karl Donfried argues,[3] to reassure those who had responded to the invitation by "buying oil" (performing good deeds) that their decision was not in vain just because they were getting older and might die (i.e. sleep) before the Bridegroom arrived. He was saying to them that what is done in this life is important. This life is the time to respond to the call of the Kingdom. One dare not postpone conversion till one's deathbed or hope for opportunities after death—perhaps even at the Last Judgment—to beg for mercy.

For us, so used to high pressure techniques of quick-sell, scare evangelism, the allegory might *seem* to support such approaches as the "Kennedy technique" in which people are asked, in the first visit of church members to their homes, "If you die tonight, do you know where you are going to go?"

Yet the allegory does not commend scaring people into the Kingdom by frightening them about what will happen to them if they don't respond to the message. The allegory is meant, rather, to reassure those who have felt moved to buy oil right now that they have made a wise and prudent decision—in fact, the necessary decision. The allegory brings a positive message, with a negative corollary; not a negative message, nor a message which is equally balanced between positive and negative elements. That is crucial. If we do not see that, our evangelistic proclamation will be unbalanced.

Yet there is the negative corollary. And that is what we must take seriously in the chapter before us. In other words, if we are to be faithful to scripture and to the people to whom we are sent, then we have to recognize that we cannot encourage people to be at ease with Jesus' message. Decision is essential; the time is now, during this life. By the decision which people make now they reflect who they are, whether wise or foolish; and their whole life-style will flow from that decision—whether it is to be the life-style of the Kingdom or the life-style of this perishing old order.

Just as those who accept the invitation find that eschatology is foreshortened—that they live eternally now, they are part of the wedding feast which is already going on in this world—so do those who fail to respond to the invitation already begin to experience the life of those to whom the door has been shut.

It doesn't take theological ability to recognize that. Any perceptive TV viewer, reader of magazine ads, or listener to ordinary conversations knows that many people in North America already experience exclusion from the wedding feast. One sees it in the compulsive consumerism that tries to substitute instant and exces-

sive gratification for long-term spiritual joy; in the anal retentive-
ness that causes many to fixate on security—on locks, insurance
policies, guns, high dividends, tax shelters, guarded all-white "lei-
sure villages" and the entire syndrome; in the sado-masochism
which makes attractive levels of violence which could not have
been tolerated a generation ago. One sees it also in the substitution of sex for love, of bigger and better orgasms for mutual
support, of voyeurism for relationship; in the substitution of short-
term purchased, contractual relationships for long-term covenan-
tal commitments—for not only bottles are thrown away in our
day, but so are spouses, elderly parents, and children with whom
one cannot get along.

But that is only to take the personal and interpersonal realms
into consideration. One can see signs of foreshortened eschatology in the social and international realms as well. Societies and
nations are also excluded from the wedding feast. In a nation
which is proud to proclaim itself (though, even on its own terms,
less and less truthfully) "Number One," what could such signs of
exclusion be? I must be a radical, or a Jeremiah, some must think,
if I take such an approach to our nation's current status. To those
who consider this charge too "radical" to be "a balanced judgment" I would say, look at our inner cities. Many of them look
like bombed-out ruins of Cologne or Dresden. They are places no
self-respecting white liberal or conservative would even like to
drive through, places no self-respecting insurance company even
thinks of insuring, places where 50 percent and more of minority
teenagers are unemployed, where a third generation of welfare
families is growing up.

Somewhat chastened, they say, We admit this, but what else?
(That one doesn't really concern us.) In response I would ask
them how they view the way the society in which they live is
maintained. Don't they see that we live under the shadow of
thousands of intercontinental missiles of destruction and damnation, that we live in a society open more and more each year to
nuclear blackmail, that we cannot get on a plane without security
checks, that even the small reliance we have thus far placed in
nuclear power has produced levels of nuclear waste we can no
longer safely deal with.

But that will not disturb the average American, who trusts that the military, when it speaks of "fail-safe technology," is being honest with them that there is no real danger; further, that we are a peaceful nation and will never get into nuclear war. The average American trusts the Atomic Energy Commission and the electric power industry to handle nuclear power safely. This argument won't move them to think that we already live in a preview-version of hell. I must be a visionary idealist, they say, to expect that we could live in a better world, with less reliance upon instruments of death and less danger to our environment from nuclear fission.

Perhaps at this point in our history it is only the pollution issue which makes people think that realized eschatology ought to be taken seriously. When Americans cannot go to beaches or eat the fish they catch in their rivers or bays, then they feel put upon. Then their life-style is threatened. But it is not enough, obviously, to force them to question deeply to what extent the type of economy to which we are committed is responsible for bringing this about, or to raise the question of whether we have dangerously committed ourselves to a type of growth and consumerism which is responsible for the plundering of the environment. The questions surface again and again, but they are not yet constant, and therefore not yet deep enough. Days when the air quality is unacceptable are relieved by days when it is satisfactory. Our sense of threat goes away as quickly as it comes, and we end up siding with the car manufacturers in saying that the standards of the Environmental Protection Administration are unrealistically tough, and we therefore postpone their enforcement for another two years.

Quick scares about the effects of chemicals added to our foods and environmental contamination of our meat and fish are relieved by predictable statements by "experts" that "the levels of contamination are within the safety range." And we go on shopping at the A & P and K-Mart to the consoling sounds of Muzak.

Our situation is something like the illustration often used in public addresses these days, that the captain of the plane has just announced that one of the engines has fallen off and there's a fuel leak in the rear, "and we've lost our bearings, but we want you to know that we're still going full speed ahead."

So levels of nitrites build up in our bodies, statistics of emphysema mount, cancer rises to epidemic levels, and nervous tension becomes more a norm than an exception. But that is what life is like, we still think.

Life is like having insecurity in our suburbs and needing to install elaborate burglar-alarm systems.

Life is like tolerating high levels of unemployment because "some people are always going to be left out of the economy."

Life is like enduring racial and ethnic tension because "when have we ever had corporate solidarity?"

Life is like being always on the short end of votes in the U.N.—"those Third World countries are just being vindictive."

Life is like always being identified with white racist regimes and repressive dictatorships. Given the choice between freedom and stability, isn't the only possible choice—and the most humane choice for the people—stability (even if it means a Pinochet, with all the torture and repression of such a regime, will be replacement for an Allende)? Given the possibility of being blackmailed over the resources we need by a popular sovereignty government versus continued assured resources and welcome for our corporations from a "somewhat elitist but benign" government, do we really have freedom of choice?

And so our options are limited. In the best of all possible worlds perhaps, we could be idealistic, humanitarian, and selfless— maybe we could even disarm. But this isn't the best of all possible worlds. This is . . . this is . . .

*   *   *

And the five who had no oil came back and begged the Bride-groom to let them in. But he said, "I really don't know you."

*   *   *

But, must we also take seriously the implication of the allegory that that's the end of it—that decisions made now, which are realized eschatologically in the present, have eternal conse-quences? Is there such a thing as eternal separation from God? Ought we to expect—and this is worse—a final destruction of all which withstands God's Kingdom ("the eternal destruction of evil and those who cling to it," as the Lausanne Response speaks of it)?

I can see no other way of faithfully reading the New Testament witness. It doesn't make me comfortable—quite the opposite— but I cannot find a solid basis for universalism in the New Testament. The only possible way this belief could be held legitimately is by positing, as some Orthodox theologians do, a two-stage process—a last judgment, involving the destruction of evil, and a final restitution of all things.

Vitaly Borovoy's contribution, prior to the Bangkok Conference, to the ecumenical discussion on salvation is a clear example of this way of dealing with the biblical texts. He considers texts which seem to point to universal salvation, such as Ephesians 1:10, Colossians 1:16-20, Philippians 2:10, II Corinthians 5:15, and Romans 3:23, over against the clear witness of scripture to a division at the judgment between the saved and the lost. He finds that these two groups of texts are contradictory unless the latter is taken to refer to "a last judgement which will not be without end," but will rather be succeeded by "the recapitulation of all things":

> If we understand these and many similar texts in the sense of a final and irreversible destiny not only of those who are saved but also of those who have to perish, without any possibility of change, then we should admit not only contradiction but even irreconcilable disagreement between the texts witnessing to universal and all-embracing redemption and what is beyond salvation, and the texts related to judgment, condemnation and discriminative selection. Usually we try to overlook this direct and obvious contradiction, or we make attempts to harmonize the interpretations.

> Given the permanent failure of such effort, we are forced to admit that there is only one possible answer: to accept the doctrine of many prominent Church Fathers and theologians of Ancient Christianity—the theory of *apokatastasis ton panton,* the recapitulation of all things. In the light of this theological interpretation there is no contradiction between universal salvation, judgment and condemnation of the sinner. In the two cases the Holy Scriptures are speaking about different eons. Only the Kingdom of God will last without end. A last judgement, "eternal punishment," torments will not be without end. From this situation there will be for everybody a transition through gradual *apokatastasis*. The transition will be multi-form and realized in several stages. The process will not start within the historical space-time of biblical salvation, but it will be outside of biblical "eternity," in the post-eschatological age to come,

with "new heavens and a new earth, in which righteousness dwells"
(II Pet. 3:13; cf. Rev 21:1).[4]

It is tempting, when one comes from a liberal Western tradition
which has asserted the goodness of God and has underplayed his
righteousness and wrath, to find consolation in a doctrine like that
which Borovoy here explicates. I would not want to distance
myself irrevocably from such a universal hope. Yet it rests, as
Borovoy himself recognizes, on the blurring in Scripture of the
distinction between "the many" and "all." Borovoy makes use of
this blurring when it is to his advantage (as in his interpretation of
Isa. 53:11) but not when it seems to argue against the likelihood
that the intention of the author of Scripture in using "all" was to
mean "many" (as I believe is the case in II Corinthians 5:15 and
Philippians 2:10). I could be convinced that the author of Ephesians literally meant "all." I could not be convinced at this stage
that any of the epistles which were indubitably written by Paul's
own hand would mean that, for Paul's concept of God's righteousness, as I understand it, involved a clear distinction between
the righteous and the unrighteous, between those who will be
saved and those who will not.

That distinction is absolutely fundamental to the Synoptic Gospels (as it is to Revelation and the Johannine writings and all strata
of the New Testament with the *possible* exception of Ephesians
and Colossians).

In this book it is the Synoptics with which we are mainly
concerned, and, in seeking to understand the import of an allegory like the one before us in its context of apocalyptic expectation,
I find that Jürgen Moltmann has more to commend himself than
Borovoy. Moltmann speaks of the meaning of a general resurrection to judgment (of which the Allegory of the Ten Young Women
speaks in the scene at the door of the wedding feast when the ten
young women "wake from sleep").

The symbol of the general resurrection of the dead, Moltmann
asserts, is a symbol of hope only for the righteous; for the unrighteous it is rather a symbol of fear. It would be better for them to
stay dead. But it is better, he says, not to speak of the resurrection
primarily in terms of human hope. The resurrection ought to be
spoken of primarily in the context of the expectation of divine

righteousness: "It represents a hope for God, for the sake of God and his right."

"Any look at world history," he contends, "raises the question why inhuman men fare so well and their victims fare so badly." The fundamental question of history, he maintains, is the question of righteousness:

> At the deepest level the question of world history is the question of righteousness. And this question extends out into transcendence. The question whether there is a God or not is a speculative question in the face of the cries for righteousness of those who are murdered and gassed, who are hungry and oppressed. If the question of theodicy can be understood as a question of the righteousness of God in the history of the suffering of the world, then all understanding and presentation of world history must be seen within the horizon of the question of theodicy. Or do the executioners ultimately triumph over their innocent victims?[5]

What even orthodox theologians are admitting by their need to posit at least two stages in the consummation is the somber and joyous reality of the righteousness of God—joyous, because we can affirm God's righteousness, somber because God's wrath is the other side of his righteousness. Orthodox theologians admit that, even if, in the farthest future, there will be a restitution of all things, in the immediate future God's justice will be done and it will involve both punishment and reward, both exclusion and inclusion.

Moltmann differs from the orthodox view in his affirmation that the "question extends out into transcendence." This is a suggestive phrase and I am attracted to it. Though not absolutely certain of what Moltmann himself means by this expression, I find that scripture requires me to say that it extends to ultimate transcendence, even unto the total renewal of creation. As the *Foundations* document states it, in Article 18 ("Consummation"):

> God's work of salvation on earth, even to the present, is riddled by the opposition of Satan and of man, and therefore remains hidden under guilt, pain, and death. So the divine activity appears as a promise and pledge that point to the future consummation of God's eternal purpose. . . .

> Then the Kingdom of God, now visible only to faith, will be revealed in all its splendor. Then the earth and its inhabitants will be completely renewed according to God's purpose. . . .

> Then Jesus Christ, who for our sake placed himself under God's judgment and who now is our king, though hidden, will be revealed in glory; as judge He will make it clear that man's decision for or against Him has been of eternal consequence.
>
> At His judgment all will be acquitted, who fully placed their hope upon the grace of God in the judgement of Christ's cross and thereby condemn themselves. They will inherit the Kingdom prepared for them from before the foundation of the world and be forever with Christ. For He returns to be glorified in His saints and to be marveled at in all who have loved His appearing.
>
> In that judgment all will be condemned who did not condemn themselves but sought the ground of their righteousness outside of the free mercy of God. He who has despised the light of grace belongs to the outer darkness of being forsaken by God.

The key phrase in this section, for our present purposes, is that "man's decision for or against" Christ is "of eternal consequence."

We do no service to the people to whom we are sent in evangelism if, out of a supposed sympathy for their sensibilities, we hide from them the dark side of God's eschatological activity or the crucial nature of the decision we are calling them to make. Jesus himself hid neither. If, out of a bias toward "positive thinking," we decide not to deal with the consequences of failure to make that decision, to respond to God's invitation, and thus do not stress the urgency of repentance, we are only proclaiming part of the message. Being "nice guys," we fail to be faithful messengers.

As the priest Ezeulu says to the British governor's messenger in Chinua Achebe's novel *Arrow of God*,[6] when the messenger has refused to report to the governor the priest's refusal to come when summoned, but says he will say, "He is indisposed": "What is this? A messenger who chooses what message he will carry?!" We cannot choose what message we will bring to God's people. We don't "know better."

If people have not repented because of our failure to bring them the whole message, their blood, as the Bible says, is on our heads (cf. Ezek. 33:1ff.).

Let it be clear that this chapter is not a call for a return to fire-and-brimstone preaching. It differs from that preaching in two important respects: (1) It is not only dealing with a far future separation from God, but with the present realization of it as well, with the signs of what the Reformers called God's "strange work"—the alienation of people from his grace; (2) it does this reluctantly, non-dramatically, without the sadistic animus which impelled many of the earlier preachers, and out of realism, rather than out of a desire either for revenge or for control, both of which have been operative at different times in our past history.

Yet it does deal with the dark side of God's grace, for—as this part of our allegory tells us—God's grace has such a dark side.

PROLOGUE: RE-IMAGING THE CHURCH FOR THE LONG NIGHT AHEAD

> The Risen Christ comes to quicken a festival in the innermost heart of humanity. He is preparing for us a springtime of the Church: a church devoid of means of power, ready to share with all, a place of visible communion for all humanity.
>
> —Taizé Council of Youth, 1975

PERHAPS THE FUNDAMENTAL INADEQUACY OF THIS BOOK IS the relative absence of ecclesiology—a doctrine of the church—from its chapters. There are two reasons for this, one intentional and one unintentional.

I have intentionally presented a non-ecclesio*centric* understanding of evangelism in this book, out of a painful awareness that, in this lamentably post-ecumenical period, "church" means denomination. I simply am not reconciled to the reduction of church growth—holistic church growth—to denominational expansion. The New Testament does not warrant us to plan for the expansion of denominations.

As a member of the National Council of Churches' Evangelism Working Group, I have seen how great the resistance on the part of denominational executives is to thinking seriously about ecumenical evangelism in these days. Denominational evangelism, on the other hand, is too liable to become triumphalistic. It is triumphalism which this book has sought to challenge, by calling the church to servant ministry. Let this point be clear: It *is* important for us to recruit people for servant ministry. But I am not convinced that membership in the institutional church today is to be identified with enlistment in servant community. Our denominational churches are too worried about their institutional survival for them to claim their members for the risky business of servant ministry.

The second reason I have not spoken centrally about the church in this book is unintentional: the allegory on which the book is based does not speak of the church (unless that be the fellowship of the five wise young women—no mention is, however, made of that).

Thus I have come to the end of the allegory, and to the end of the book, without having dealt with the church, except in passing. This is not my normal theological style. Those who know my previous writings know that I believe the church is central to God's plan, crucial for any approach to evangelism—both as the base from which evangelism takes place and as part of the goal of evangelism. As I said in quoting Athol Gill earlier, the grace of new community is part of the message. The fellowship of the church is a proximate goal, an intermediary goal, on the way toward the goal of a restored human fellowship, but it is a sign of the partial realization already in this present order of God's eschatological purpose.

And yet what is the church? I sense that the models we have of what "church" means fail to express adequately the concept of mission about which I have spoken.* I am far from certain what such models will look like when we find them. I think we have a lot of work to do to try to re-image such models. And that is why I have designated this chapter a "Prologue" rather than an "Epilogue," for we are barely beginning to imagine an adequate ecclesiology for North America to accord with the new age that is fast upon us.

That age, our foundation allegory tells us, is characterized by darkness—it will be a long time till dawn. In the immediate future the church will have to devise a style of life which will enable it to wait patiently and minister effectively in the midst of increased international and domestic turbulence, in the face of continued oppression of the weak and heightened repression of those who challenge the status quo. Such a heightening of repression Berkhof calls the re-assertion of the "anti-forces," who, sensing that their doom is clear now that God's Kingdom has drawn near,

*See Chapters 5 and 6.

exert their strongest rebellion in an attempt to defeat the Kingdom.

What will be appropriate ways of imaging the church in such a time as this? We will be helped by four metaphors of the church: as a center of resistance, as a witness to transcendence, as a loyal opposition, and as a servant community. These images have come to me from groups with differing perspectives within the contemporary church. The vision of the church as a center of resistance comes from the radical evangelicalism of *Sojourners* magazine, of Daniel Berrigan and William Stringfellow and, originally, from the Confessing Church in Nazi Germany.

The image of the church as a witness to transcendence brings to mind the emphasis on transcendence made by the authors of the Hartford Appeal for Theological Affirmation.

To speak of the church as a loyal opposition—as both in and committed to society, while not being of society, and sensing itself called to oppose society for society's sake—would be a way of expressing the vision I have received from Dutch theologians like Hendrikus Berkhof, many in the British churches whose writings have been shared with me largely by John Poulton,[1] and from many church people in this country.

To speak of the church as a servant community is to use the language of the ecumenical movement of the last decade and more; it brings to mind Bonhoeffer's understanding of Christ as "the man for others" and concomitant images of the church as a "church for others"—or, to use Hoekendijk's phrase, "The Church Inside Out."[2]

That these images seem to come from rival parties does not faze me. I believe each is a gift of God, and that without one or more of these gifts the others cannot function. A truly contemporary biblical ecclesiology cannot be less than multi-dimensional. In addition, I may be found guilty of poor interpretation of these images. If so, I plead *nolo contendere*. I feel no compulsion to interpret the images exactly as the originators did. Each image suggests something to me which I find crucial to a balanced understanding of the church. No one has a patent on any of these images. Somewhat selfishly, I would like to garner them all into my basket. In this time of "prologue," we all need to do a lot of borrowing. Without new combinations and re-combinations, we will never make it.

So then I will proceed without further apology to elucidate each of the images in turn, and then to conclude by sharing a manifesto, "Toward a Church of the Beatitudes," which expresses what I think will be a type of church commitment increasing numbers of Christians will feel compelled to make in the next years, as the darkness deepens.

(1) A Center of Resistance

If you are scoring these images on Richard Niebuhr's typological score-sheet (the one he provided so memorably in *Christ and Culture*),[3] this one is surely to be labelled "Christ Against Culture." It is the position which has traditionally been taken by Anabaptists and various sects.

Here the church understands itself as locked in struggle, on behalf or at the behest of God, with culture gone amok. The culture may be epitomized by the state—which will then be called the Beast—or the state might be relatively unrelated to the issue, a mere tool in the employ of a culture which far transcends it. Perhaps in that case, one would be interpreting the Book of Revelation correctly by applying the image of the Beast to the culture itself and not the state, saying that it is with the culture that the church is locked in combat, that it is the culture which the church is called to resist.

When I speak of culture here I speak of it in the sense in which Oscar Lewis coined the phrase "the culture of poverty."[4] I am not speaking of the folkways, arts, and character of a distinct "culture group," but of a culture which transcends group boundaries. The culture I think the church in the North Atlantic world is called to resist is "the culture of fear and oppression"—the culture which owns the vast technological infrastructure, controls the media, manipulates the economic system, and dominates the world of education. It is the culture which says to the world, in the words of Burger King, "Have it your way"—holding up before it the idols of consumerism—while alienating from people whatever power they ever had.

Against this culture, which far transcends the individuals who make it up (I am not just speaking of a "power elite," but of a culture which controls even that power elite which undoubtedly exists), the church is summoned to resist. Just as Christ was sent to engage in battle with the principalities and powers, so are we. John Howard Yoder has a helpful way of describing how Christ in fact "disarmed" the powers: it was by "depriving them of the weapon from which they had derived their power, the power of illusion, their ability to convince men that they were the divine regents of the world, ultimate certainty and direction and happiness and duty." Christ revealed to humanity that "we have a higher destiny, higher orders to follow." Where the cross is preached, Yoder goes on, the "disarming" of the Powers continues to take place.[5]

The church is called to resist the continued alienation of power from God's people by those who wish to exploit the people for their own ends, whether the power to be resisted be identified as "the international capitalist class" or "the military/industrial/scientific complex," "materialism," or "covetousness." The church is called, first of all, to *be* a community of people who remain free from the powers—not conformed to the world—and who can therefore, secondly, deprive the powers of their essential strength, the power of illusion, through proclaiming to the people the gospel of God, a gospel which will liberate them from the control of the powers. This is the role of the church as proclaimer of truth.

We must recognize that to speak of the church—the total institution of the church across North America—as free from the sway of the culture's illusions and therefore its power, is manifestly untrue. The church is simply not that free—the culture has taken most of the church captive. Not only are most of the dominant myths of our time accepted by the church, but many of them are baptized by the church, just as they were earlier when the missionary mandate was confused in the late 19th and early 20th centuries with "Manifest Destiny." I write this chapter on the eve of Thanksgiving, knowing that thousands of prayers of thanks will be given in American churches tomorrow for the "benefits" of consumerism, for our "high standard of living," that we live in "a free country," that we are "Number One in the world." The sense of well-being in our society is still strong despite a long recession and high unemployment. Few in the churches even hope for an alternative or think things could be better, much less understand themselves as called to resist the present order.

The model of the church as a center of resistance applies therefore, in the first instance, only to a tiny segment of the church, an *ecclesiola in ecclesiae,* a remnant, a "company of the committed."

With Karl Barth we can say, however, that this is what the church in its essence *is* and our message to the church must be more than "Be converted." It must be "Become what you are." The Bride of Christ has been bought with a high price. Her freedom has been purchased. She is under no obligation to the principalities and powers. She stands free.

But it will be the task of the conscious remnant to be the vanguard of the church's new life, to insist that the church enter upon its inheritance, that it become a resistance. This is a role properly played, both as *pars pro toto* and as a conscientizing leaven within the whole, by the Christian community movement, by the base church, by various house churches and "liberation churches," and—the juxtaposition may surprise many of those in the first list—by the national and regional bureaucracies of the denominations, as well as by the theological seminaries.

The bureaucracies have—I say this after five and one half years of working in one—a certain freedom from the workaday world of the parish that enables a number of officeholders to play an extraordinarily creative role in feeding the minds of both church and nation. Some of the most exciting examples of "demystification" I have seen in the last years have come not from community movements but from people employed by denominations which are not recognizable, at least at the parish level, as part of any vanguard. Both in their own research and development, and the position papers which emerge therefrom, and in the consultations and conferences which they have convened—both denominationally and ecumenically—the "bureaucrats" have made a continuing substantive contribution to the disarming of the principalities and powers. The freedom which such officeholders have is a stewardship which they exercise on behalf of the church as a whole, and it would be a mistake for them to seek to reinterpret their ministry as a consensus ministry: they are called to lead.

I think of the actions of the denominations against the multi-national corporations, the abuse of human rights, arms sales, the plutonium economy, world hunger, the corruptions and in-adequacies of the welfare system, the exploitation of people by the media, and so many other examples of human alienation. The pronouncements, studies, and front-line actions of the bureau-cracies provide a first-class example of the meaning of resistance.

But let us not be deceived. Much of this is done at the local level as well. Parish churches which in many ways are acculturated have in other ways demonstrated remarkable freedom and initia-tive, working as advocates of the poor and downtrodden, raising a strong "no" when it is needed in the community, creating alterna-tive models of how to deal with human problems, getting people out to the polls on important issues.

Bishop David Sheppard of the Church of England, in his book *Built as a City,*[6] describes how he has gained from the churches of his diocese an understanding of how they can be committed to the pursuit of "limited"—but crucial—"aims in the city where we live":

> . . . We are to encourage Christian expectations in the city; love really is the toughest commodity in the world; life comes through our smaller "death," as it does through his Cross; people can be enabled to achievements far beyond what they expect, and we can be set free from some of our present day enslavements.
>
> . . . we should not try simply to come to terms with some patterns of urban community, because when we look at them carefully we shall see that they are expressing non-community and non-life. For example, we are not simply to teach people how to fit in to some huge new housing development or to the jobs which industry offers. The Kingdom of right relationships challenges people to believe that they can bring about changes in community and in industry. Then people can be people, families can be families, neighbours can be neighbours and workers can be workers.
>
> We must hold on to the dream that it is possible for a place to be built as a city, and to know in the thick of its life right relationship between men with God.[7]

In my experience, once people in a parish become open to one such action, to one type of advocacy, to one example of resistance—say to the support of the United Farm Workers' boycotts—they become open to other actions as well: a new self-understanding develops and they begin to put themselves on the line for other causes as well. According to the jargon, they become "radicalized."

Samuel Parmar of India believes that a middle-class church can, without ceasing to be a middle-class church, begin working on a regular basis with the poor, as unlikely but actual partners in bringing about revolutionary change.[8] Karl Barth's biblical realism would encourage us to maintain that hope, far-fetched though it may seem, and to resist elitism in the social action movement, never despising the local, the parochial, knowing that in the end, unless the whole Body of Christ is mobilized, we will never get beyond resistance to the kind of meaningful social change for which we are licensed to hope.

And yet we must be careful lest we seek to import into the conscientization/action process a less than biblical understanding of how social movements develop. Benton Johnson, in a highly perceptive study of the social action movement of modern Protestantism[9] (which he calls "the new piety"), points out the differences between the "inner-worldly asceticism" of earlier Protestantism—which did really change the world—and the "new variety of inner-worldly asceticism" which is found in the social action movement of today. The old version, as Max Weber realized, offered "unique incentives" to people to change their life-style: the hope of salvation and the strength of discipline within the church.

But the new activism, Johnson notes, offers no discipline and little sense of fellowship in the church and has the "fatal theological shortcoming" of "failing to tap the inner reservoirs of human motivation," by creating "no desperate sense" of being bound "and therefore no real need for release." Instead, Johnson writes, it relies "mainly on appealing to disinterested love and to a middle-class sense of duty. . . . There is no hope of glory in the new piety. . . . The new piety implies radical change but it denies the core of all the old doctrines and offers no doctrine of comparable power as a substitute." The "spokesmen" for the new piety, Johnson argues, need to "invent or borrow a theoretical framework that is as powerful and compelling as the old Christian gospel."

The reader will by now recognize that my reply will be that "the old Christian gospel" is still there, that no "new theoretical framework" is required to replace it, that the Holy Spirit is still around, and no new source of power need be found. But I cite Johnson at length because I believe that he has made a telling critique of why the "new piety" of social action has failed to be as revolutionary as it might: we have sought to maintain the direction of change, indeed to radicalize it, while discarding the substance of faith. The key to the persistence of any resistance movement is that it can tap the deepest human motivations of the grace of God and the love of the fellowship. These are essential for any Christian community or base church to continue; they are even more crucial as we seek to bring sizable portions of the standard churches into the movement. We can only call people to resist the culture when they are being renewed daily in their innermost being by a force that transcends culture and offers an alternative to conformity (cf. Rom. 12:1f.).

And that brings us naturally to consider our second model of the church.

(2) Witness to Transcendence

As I noted above, the word "transcendence" has come to the center of the church's dialogue largely through the efforts of the Hartford Appeal,[10] which noted "an apparent loss of a sense of the transcendent" and laid on that loss the responsibility for "undermining the church's ability to address with clarity and courage the urgent tasks to which God calls it in the world."

It may seem strange for me to be citing the Hartford Appeal positively. I was uneasy from the start with the way in which the Hartford Group, in calling for transcendence, seemed—both within the Appeal and in subsequent writings—to be identifying transcendence with another realm, to be implying that "the religious" is a sphere unto itself, thus vitiating the witness of the New Testament church to the incarnation. Some of the Hartford signers have clearly dissociated themselves from any such intention; others have not. The debate as to their intention goes on, particularly in the aftermath of their publication of a book of essays, *Against the World for the World*,[11] attempting to carry further and provide greater depth to their thought.

I will not argue that case here, but seek rather (a) to state my impression that Hartford touched a vital nerve, that we must deal with the issue of transcendence; and (b) to clarify what I believe the New Testament encourages us to think of as transcendence, as it applies to this current day.

I would in some respects associate myself with Charles Davis who, in a review of *Against the World for the World*,[12] wrote:

> I myself would attribute the decline of religious faith and the absence of an assured theology to a loss of immanence and a false concept of transcendence. The order of the day should not be a direct emphasis upon transcendence, which in the present situation would simply be misunderstood and reinforce the false transcendence that plagues religious thinking and practice. More to the point is to meet the superficiality of modern culture by a stress on the depths immanent in every area of human experience. . . .

> Much of what passes for transcendence and otherworldliness in religion and theology is the distorted counterpart of the positivism and objectivism of the dominant culture. Despite all the clumsiness and exaggeration accompanying it, the worldly turn of faith and theology, the emphasis upon secular and political concerns, is a reaction in the right direction.

I would associate myself with Davis's critique of Hartford's concept of transcendence; I would not wish at this stage to associate myself with his understanding of immanence. I myself prefer the concept of incarnation, for I believe it maintains the sense of God's otherness—the world *is* apart from God, both by creation and by fall—but the world is in the process of being "transformed," through the incarnation and the ascension, into the Kingdom of God. The reason there is no demarcated religious sphere is that the gulf between the sacred and the secular has been overcome by an act of God—the incarnation. A "genuine transcendence," as opposed to a spurious one, affirms that what we have already seen of God's action points beyond itself into the future of God's Kingdom.

Denis Goulet is, to my mind, the writer who has most satisfactorily taken up the call to affirmation of transcendence in terms of the call of the church to ongoing incarnational engagement in the project of world-transformation. "One betrays the cause of history," he writes, "by forgetting that what makes human history important is its unrelenting drive towards transcendence":

> The dialectic of existence is served neither by reductionist sec-
> ularism nor by alienating supernaturality, but by the living tension in
> which human beings . . . find an issue or a way out of the impasses
> attaching to their finiteness and contingency.[13]

He goes on, expanding on the thought of Teilhard and Lebret:

> Eternal life, whatever it may mean, ultimately begins within time.
> Otherwise it is sheer fantasy. Yet, although secular history is an
> ultimate end having its own self-justifying finalities, it is a *relative*,
> not an *absolute* ultimate end. Within its own order . . . it stands as
> the last word. . . . Nevertheless, it is the belief of Christians that
> history is not an absolute ultimate end. Human history does not
> exhaust the totality of being's mysterious possibilities. Hence, the
> cosmic order may not be the final All.[14]

He therefore sees a need for "mystical messianisms" to complement "political messianisms" in bringing about the revolution
the world needs. True revolution must be cultural as well as
political. It is not enough to think of a "greening of America" or a
"revolutionary new consciousness."

> . . . unless the psychic revolution "bites on" social structure, it will be
> escapist. And unless advocates of political revolution learn to under-
> stand the deep, cosmic yearning of alienated, technologized 20th
> century Americans for a level of meaning and depth beyond mere
> political programs, the cultural revolution will abort. True revolution-
> ary accomplishment consists in creating new realities, where mysti-
> cal and political messianisms fructify each other and lead to unimag-
> ined innovations in the social order.[15]

Reading Goulet draws me back to Reinhold Niebuhr's *Beyond
Tragedy*.[16] Although I had—I think legitimately—been warned of
Niebuhr's "Christian realism" in so far as it involves compromise
with power structures, I found Niebuhr's approach to the tragic in
history deeply meaningful. Niebuhr has an understanding of the
effects of the fall which must inform our hopes for the human
animal, lest we fall into a romantic idealization of human nature, as
we often do when we think of the "purity" of those who are
seeking liberation. Read this warning, for example:

> The weak will not only sin when they become mighty, but they sin in
> prospect and imagination while they are weak. . . .
>
> No class which resists the sins of the mighty and the noble ever does
> so with a purely messianic consciousness. Compounded with its

> purer sense of destiny is a baser metal of wounded ego and com-
> pensatory pride and vindictiveness. The disinherited are human, and
> therefore subject to basic human sins. . . .
>
> Each civilization will imagine that it has overcome the weaknesses
> and sins which brought death to its predecessors; and it will illustrate
> the quintessential form of those weaknesses in that very conviction.[17]

If the changes we are seeking are not to become new Babels, we must recognize, Niebuhr is saying, that "every civilization and every culture is a Tower of Babel." A sense of the transcendent will make us "profoundly uneasy" about even our highest social values, since we have the knowledge that the God whom we worship "transcends the limits of finite man, while this same man is constantly tempted to forget the finiteness of his cultures and civilization and to pretend to a finality to them which they do not have."

Goulet is concerned lest the affirmation of the finiteness of the present order and the transcendence of the infinite proves alienating, as indeed it often has, when people are led to conclude that the transcendent is in another realm and will only be attainable through God's action in God's time. This can lead to quietism, to acquiescence in present injustice, to a failure to take charge of the situation in the way God intends us to. As J. G. Davies writes, this would be to expect God to act while depriving him of his normal way of action, through human agents.[19]

Colin Williams, in a talk about Paul's letter to the Galatians, understands transcendence, however, in a non-alienating way:

> What Paul is saying is, "Look, the transcendence I'm talking about, that life that is above, that life which is hid with Christ in God, is the life which you are asked to lead. When you're in Christ you've got to start to live as he revealed life, that transcendent life which is able to transcend all the terrible hostilities, conflicts, and institutional separations. That is, therefore, the new quality of transcendent life which breaks through in the middle of history.

He says we had that insight in the sixties, but then ran out of steam and ended up copping out,

> because when we ran against the full depths of the limits of human nature and the full power of our institutions to resist, we simply didn't have the resources to deal with it. We were too optimistic about our capacity to live the transcendent life in Christ. We didn't take seri-

ously the way in which the biblical story talks about the meaning of God appearing in the events of history but finishes it up always with the insistence that the attempt to live it ends up. on a cross.

The story goes on, however, Williams says, to affirm that

that transcendent life of Christ can break through those terrifying limits. There is a resurrection. . . . But the story of Christians in history is always a *theologia crucis,* a theology of the cross, never a *theologia gloriae,* a theology of glory.[20]

We live, however, through justification by grace through faith alone. We are "never going to be able to translate the life of Christ with anything like completeness into the institutions of the world," Williams says, "or into the structures of our own existence, but nevertheless we are given the capacity to live in the midst of that."

Those from more liturgical traditions think immediately at this point of the sustaining power of the sacraments. They are, in and of themselves, "witnesses of transcendence."

Father Georges Florovsky writes,

The Church is more than a company of preachers. It has not only to invite people, but also to introduce them into this New Life, to which it bears witness. . . . The aim of its missionary activity is not merely to convey to people certain convictions or ideas, not even to impose on them a definite discipline or a rule of life, but first of all to introduce them into the New Reality, to convert them, to bring them through their faith and repentance to Christ Himself, that they should be born anew in Him and into Him by water and the Spirit. Thus the ministry of the Word is completed in the ministry of the Sacraments.[21]

I have at times tended to rebel at the words with which the elements are administered in many communion services—"This is the body of Christ which is given to preserve thy body and soul unto everlasting life." It seems alienating, pointing me away from life here and now. It seems like sacramentalism, attributing to the elements a "medicinal" quality which, as a Reformed Christian, I cannot accept. Nevertheless I think it is not without significance that even in "low church" traditions there has been an efflorescence of communion celebrations these last years. It seems as if we have been bearing witness to the inadequacy of the myth of "autonomous man" and looking for a power beyond our own, for an affirmation that we are moving toward a resurrection which is not just immanent in our experience. "Take this sacrament to thy comfort," we are told, and we seem to be doing just that. "Feed on Christ in your innermost heart with thanksgiving," we are told, and we seem to find such eucharistic praise very much a feeding.

But enough of this. This section is not entitled "God's Transcendent Witness to Us" but "Witnesses of Transcendence," meaning that the accent in the end falls on what we as a church do when we are fed. We witness to others of the transcendence we have seen and heard and experienced, in the hope, as I John 1:1-4 puts it, that we might come into communion, or fellowship, with those to whom we witness. Mortimer Arias of Bolivia put it well at the Nairobi Assembly: "New Testament evangelism is a true *communication* of a *community* which calls to *communion.*"[22]

As witnesses to transcendence, we are not to be turned in upon ourselves. As Bishop Arias said in a United Church of Christ meeting in November, 1976, that is the worst of failures of understanding of Jesus' intention in the Lord's Supper. "For as often as you eat this bread and drink this cup," Paul wrote, "you *proclaim* the Lord's death till he comes." Our liturgical activity, Bishop Arias reminded us, is proclamatory activity. Our eucharist is not the closed feast of a select community, but the open proclamation of the coming of Christ. Our deepest yearning must be to communicate his message in such a way that others, too, will come to know it and follow him.

That will take place in many ways, but mostly, I think, side by side. Top-down communication is still possible in a hierarchically structured world, but the Christian communication which follows the model of Christ will eschew all attempts to speak down to others. Shoulder to shoulder communication is more the model of the Galilean carpenter. Nestor Paz, a young Colombian Roman Catholic, who joined the abortive liberation struggle in his country in the sixties, thought of his presence in the guerilla army as a witness to what Christians believe:

> I think my presence in the column, especially in the vanguard, has been beneficial. . . . It makes me happy to realize that all my previous formation and what we learned together is helping to make us more human. I think that people see this, and I'm glad . . . because it is a fundamental, inescapable service we must do for others: to show with our "life," our example, what we believe and desire, and to have an even spirit. . . .[23]

Most of us will not feel called to make our witness as Paz made his. Some of us would even take issue with his decision as a Christian to become a guerilla. But his example—he died of starvation in the pursuit of his convictions—forces us to ask, In what way are *we* witnessing to a Person, to a Life, to values, to a world, to a Kingdom which transcends this present one? And who is perceiving our witness? Are we witnessing to a transcendent future which impinges upon this present world order and brings it under judgment, calling it beyond itself, to transformation? Or are we witnessing to a life "above" which reduces the ultimate significance of this present life and the struggle to create a more human order?

I find myself driven back to Lebret when I ask these questions. Are we, he would have said, witnessing to humanity's need for self-transcendence? And does that transcendence include, not an ahistorical but a metahistorical transcendence?[24]

(3) A Loyal Opposition

It was in the British parliamentary system that the concept of a *loyal* opposition grew up. The concept is the antithesis of the "zero sum game," in which every gain of yours is a loss of mine.

There is a sense that "We're all in this together," and that— even if we are opposed to you within Parliament—we still are within Parliament: we don't "pick up our marbles and go home." The game transcends both of our parties.

This is not, as I understand it, to be equated with the "bipartisanship" of the American Congress on certain issues. The *loyal* opposition is clearly an opposition. It will not paper over its differences with the ruling party. The issues are too crucial for that to be.

When applied to the church, the term loyal opposition therefore expresses both solidarity in society and opposition to society. As such, I think it has a lot to commend itself as our third image of the church.

For one thing it keeps us from fastening too much on the concept of a resistance. That concept expresses part of the church's mission, but not all. In some societies the church may need to become totally a resistance, but, as Calvin expressed it, in the light of the ascension of Christ that is the atypical, abnormal situation. In some societies—I think particularly of Tanzania—the church may be called to a great degree of identification with the dominant culture. This side of the *parousia* that, too, is atypical. In most societies for most purposes the church might best think of itself as a loyal opposition.

I think that is true at the present time in the United States of America. Though the church is called to resist the principalities and powers in every encroachment they make on our national life, I do not believe the church is called in America this day to total opposition, total resistance. I cannot be among those who— perhaps out of a more perceptive reading of Scripture than my own—apply to the USA the title "the Beast." Nor will I easily be moved to follow the example of those who, out of their studies of fascism, feel moved to spell America with a "k."

If that means I run the risk of falling into "civil religion," I'm willing to run that risk—confident that the Holy Spirit will keep me from falling into it—for the sake of what I believe a loyal opposition can do to transform what is certainly an imperialistic, over-weeningly proud nation, with demonstrated failures of justice, into a nation which reflects in some significant ways more of God's righteousness and concern for world community.

I am not "bullish on America." My hope is in the transforming power of the gospel. It is not a naive, optimistic hope, but a chastened hope. I believe that, even in the face of the deepening darkness, the gospel can transform America in the late 20th century. It did that at other periods in our history, and it can do it today, as it once again forces and frees us to hope. Our hope is for resurrection, not for vindication. Such a hope cannot be held forth by an unquestioning supporter of our system, but only by an opposition, a paradoxically loyal opposition.

A loyal opposition, as I understand it, will resist the temptation of a president of an Eastern Bible college when, in his inaugural address, he said that the college stood for "the three p's—the preeminence of Christ, the philosophy of Christian education, and patriotism." It will rather, in the words of Walter Rauschenbusch, "disturb the patriotism and loyalty of citizens for their country" by awakening "slaves to a sense of worth and longing for freedom," women to "break down the restraints of custom and modesty," exploited workers to "throw down their tools and quit work." It will be a leaven spreading "not only sweet peace and tender charity, but the leaven of social unrest."[25]

Rauschenbusch goes on:

> No great historic revolution has ever worked its way without breaking and splintering the old to make way for the new. New wine is sure to ferment and burst the old wineskins. Moreover, it is likely to taste sour and yeasty, and some will say, "The old is better." . . . Jesus came to cast a fire upon the earth. . . . But he was willing to pay the cost of the Kingdom of God in tears and blood if need be.

"The major advances in civilization," Alfred North Whitehead philosophized, "are processes which all but wreck the societies in which they occur." Society in its official expression will therefore resist such advances. It is the task of a loyal opposition to force the pangs of new birth, not to allow the society to recoil from that which causes pain.

"We are stranded," Henry Kissinger stated in one of his more philosophical moments in 1976, "between old conceptions of political conduct and a wholly new conception, between the inadequacy of the nation-state and the emerging imperative of the global community." Except perhaps in opening relations with China, Kissinger did little to get beyond the strandedness which he lamented. It is the duty of the church as a loyal opposition to force the nation to step out of its lonely quagmire and into the future.

Abraham Lincoln recognized the problem. The times were changing rapidly, but the nation was "still under the sway of inflexible dogmas." His remedy for our survival, for our recovering greatness as a nation, was expressed in somewhat mystical language: "We must disenthrall ourselves," he said. We are under a kind of spell. The task of a loyal opposition is to challenge "inflexible dogmas," sacred cows, false consciousness. In evangelism the church has a truth-telling function, and it is that truth which alone will make humanity free.

"The church," P.T. Forsyth wrote in Britain a couple of generations ago, "has in its holy gospel the only spiritual power which can regenerate society."[26] It cannot think of that power as for itself alone. "Christian love will take the form of a demand for social justice and an insistence that if the present industrial order stifles the Christian life and rides roughshod over Christian values, the order must be changed."

Adrian Hastings has similar views of the importance and universality of the Christian message:

> If the gospel is true at all, it is both important and universal—universally important. By definition it is not a geographically, culturally, racially or sexually limited thing, but a geographically, culturally, racially and sexually transcending thing. It is a message from Adam to Adam. If it is not received by the whole human race, something must be—gospelwise—greatly amiss, and satisfaction with such a situation in principle is intrinsically a denial of the meaning of the gospel.[27]

I go back again to the *Foundations* document for the sense of the whole:

> The Church of Christ is separated from the world and incorporated into Christ. Therefore she must not become conformed to this world. . . .
>
> At the same time the Church of Christ is sent out into the world. Incorporated into Christ who loved the world, she loves the world for Christ's sake. Therefore it is not her mission to condemn but to save. . . . She will never conceal her intrinsic opposition to the world, nor will she acquiesce in an external antithesis to the world.
>
> The Church is not the Kingdom of God. She is the foretoken and herald of the new world and the new humanity.[28]

When we read such language we must say to the church, "Be what you are." We must call the church to give up its cheap accommodation to the ways of the world, its hopelessness for meaningful change. We must call it to ask now the questions which will be asked of it when God's new order has come. At that time the church will be asked, "Did you speak out for that new order? To what extent did you oppose society for society's own sake, because you had hope for what God could do to transform society?"

Those questions are being asked world-wide whenever a revolution is taking place. The church must learn to ask itself those questions before the revolution takes place, questions such as Tissa Balasuriya of Sri Lanka asks concerning the performance of the Catholic Church in South Vietnam, now that change has come to South Vietnam against its will:

In the light of what has happened in Indochina, we have to ask ourselves what meaning there was in the type of mission activities which were carried out earlier. What relevance did the presentation of the word of God in preaching and in catechesis have to the exploitation of the people—both by the local elite and the foreign powers?

Even if Christians were opposed to the immorality of public life, how strongly did they contest it? . . . What meaning did the elitist schools run by Christian missions with great dedication have for the formation of youth within the situation of inequality and injustice? Likewise what was the adequacy of social services of a person-to-person nature, however necessary and good they were, to meet the total problem of a society which the liberation forces were contesting?

We must similarly question the theology of the Churches which formed a clergy, religious and laity in large measure incapable of reading the signs of the times and being not in sympathy with the anguish of the masses. . . .[29]

A moving example of how the church has been called to such awakening in our country in the present time is in the *Pastoral Letter on Powerlessness in Appalachia*[30] by the Catholic bishops of that exploited and depressed region. I quote from its final words:

Dear sisters and brothers,
we urge all of you
not to stop living,
to be a part of the rebirth of utopias,
to recover and defend the struggling dream
of Appalachia itself.
For it is the weak things of this world,
which seem like folly,
that the Spirit takes up
and makes its own.
The dream of the mountains' struggle,
the dream of simplicity
and of justice,
like so many other repressed visions,
is, we believe,
the voice of the Lord among us.

In taking them up,
hopefully the Church
might once again
be known as

—a center of the Spirit,
—a place where poetry dares to speak,
—where the song reigns unchallenged,
—where art flourishes,
—where nature is welcome,
—where little people and little needs
come first,
—where justice speaks loudly,
—where in a wilderness of idolatrous destruction
the great voice of God still cries out
for Life.

In a "wilderness of idolatrous destruction" we are called to speak the "No" which must be spoken in order that the "Yes" of God might still be heard. We are also called to be a servant community.

(4) A Servant Community

It might seem that this last section might be answered simply by referring to Chapter 7 and Thomas Klise's "Silent Servants of the Used, Abused, and Utterly Screwed Up." That is part of what is to be said. It can also be said in the words of a much older document than *The Last Western,* the early Christian "Letter to Diognetus," which describes Christian citizenship as servanthood:

Christians are not distinguished from the rest of mankind by nationality, speech or culture. They do not establish cities of their own; they speak no particular dialect; they follow no particular mode of life. . . . they conform to the customs of the land in dress, food and living habits. Yet through it all they demonstrate the wonderful and admittedly striking character of their citizenship.

Christians live in their native countries as aliens or pilgrims. They participate in affairs as good citizens, but they put up with all things as strangers. Every foreign country is their home and every home is a foreign country. . . . They observe the established laws but in their private lives they rise above the laws. They love all men but suffer persecution from all men.

No one knows much about them, yet they are condemned. They are put to death, yet they are restored to life. They are poor, yet they make many rich. They lack everything, yet they abound in everything. They are dishonoured, yet in their very dishonour they are glorified. They are slandered, yet they are vindicated. They are reviled, yet they bless. When they are insulted they pay it back with honour. When they do good they are punished as evildoers. When they are punished they exult as men who receive life. Those who hate them cannot really explain their hatred. In short, what the soul is in the body, Christians are in the world.[31]

Few of us recognize the church we know in the words Diognetus read. Yet there are individual Christians we have known, and perhaps some Christian communities as well, who embody these characteristics visibly. For most of us, however, it is an ideal to be striven after, not a description of what exists.

What characterizes that ideal? It seems to me it is the selflessness of Christians therein described—their lives are exocentric rather than egocentric. A generation ago we all referred to this with the Greek word *agape,* which was defined as "suffering love" or "love for the other for the other's sake" or "self-emptying love." Love is not on the Top Ten today. Righteousness and concern for justice are. But love is not opposed to righteousness. Righteousness, as Forsyth said, is "the public form of love."[32] And yet somehow love loses out when we do not call it by its own name. Let us therefore say that what we are called to do as a servant people is to "live in the Spirit . . . radiating the divine *agape* in the fellowship of a community."[33] Love is of the essence of our servanthood. An American Lutheran theologian, William Lazareth, speaking at the Catholic Eucharistic Congress in 1976, described servant ministry in terms of the church's *leitourgia:*

> The Church itself is a *leitourgia,* a ministry, a calling to act in this world after the fashion of Christ, to bear testimony to Him and His Kingdom. The eucharistic liturgy, therefore, must not be approached and understood in "liturgical" or "cultic" terms alone. Just as Christianity can—and must—be considered as the end of religion, so the Christian liturgy in general, and the Eucharist in particular, are indeed the end of cult, of the "sacred" religious act isolated from, and opposed to, the "profane" life of the community. . . .

> The Eucharist is a sacrament . . . the entrance of the Church into the joy of its Lord. And to enter into that joy, so as to be a witness to it in the world, is indeed the very calling of the Church, its essential leitourgia, the sacrament by which it "becomes what it is"—the servant body of the Servant Lord.[34]

Bishop J.A.T. Robinson, author of *Honest to God,* preaching at Riverside Church, New York, in August, 1976, expressed his belief that the time has now drawn closer when the church can be a servant again. "In these years God has stripped us down," he said. "Triumphalism is out now. We used to think we could vote in a new church. We have, however, come to recognize that change will not come about just through reform and renewal. We have learned the hard way that the way to new life is through death and resurrection. God *gives* us our new form. We don't make it. I have less optimism," he concluded, "than twenty-five years ago, but deeper hope."[35]

It was on the question of optimism and hope that I began this book. We have now come full circle. In speaking of the church as a servant community we are really describing the church as a servant of hope.

I do have such hope. It is not a general optimism, but the hope to which the Allegory of the Ten Young Women calls us, to be patient in well-doing as we wait for the revealing of our hope. We wait, as did the young women, in the darkness. The dawn has not yet come. But we are called to a poor but joyous feast as we wait, our lanterns and our oil in hand.

No one has expressed better for me at this time what the style of such waiting might be than those who wrote the pledge "Toward a Church of the Beatitudes," a pledge the signing of which changed my life:

> Recognizing that Christ's Gospel of love, liberation, justice and peace is either promoted or obscured by the life-style and manner of exercising power in Christian communities and gatherings,
>
> And that Christ calls his people to a spirit of profound repentance and love, to put apathy behind, and to participate fully in the ongoing responsibility of God's loving community,
>
> We pledge ourselves to accept God's claim on our personal and corporate lives and to encourage our church communities in these directions:
>
> 1. To be poor in fact, adopting new and radically simpler life-styles, refusing to increase our affluence until all other persons and human communities have essentials.
>
> 2. To be poor in spirit, renouncing identification with worldly wealth and power, thus nurturing our obedience to the spirit of the living Gospel.
>
> 3. To preach, teach and practice Gospel simplicity within our

church institutions, urging the church to use its resources to bring justice to the hungry, poor and oppressed.

4. To develop co-operative and participative patterns of living, sharing, working and relating.

5. To take up Christ's role of humble service and gentle love in leadership and decision-making, and to resist abusive power relationships.

6. To work for ending racism, sexism and age and class discrimination in our church communities, so that through loving and non-violent action the church can effectively contribute to healing these sins in the world.

7. To proclaim prophetically the need for a just world distribution of power, wealth and natural resources.

8. To accept the cross, and the joys and pain of discipleship, ready even to be persecuted for justice.[36]

NOTES

Chapter 3

1. Quoted in H.R. Niebuhr, *The Kingdom of God in America* (New York, 1937), p. 142.
2. Samuel Harris, *The Kingdom of Christ on Earth* (Andover, MA, 1874), p. 225.
3. American Board of Commissioners for Foreign Missions, *Annual Report, 1881* (Boston, MA), pp. xiiff.
4. Ibid.
5. Ibid.
6. Robert Heilbroner, *An Inquiry into the Human Prospect* (New York, 1975), p. 13.
7. Ibid., 136.
8. Ibid., 169.
9. Ibid., 138.
10. Karl P. Donfried, "The Allegory of the Ten Virgins as a Summary of Matthean Theology" in *Journal of Biblical Literature,* Vol. 93, No. 3 (Sept., 1974), p. 245.
11. Ibid., 427.
12. "The Liberation of White Theology" in *Christian Century,* Vol. 91, No. 11 (March 20, 1974), p. 318.
13. Quoted in the *New York Times,* Feb. 16, 1975, p. 15.
14. Quoted in Dale Brown, *The Christian Revolutionary* (Grand Rapids, 1971), p. 122.
15. Ibid., 122f.

Chapter 4

1. Reported by John J. O'Connor in the *New York Times,* Summer, 1975 (exact date not available).
2. "The Way that Leads to Peace," *Responsibilities of the Mass Media,* mimeographed.
3. Ecumenical Consultation on Domestic Hunger, reported in press release, National Council of Churches, Sept. 15, 1975.
4. Jacques Ellul, *The Technological Society* (New York, 1964), p. 14.
5. Ibid., xxxiii.

6. Ibid., 74
7. Ibid., 80.
8. Ibid., 85.
9. Ibid., 87.
10. Ibid., 89
11. Ibid., 96.
12. Ibid., 96.
13. Ibid., 96f.
14. Ibid., 111.
15. Ibid., 116.
16. Heilbroner, op. cit., 78.
17. Robert Bellah, *The Broken Covenant* (New York, 1975), p. 133.
18. Ibid., 132.
19. *Right On!* Nov., 1975 (Berkeley, CA), p. 5.
20. Max Weber, *The Protestant Ethic and the Spirit of Capitalism* (New York, 1958), p. 181.
21. Johanna Steinmetz, "Mr. Magic—The TV Newscast Doctor" in the *New York Times,* October 12, 1975, Section 2, pp. 1ff.
22. Quoted in *Emile Durkheim on Morality and Society,* ed. Robert Bellah (Chicago, 1973), p. xlvii.
23. Quoted in Ernest Wallwork, *Durkheim: Morality and Milieu* (Cambridge, MA, 1972), p. 49.
24. Robert Bellah, *The Broken Covenant,* p. 145.
25. Ibid.
26. Ibid.
27. Robert Nisbet, *The Sociology of Emile Durkheim* (New York, 1974), p. 269.
28. Bellah, op. cit., 142.
29. Wallwork, op. cit., 125.
30. Ibid., 109.
31. Bellah, op. cit., 163.
32. Wallwork, op. cit., 129.
33. Ibid., 110.
34. Ibid., 111.
35. Bellah, op. cit., 195.
36. Ibid., 1.
37. Cf. Bellah, p. xlvii.
38. Qu. 114.
39. Jonathan Edwards, *Works,* IV, pp. 120f.
40. Cf. Isaac Rottenberg, *Redemption and Historical Reality* (Philadelphia, 1964), pp. 171f.
41. Hendrikus Berkhof, *Christ the Meaning of History* (Richmond, VA, 1966), p. 199.
42. Leszek Kolakowski, *Toward a Marxist Humanism: Essays on the Left Today* (New York, 1968), pp. 25, 33, 66, 187.
43. *Foundations and Perspectives of Confession* (New Brunswick, NJ: New Brunswick Theological Seminary, 1955), Art. 18, p. 29.

Chapter 5

1. Jose Miranda, *Marx and the Bible* (Maryknoll, NY, 1974), p. 245.
2. "A Preliminary Dialogue with Gutierrez' *A Theology of Liberation*" (from dialogue between United Methodists and Evangelicals for Social Action, Washington, D.C.), p. 29.
3. Krister Stendahl, "The Apostle Paul and the Introspective Conscience of the West" in *Harvard Theological Review,* Vol. 56 (July, 1963), pp. 199ff. (I am grateful to Dr. John Howard Yoder for leading me, in his book *The Politics of Jesus,* to this article.)
4. Ibid., 202.
5. Ibid., 205.
6. Ibid., 205f.
7. Ibid., 206f.
8. Ibid., 214f.
9. Tjaard G. Hommes, "Deus Ludens: Christianity and Culture in the Theology of A. A. Van Ruler" in *Reformed Review,* Winter, 1973, p. 90.
10. Hans Küng, "What Is the Christian Message?" in *Mission Trends,* No. 1, ed. G. Anderson and T. Stransky (New York and Grand Rapids, 1974), p. 109.
11. John V. Taylor, *CMS Newsletter,* London, 1971.
12. Alfred C. Krass, prepared for presentation on the Theology of Mission, Eden Theological Seminary, St. Louis, MO, Nov. 8, 1974.
13. D.T. Niles, Inaugural Sermon, Union Theological Seminary.
14. Wallace Stevens, quoted in *The Ridgeleaf,* No. 89, June, 1975 (Kirkridge, PA).
15. Nikos Nissiotis, "The Gospel Message in a Time of Revolution," *One World,* Sept., 1975 (Geneva), pp. 16-18.
16. Ibid., 17.
17. Ibid., 17.
18. Hugo Assman, quoted in D. Goulet, *A New Moral Order* (Maryknoll, NY, 1974), p. 121.
19. The Chicago Declaration has been reprinted in *The Chicago Declaration,* ed. Ronald Sider (Creation House, Wheaton, IL, 1974).
20. Richard Mouw, "Weaving a Coherent Pattern of Discipleship," *Christian Century,* Aug. 20-27, 1975, pp. 728-731.
21. Reprinted in *Let the Earth Hear His Voice,* International Congress on World Evangelization, ed. J.D. Douglas (Minneapolis, 1975), pp. 3-9.
22. Boston Industrial Mission, 56 Boylston St., Cambridge, MA 02138.
23. Lewis Smedes, "From Hartford to Boston," *The Reformed Journal,* Vol. 26, No. 4 (April, 1976), pp. 2f.
24. Billy Graham, "On Religion," *Philadelphia Inquirer,* May 11, 1977.
25. Mircaea Eliade, "Sacred Time and Myths," *The Sacred and the Profane* (New York, 1959).
26. Daniel Berrigan, "The Man Who Couldn't Say Yes or No," *Radix,*

Vol. 8, No. 1 (July-Aug., 1976) (Berkeley, CA), pp. 5ff.

27. *Let the Earth Hear His Voice* (Minneapolis, 1975), pp. 1294ff.
28. Ibid., 1294.
29. Ibid.
30. Reprinted in *A Monthly Letter About Evangelism,* World Council of Churches, Feb., 1975, p. 8.
31. Ibid., 4.
32. *Catholic Committee of Appalachia,* Prestonsburg, KY.
33. I am grateful to my friend, Dr. Orlando Costas, for insisting that I resist the temptation to speak of evangelism-in-general and go on to develop an evangelism specifically for North American middle-class society today.

Chapter 6

1. Michael Clark and Leah Margulies, Interfaith Center on Corporate Responsibility, 1976.
2. Reprinted in *SCAN,* Partnership in Mission, Vol. 1, No. 2 (May, 1976) (Abington, PA).
3. Ibid.
4. Ibid.
5. Ibid.
6. Ibid.
7. Ibid.
8. Geiko Müller-Fahrenholz, "Overcoming Apathy: The Church's Responsibilities in Face of the Threats to Human Survival" in *Ecumenical Review,* Vol. 27, No. 1 (Jan., 1975), pp. 48-56.
9. Ibid., 50f.
10. Ibid., 55f.
11. Ibid., 54f.
12. Ibid., 56.
13. Ibid.
14. Ibid.

Chapter 7

1. M.M. Thomas, *Religion and Society,* Vol. 19, No. 1 (March, 1972), pp. 72f.
2. *Risk,* Vol. 9, No. 3 (1973), pp. 36f.
3. From an interview with Sharon Gallagher in *Right On!,* Sept., 1975, (Berkeley, CA).
4. Ibid.
5. John J. O'Donnell, "The Cross in a Secular World," *Commonweal,* April 9, 1976, pp. 234ff.
6. *Let the Earth Hear His Voice,* p. 5.

7. Kazoh Kitamori, *Theology of the Pain of God* (Richmond, VA, 1965).

8. Ibid., 20.

9. Ibid., 147.

10. Jürgen Moltmann, *The Crucified God* (New York, 1974), pp. 4f.

11. Ibid., 7.

12. Ibid., 27.

13. Ibid., 273f.

14. Ibid., 85f.

15. Ibid., 263.

16. Ibid.

17. Ibid., 107.

18. Ibid., 5.

19. Ibid., 170f.

20. Ibid., 120.

21. Ibid., 4.

22. Kosuke Koyama, *Waterbuffalo Theology* (Maryknoll, NY, 1974), pp. 68f.

23. Thomas Klise, *The Last Western* (Niles, IL: Argus Publications, 1974).

24. Ibid., 150.

25. Ibid., 38-52.

26. C.H. Dodd, *The Founder of Christianity* (New York, 1970).

27. Ibid., 41.

28. Ibid., 68.

29. Ibid., 115.

30. Ibid., 126.

31. Moltmann, op. cit., 120f.

32. Dodd., op. cit., 90.

33. Ibid., 99.

34. Ibid., 105.

35. Ibid., 106.

36. *Let the Earth Hear His Voice,* p. 5.

37. "Christian Social Responsibility" in *The New Face of Evangelicalism,* ed. C. Rene Padilla (London, 1976), p. 97.

38. I am indebted for this insight to Jose Miranda, *Marx and the Bible,* (Maryknoll, NY, 1974), p. 240.

39. *Risk,* Vol. 9, No. 3, p. 49.

40. Roger Garaudy, *The Alternative Future: A Vision of Christian Marxism* (New York, 1974), p. 85.

41. Ibid.

42. Cf. W.A. Visser 't Hooft, *The Kingship of Christ* (New York, 1948), pp. 84f.

43. *Foundations and Perspectives of Confession* (New Brunswick, NJ: New Brunswick Theological Seminary, 1955).

44. John Baillie in *The Belief in Progress* (New York, 1951) quotes Oliver

Quick on this point, to the effect that in the theology of the Middle Ages, "The resurrection of Christ Himself is thought of less as the first fruits of the new world . . . than as the assurance that the faithful soul, like its Lord, will rise into heavenly glory after death. . . . A mainly individualistic eschatology has replaced the mainly cosmic eschatology of the Bible. . . . Time is thought of less as the process of events whereby God is bringing this world to an end in order to establish . . . the world to come; it is thought of more as the process whereby each individual soul reaches its destiny in heaven or hell. . . . The great transformation of the universe at the last day . . . seems almost to become an irrelevance" (pp. 202f.).

45. Commentary on Philippians 2:10, C.R. 80, p. 29.
46. Thomas Torrance, *Kingdom and Church* (Edinburgh, 1956), p. 156.
47. Ibid., 121.
48. Ibid., 137.
49. Ibid., 161.
50. Ibid., 161f.
51. Ibid., 161.
52. Ibid., 153.
53. Ibid., 159.
54. Ibid., 158.
55. Ibid., 158.
56. *Institutes of the Christian Religion,* ed. J.T. McNeill, Vol. 1 (Philadelphia, 1960), p. 351.
57. Ibid., 348.
58. Ibid., 358.
59. Ibid., 36f.
60. Torrance, op. cit., 156.
61. Ibid., 105.
62. Ibid., 89.
63. Cf. J.P. Martin, *The Last Judgment: From Orthodoxy to Ritschl* (Grand Rapids, 1966), pp. 82ff.
64. I am indebted to Dr. Edward Huenemann for pointing me toward the socio-historical significance of the Heidelberg Catechism.
65. W.A. Visser 't Hooft, *The Kingship of Christ* (New York, 1948), p. 136.
66. Ibid., 136.
67. Ibid.
68. Ibid., 138.
69. Ibid., 137.
70. Ibid.
71. The English translation was published by New Brunswick Theological Seminary, New Brunswick, NJ, 1955.
72. Visser 't Hooft, op. cit., 123.
73. Tjaard G. Hommes, in *Reformed Review,* Winter, 1973, pp. 90f.
74. Ibid., 94.
75. Ibid., 122.

76. Isaac Rottenberg, *Redemption and Historical Reality* (Philadelphia, 1964), p. 171.
77. I. John Hesselink, "Introduction to Winter," *Reformed Review,* 1973, pp. 54f.
78. A.A. Van Ruler, *The Greatest of These Is Love* (Grand Rapids, 1958), p. 96.
79. Ibid., 97.
80. A.A. Van Ruler, *Gestaltwerdung Christi in der Welt,* p. 7.
81. Hendrikus Berkhof, *Christ the Meaning of History* (Richmond, VA, 1966).
82. Ibid., 133.
83. Ibid., 169f.
84. Ibid., 173.
85. Ibid., 170.
86. Ibid., 170f.
87. Ibid., 175.
88. Ibid., 178.
89. Ibid.
90. Ibid., 181.
91. Ibid.
92. Ibid.
93. Ibid., 199.
94. Ibid.
95. Ibid.
96. Ibid., 204.
97. James Martin, *The Last Judgment in Protestant Theology* (Grand Rapids, 1966), p. 21.

Chapter 8

1. Quoted in review of *The Church and I* (New York, 1974) by William Buckley, Jr., *New York Times Book Review,* Sept. 8, 1974, p. 2.
2. A.C. Krass, *Beyond the Either/Or Church* (Nashville, TN, 1973), Ch. VII, "Signs of Hope."
3. Hendrikus Berkhof, *The Doctrine of the Holy Spirit* (London and New York, 1964), p. 96.
4. Paul Fries, "Van Ruler on the Holy Spirit and the Salvation of the Earth," *Reformed Review,* Winter, 1973, p. 131.
5. Ibid., 130.
6. Ibid., 132.
7. Ibid., 128.
8. I. John Hesselink, in *Reformed Review,* 1973, pp. 54f.
9. Tjaard G. Hommes, in *Reformed Review,* Winter, 1973, p. 95.
10. Ibid.
11. Ibid., 120.
12. Ibid., 90.

13. Ibid., 94.
14. Ibid., 92.
15. Ibid., 93.
16. A.A. Van Ruler, *The Greatest of These is Love,* pp. 90f.
17. Arthur Ainger, 1841-1919.
18. Thomas E. Clarke, "Societal Grace: For a New Pastoral Strategy" in *Soundings,* Center of Concern, Washington, DC, 1974, pp. 15f.
19. Ibid.
20. Ibid.
21. Cf. the excellent essay by Norman Birnbaum, "Beyond Marx in the Sociology of Religion?" in Glock, C., and Hammond, P., eds. *Beyond the Classics?* (New York, 1973), pp. 3-70. The chapter contains an excellent bibliographical section for those wishing to pursue recent Marxist thought.
22. Cf. Goulet, *A New Moral Order,* pp. 109f., 124-126.
23. Ibid., 119f.
24. Ibid., 119.
25. M.M. Thomas, *Man and the Universe of Faiths* (Madras: Christian Literature Society, 1975), pp. 127f. This volume, though I have quoted directly from it only at this point, has been one of the formative books which I have read in preparing this book. I highly recommend it as a brief guide to comparative religious study in the light both of recent developments in world religions and of the struggle for liberation and development.
26. Leszek Kolakowski, *Toward a Marxist Humanism,* pp. 144f.
27. Ibid., 145.
28. Ibid., 146.
29. Goulet, op. cit., 133.
30. Ibid., 132.
31. Goulet, op. cit., Chapter II, 23-49.
32. A.C. Krass, *Frontier,* Spring, 1970.
33. Thomas Suavet, *Actualite de L.-J. Lebret* (Paris, 1968), p. 33.
34. L.-J. Lebret, editorial in *Développement et Civilisations,* No. 26 (June, 1966), p. 49.
36. L.-J. Lebret, *Mystique d'un Monde Nouveau* (Lyons, 1941), p. 38.
37. Ibid.
38. Goulet, op. cit., 41.
39. L.-J. Lebret, *Mystique d'un Monde Nouveau,* p. 38.
40. Goulet, op. cit., 42.
41. Suavet, op. cit., 32.
42. Ibid., 24.
43. L.-J. Lebret, *The Last Revolution* (New York, 1965), pp. 3f.
44. Ibid., 4.
45. Ibid., 137.
46. L.-J. Lebret, editorial, *Développement et Civilisations,* March 25, 1966, pp. 3f.

47. Ibid., 4.
48. Ibid.
49. Ibid., 5.
50. Suavet, op. cit., 26f.
51. L.-J. Lebret, "Développement Harmonisé" in *International Development Review,* Vol. 8, No. 4 (December, 1966), p. 23.
52. Ibid., 24.
53. Ibid.
54. Goulet, op. cit., 40f.
55. L.-J. Lebret, *The Last Revolution,* p. 171.
56. Ibid., 178.
57. Ibid., 181f.
58. Suavet, op. cit., 33.
59. Goulet, op. cit., 38.
60. Ibid., 36.
61. L.-J. Lebret, *The Last Revolution,* p. 4.
62. Ibid., 163.
63. *Développement et Civilisations,* loc. cit., p. 6.
64. L.-J. Lebret, *The Last Revolution,* 4.
65. Ibid., 213.
66. Ibid., 199.
67. Boston Industrial Mission, op. cit.
68. Robert Middleton, "The Bosford Declaration" in *Christian Century,* Vol. 93, No. 26 (Aug. 18-25, 1976), pp. 704-8.
69. Robert Bellah, *The Broken Covenant,* p. 153.
70. Hendrikus Berkhof, *Christ the Meaning of History,* pp. 180f.
71. Ibid., 188.
72. Ibid., 168.

Chapter 9

1. Richard Niebuhr, *The Kingdom of God in America* (New York, 1959), p. 193. Niebuhr described liberalism with the following words: "A God without wrath brought men without sin into a kingdom without judgment through the ministrations of a Christ without a cross."
2. *Let the Earth Hear his Voice,* p. 1294.
3. Karl Donfried, *JBL,* Vol. 93, No. 3 (Sept., 1974), p. 425.
4. Vitaly Borovoy, "What Is Salvation?—An Orthodox Statement" in *International Review of Mission,* Vol. 61, No. 241 (Jan., 1972), p. 41.
5. Moltmann, op. cit., 175.
6. Chinua Achebe, *Arrow of God* (Garden City, NY, 1969).

Prologue

1. See his *Jesus in Focus* (London, 1975); *A Today Sort of Evangelism* (London, 1972); and *Dear Archbishop* (London, 1976).
2. Hoekendijk, *The Church Inside Out* (Philadelphia, 1966).
3. Richard Niebuhr, *Christ and Culture* (New York, 1951).
4. Oscar Lewis, *La Vida* (New York, 1965-1966), pp. xlii-lii.
5. John Howard Yoder, *The Politics of Jesus*, pp. 149f.
6. David Sheppard, *Built as a City* (London, 1974).
7. Ibid., 356.
8. *One World*, Geneva, July/August, 1976.
9. Benton Johnson, "Max Weber and American Protestantism" in *Sociological Quarterly*, Vol. 12 (Autumn, 1971), pp. 473-485.
10. Available in *Origins*, Vol. 4, No. 33 (Feb. 6, 1975) (National Catholic News Service).
11. *Against the World for the World*, ed. Peter Berger and Richard Neuhaus (New York, 1976).
12. Charles Davis, review of *Against the World for the World* in *Commonweal*, Vol. 103, No. 23 (Nov. 5, 1976), pp. 733ff.
13. Denis Goulet, *A New Moral Order*, p. 132.
14. Ibid., 131.
15. Denis Goulet, "Needed: A Cultural Revolution in the United States" in *Christian Century*, Vol. 91, No. 30 (Sept. 4-11, 1974), pp. 816ff.
16. Reinhold Niebuhr, *Beyond Tragedy* (New York, 1937).
17. Ibid., 219, 224.
18. Ibid., 28.
19. J.G. Davies, *Christians, Politics, and Violent Revolution* (London, 1976), p. 160.
20. Colin Williams, from an address, "Is It Too Late for Evangelism?" given Dec. 6, 1975, EVCOM Workshop, Columbus, OH (mimeographed, Office of Communication, United Church of Christ).
21. Georges Florovsky, *Bible, Church, Tradition: An Eastern Orthodox View* (Belmont, MA, 1972), p. 69.
22. Mortimer Arias, "That the World Might Believe" in *International Review of Mission*, Vol. 65, No. 257 (Jan., 1976), p. 23.
23. Nestor Paz, *My Life for My Friends, The Guerilla Journal of Nestor Paz, Christian* (Maryknoll, NY, 1975), p. 56.
24. Goulet, op. cit., 41.
25. Walter Rauschenbusch, *Christianity and the Social Crisis* (New York, 1907), pp. 139f.
26. A.M. Hunter, *P.T. Forsyth* (London, 1974), pp. 98f.
27. Quoted in John Poulton, *Jesus In Focus* (London, 1975), p. 113.
28. *Foundations and Perspectives of Confession*, pp. 23f.
29. Tissa Balasuriya, "Theological Reflections on Vietnam" in *Commonweal*, Vol. 102, No. 14 (Sept. 26, 1975), pp. 426ff.
30. *Pastoral Letter on Powerlessness in Appalachia* (Prestonsburg, KY: Catholic Committee on Appalachia, 1975).

31. Found in *Teachings of the Twelve Apostles,* translated and annotated by James A. Kleist (Westminster, MD, 1948).
32. Hunter, op. cit., 99.
33. "Looking Towards World Evangelism," Declaration of the International Theological Conference on Evangelism and Dialogue in India, 1971 (IDOC 1973), p. 49.
34. William Lazareth, "The Eucharist as Lived," 41st International Eucharistic Congress, Philadelphia, August 5, 1976 (mimeographed). (mimeographed).
35. These words are transcribed as recorded by hand from a radio broadcast on WRVR, New York, same date.
36. "Toward a Church of the Beatitudes," available from Liberty to the Captives, Box 12236, Philadelphia, PA 19144.